Piaget's Theory of Cognitive and Affective Development

Foundations

of Constructivism

Fifth Edition

Barry J. Wadsworth

Mount Holyoke College

With Drawings by the Author

Longman *Publishers USA*

Piaget's Theory of Cognitive and Affective Development:
Foundations of Constructivism, Fifth Edition

Copyright © 1996, 1989, 1984, 1979, 1971 by Longman Publishers USA.
All rights reserved.
No part of this publication may be reproduced,
stored in a retrieval system, or transmitted
in any form or by any means, electronic, mechanical,
photocopying, recording, or otherwise,
without the prior permission of the publisher.

Longman, 10 Bank Street, White Plains, N.Y. 10606

Associated companies:
Longman Group Ltd., London
Longman Cheshire Pty., Melbourne
Longman Paul Pty., Auckland
Copp Clark Longman Ltd., Toronto

Acquisitions editor: Virginia L. Blanford
Assistant editor: Chris Konnari
Production editor: Linda Moser/Electronic Publishing Services Inc.
Cover design: Robin Hoffmann
Production supervisor: Richard Bretan
Compositor: Electronic Publishing Services Inc.

Library of Congress Cataloging-in-Publication Data
Wadsworth, Barry J.
   Piaget's theory of cognitive and affective development :
Foundations of constructivism / Barry J. Wadsworth : with drawings by
the author.—5th ed.
      p.   cm.
   Includes bibliographic references and index.
   ISBN 0-8013-0773-2
   1. Cognition in children.   2. Emotions in children.   3. Piaget,
Jean, 1896- . I. Title.
BF723.C5W33 1996
155.4'13'092—dc20

                                     95-14394
                                     CIP

1 2 3 4 5 6 7 8 9 10-MA-9998979695

To Eva Risley Clark, West Side School

Contents

Preface

This book evolved out of the first four editions of *Piaget's Theory of Cognitive and Affective Development*. Its aim remains the same as that of the four earlier editions: to introduce the education or psychology student to Jean Piaget's theory in an undistorted, conceptual manner. Although the first two editions focused primarily on Piaget's work on cognitive or intellectual development, the third edition and this volume also examine Piaget's extensive studies on affective development, a rich body of work largely overlooked by psychologists and educators. I have also incorporated the most important developments in Piagetian theory of the last several years. My goal is to show the reader that there are many rewards in understanding Piaget's work.

Piaget painted a compelling picture of how children construct and acquire knowledge. This conception was based on 60 years of rigorous observation, thought, and research by one of the most creative and insightful minds of this century. Scientists generally agree that Piaget pushed the frontiers of psychological thought as far as any one person ever has. Educators and child psychologists agree that he has led us to an important new understanding of children's development. Regardless of their professional position, those who work with children (and with adults) can be more effective if they understand how and why children behave as they do. Piaget and his advocates have contributed much to that understanding.

As an elementary school teacher initially, I had doubts about some of the educational practices I engaged in. My intuitions often took a direction that my peers and tradition did not want to follow. Because of my discovery of Piaget's work, I have developed a better understanding of children, the educational process, and where my intuitions properly fit. My hope is that this book will similarly assist you.

I began to write about Piaget's work in 1969 as a college teacher who believed it important for education and psychology students to become familiar with Piaget's ideas. When I was working on the original edition of this book, Piaget was just becoming a buzzword in American psychology and education. Twenty-five years later, Piagetian theory is no longer in vogue, less a novelty, and even dismissed by many as "old hat" and inadequate. I and others feel strongly that Piaget's theory has as much to offer psychology and education today as in earlier years. For me, Piaget's theory is as exciting today as in the 1960s and it continues to be the most useful guide to my thinking and efforts to make sense of issues in education. It is not my only guide, but a highly valued one.

My understanding (my construction) of Piaget's theory has changed (developed) over these 25 years. The theory has changed, as all theories do and must. I am embarrassed by some of the interpretations I made and committed to print in the 1970s, but heartened by my recognition that they were reasonable given my understanding at that time. If I have improved qualitatively my understanding (my construction) of Piaget's theory, then my current interpretations should be more valid. That, as Piaget would have us believe, is what construction of knowledge is all about.

In the 1960s and 1970s, most Piagetians focused on cognitive development, equating it with intellectual development. We were wrong. Piaget told us that there was more to intellectual development than cognition, but we did not hear. He always maintained that, in addition to cognition, development has an affective component, a social component, and an ethical or moral component.

I would like to thank the following people who reviewed the manuscript for the fifth edition and provided helpful comments:

Kay Alderman, University of Akron

Helmut W. Bartel, Temple University

James A. DeRuiter, University of Northern Colorado

Yoko Ishigaki Karjala, San Jose State University

Janice Patillo, Stephen F. Austin State University

Charles Temple, Hobart & William Smith Colleges

THE ORGANIZATION OF THE BOOK

One of the difficulties encountered by the uninitiated in reading Piaget's works is the number of unique concepts he used to conceptualize behavior. It is necessary to understand these concepts before his works can be understood. The Introduction provides a brief historical overview, including a biography of Piaget and a discussion of his approach to research. Chapter 1 describes four concepts that are central to all Piaget's work: schema, assimilation, accommodation, and equilibration. Chapter 2 deals with the components of intelligence and the factors affecting its development, the three types of knowledge, Piaget's levels of development, and affective development.

Chapters 3 through 6 each deal with one of the four levels of cognitive and affective development. Chapter 7 discusses the relationship of cognitive and affective development to adolescent behavior. Chapter 8 summarizes the previous chapters and discusses some of the broad implications of Piaget's works for child training and education.

Chapter 9 discusses Piaget's constructivist concepts in relation to mathematics education, reading and writing instruction, and the field of learning disabilities.

Prior editions of this book have been criticized for not including more coverage of research and reviews of the work of theorists who have presumably moved beyond Piaget (neo-Piagetians). In deciding what to include in this edition, I have chosen not to cover everything, as textbooks often try to do, but to focus on the theory of Jean Piaget, which has stood the test of time as a powerful and useful view of intellectual development. In addition, I have attempted to address what I see as common shortcomings in understandings of the theory, and to do so clearly and concisely.

In addressing educational practice, recognizing that the principles guiding constructivist practice do not vary from one content area to another, I have included in the last chapter discussions of the teaching of mathematics, reading, and writing only where I feel practice is most in need of revision. I hope an understanding of Piaget's theory and the principles of constructivism will provoke readers to pursue further their questions. Construction of knowledge is never complete. This book is but a beginning.

Barry J. Wadsworth

Introduction

Jean Piaget's college and university training was in the natural sciences. His main interests originally were in biology. Early in his career, he became interested in children's intellectual development, and he spent the last 60 years of his life gathering an impressive amount of research information pertaining to mental development. His work produced an elaborate and comprehensive theory of how intelligence develops.[1]

In America, Piaget is thought of primarily as a child psychologist and educator. In the strict sense, he was neither. His work was not directly concerned with predicting behavior, as the psychologist's often is, nor was he directly concerned with how to teach children. He preferred to be classified as a genetic epistemologist.[2] His work was primarily concerned with describing and explaining in a very systematic way the growth and development of intellectual structures and knowledge. It is not surprising that his work has had a great impact on education and psychology, both here and abroad.

Piaget's publications, over 50 books and hundreds of articles, all written originally in French, took many years to cross the Atlantic. Only since the 1960s have Piaget's works and Piagetian concepts spread quickly throughout American educational and psychological thought. L'Abate's 1968 frequency of citation study[3] is a measure of the impact of Piaget's works on American thought. L'Abate's search of journals and textbooks in the child development field during the 1950s and 1960s

---

[1] In this book, the terms *intellectual* and *mental* are used interchangeably.

[2] *Genetic epistemology* is the science of how knowledge is acquired.

[3] Two journals, *Child Development* (1950-65) and *Journal of Genetic Psychology* (1957-58, 1960-65), were searched, along with 12 popular and current textbooks on child development.

found Piaget to be the most frequently cited author. A more recent study, undertaken in 1979 by the author of this book and similar to L'Abate's, also found Piaget to be the most frequently cited author.

THREE TYPES OF PSYCHOLOGICAL THEORIES

There are three major streams of psychological and educational thinking, each forming a theoretical position resting on a different set of assumptions (Langer 1969; Kohlberg and Mayer 1972). The assumptions of each theoretical position form the core around which each theory is constructed. Each evolves a different concept of the child. Each suggests different ways of "educating" the child. The three broad theoretical positions are outlined here as *romanticism-maturationism, cultural transmission-behaviorism,* and *progressivism-cognitive development* (Kohlberg and Mayer 1972).

Romanticism–Maturationism

Romanticism has its roots in the writings of Jean-Jacques Rousseau. It is primarily a maturationist concept of development. Experience or the environment is important only insofar as it affects development by providing the necessary nourishment for the "naturally" growing organism. Genetically predetermined stages are seen as unfolding naturally. Stages can be *fixated,* or arrested by experience, but the *course* of development is assumed to be innate, inborn, inherited, or genetically predetermined.

Maturationists such as Freud and Montessori hold that what comes from within the child is the most important aspect of development; therefore, the pedagogical (educational) environment should be permissive enough to allow the inner "good" (abilities and social virtues) to unfold and the inner "bad" to come under control (Kohlberg and Mayer 1972). Thus, the child is conceptualized as a plant. It is begun

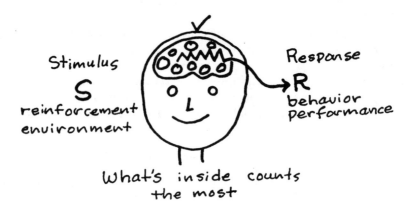

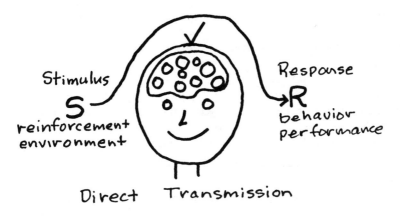

from a seed and all the characteristics that it can evolve are predetermined and contained within the seed. The plant needs sunshine, air, and water (a good environment) in which to grow, but beyond retarding or maximizing growth, environmental factors do not have major effects on the primary characteristics of the plant. It is what is inside the individual that contributes the most.

Cultural Transmission—Behaviorism

The traditional education practiced in the United States and most Western societies is rooted in the concept that the job of education is the direct transmission of bodies of information, skills, and the values of the culture to the child. In the Soviet Union, this idea has been institutionalized as an explicit state policy.

The cultural transmission concept of development views the mind as a machine.[4] There are environmental inputs and behavioral outputs, but the concept implies that the organism has little to do with its own development. The environment is assumed to be responsible for development. Underlying this mechanistic concept of development are such associationistic concepts as *stimulus and response* and *reinforcement,* which have their roots in the works of John Locke, Ivan Pavlov, John Watson, A. H. Thorndike, and most recently B. F. Skinner. Development of the child's mind, moral values, and emotions is seen as a result of specifically acquired associations under the control of the environment (reinforcement).

---

[4] In my experience as a teacher of psychology and education, I have found that many students reject the cultural transmission–behaviorism concept purely on emotional grounds. They are disturbed by the notion of considering themselves "machines" or even machinelike. Although the position of this book lies in large part in opposition to the behaviorist concept of development, one must be cautioned against rejecting ideas for purely emotional reasons. One is of course free to do so, and from certain perspectives, it is perfectly valid to do so. But such a rejection is not based on the psychological truth or falseness of the question whether a human being is a "machine," a genetic map, or a unique organism playing a part in his or her own development.

Current educational innovations based on the cultural transmission rationale are *educational technology* and *behavior modification*.[5] In these views, external experience (or reinforcement) is considered critical in shaping or determining the course of learning and development. Maturation or genetic predeterminism is generally considered to be of little significance.

The cultural transmission–behaviorism model suggests that children can learn only through direct instruction. The teacher must teach the child. This is most efficiently carried out when the teacher (or parent) controls the reinforcers that work for a specific child and makes the receipt of reinforcement contingent on learning desired responses. Motivation for learning is viewed as external.

Progressivism–Cognitive Development

In the progressive-cognitive development conception of learning and development, both maturation and the environment are central (although the importance of the environment and maturation is construed entirely differently from the constructions in the other two models). This is an interactionist viewpoint. Mental development is seen as the product of the interaction of the organism (the child) and the environment. This position was first elaborated by Plato, then early in this century by John Dewey and most recently by Heinz Werner, Lev Vygotsky, and Jean Piaget.[6] The child is viewed neither as a product of maturation nor as a machine completely controlled by external agents. The child is a scientist, an explorer, an inquirer; he or she is critically instrumental in constructing and organizing the world and his or her own development.[7] Motivation for learning and development is primarily internal.

---

[5] *Educational technology* sounds like it means more than it does. Basically, educational technology is the application of technological innovations to educational practice. This includes such things as computer-assisted instruction, teaching machines, programs, television, and other audiovisual devices. The assumptions underlying these techniques are generally the same as those of the cultural transmission concept of learning.

Behavior modification is the application of reinforcement techniques to educational or therapeutic practice. The term *behavior modification* is misleading because it refers to a specific technique among many techniques. Indeed, all people in education, regardless of the techniques they are using, are involved in modifying behavior whether they call it that or not.

[6] Piaget was obviously not the only person working in developmental psychology in this area. Hundreds of others have made important contributions in recent years. Nevertheless, with the possible exception of Heinz Werner and Lev Vygotsky, Piaget stood alone in the magnitude of his research over 60 years and in having generated a cohesive theory.

[7] A caution was previously made regarding the rejection of psychological theories on emotional grounds. Similarly, one must caution against accepting psychological theories for emotional reasons. My experience has been that most people like Piagetian theory. They like the picture Piaget painted. Again, this is not evidence for the correctness or incorrectness of assertions or adequate logical grounds for the acceptance of a theory. No doubt, it is important for teachers to like and feel comfortable with whatever they use, however.

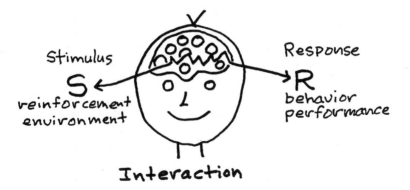

BIOGRAPHY

Jean Piaget's life was one of scholarship and hard work. He was born in 1896 in Neuchâtel, Switzerland. By his own admission, he was an intellectually precocious youth. At age 10, he managed his first publication, a description of a partly albino sparrow he observed in a public park. To some extent, the direction and rigor of Piaget's efforts were determined early in his life. At age 15, he decided to direct his work toward a biological explanation of knowledge, a goal that is clearly reflected in his later work.

In 1915, at age 18, Piaget received his baccalaureate from the University of Neuchâtel. Three years later, he received a doctorate in the natural sciences from the same school. Much of his study was in philosophy. During this period, Piaget studied the development of mollusks in the many lakes around Neuchâtel. He was interested in how mollusks adapted to being transferred from one environment to another. He discovered that their shell structure was affected by rough or calm lake water; the shell structure changed as the environment changed. By age 21, he had published 25 professional papers (mostly on mollusks) and was considered one of the world's few experts on mollusks.

His intensive work in biology led him to conclude that biological development was due not only to maturation (and heredity) but also to variables in the environment. He observed in successive generations of mollusks certain structural changes that could be attributed only to movement from large lakes with much wave action to small ponds with little or no wave action. Such observations convinced Piaget that biological development was a process of adaptation to the environment; it could not be explained by maturation alone (Piaget 1952b). These experiences and convictions contributed to Piaget's later view of mental development as primarily a process of adaptation to the environment and an extension of biological development.[8]

Piaget moved from biology to philosophy and eventually to psychology early in

---

[8] Mental development as a form of adaptation in the biological sense, one of Piaget's revolutionary and most important concepts, is discussed in Chapter 2.

his life. In 1918 he published two works that appear to be evidence of this transition and reveal some fundamental beliefs that were part of the roots of his later work in intellectual development. One publication was a brief paper titled "Biology and War," and the second was an autobiographical novel, *Recherche*.[9]

In "Biology and War," Piaget examined and rejected both the Darwinian and Lamarckian positions, which conclude that for biological reasons, wars are inevitable. Piaget argues that human development and the effort to understand move humans toward cooperation and altruism—and away from war. This position is an early statement of Piaget's later formulation that development is a process of interaction between the biological individual and the environment.

Recherche novelizes Piaget's struggle with science and faith and touches on a number of social issues, including feminism. The book depicts the crisis, and Gruber and Vonèche (1977) write of the resolution:

> Then the "blinding discovery": "science gives knowledge of good and of evil." It can explain everything, but it says nothing about values. It is faith that speaks of them. Faith is not knowledge, it is action. The contradiction between faith and knowledge is thus resolved. The final phase of the search is reconstruction: science gives laws of the world, faith is its engine. (p. 43)

About to take up the quest for understanding human intellectual development, Piaget resolves the conflict between science and faith by arguing the place for both intelligence (science, knowledge) and values or affectivity (faith) in human development. Again, this theme plays a central role in Piaget's theory, as we see in the chapters ahead.

In 1918 Piaget also completed his doctorate in biology, and he turned to psychology. He had become convinced that there were severe limits to philosophy. He was most concerned that philosophical solutions to problems could not be verified without experimental work. For several years, he had been reading and taking classes in psychology, and he had become increasingly interested in the field. In 1919 he went to Zurich, where he studied and worked in psychological clinics, immersing himself in psychological experimentation. Later in 1919, he went to Paris and spent two years at the Sorbonne. While in Paris, he had a chance to work in Binet's laboratory (a grade school), standardizing several tests.[10] Unenthusiastic at first, he became intrigued with the incorrect answers children gave to questions on the tests; shortly thereafter, he was hard at work examining the reasoning processes underlying children's responses.

Piaget had found his research interest. He was convinced that the development of children's intelligence could be studied experimentally by studying their thinking and reasoning. For two years, he continued testing children, examining the development of their thought.

---

[9]   *Recherche* translates as *search* or *research*. Both of these publications can be found translated in Gruber and Vonèche (1977), *The Essential Piaget*.

[10] Binet is considered the progenitor of intelligence testing. He developed the Binet Intelligence Test, from which current forms of the Stanford–Binet Intelligence Scale were derived.

At last I had found my field of research. First of all it became clear to me that the theory of the relations between the whole and the part can be studied experimentally through the analysis of the psychological processes underlying logical operations [logical reasoning]. This marked the end of my "theoretical" period and the start of an inductive and experimental era in the psychological domain which I had always wanted to enter, but for which until then I had not found the suitable problems. (Piaget 1952b, p. 245)

In 1921, Piaget was offered the directorship of studies at the Institut J. J. Rousseau in Geneva, a position that proved to be the perfect environment for his studies. He was launched on a course of research that did not change: the investigation of the mental development of children. Piaget's research and writing on this issue filled most of his professional work for the next 60 years.

By the time he was 30, Piaget was famous for his works in psychology.[11] Through the years, he conducted continuous research and taught at the University of Geneva. A prolific writer, he published many books and hundreds of journal articles, many in conjunction with the colleagues he assembled in Geneva. He attributed much of his productivity to those who worked with him over the years.

Piaget was an untiring worker. Until his death in 1980, he followed a strenuous, self-imposed work schedule. Each summer, when the school year ended, he collected his research findings for the year and headed for an abandoned farmhouse in the Alps, where he spent the summer in isolation, writing and walking, his whereabouts unknown but to a few friends and his family. When the summer ended, he returned from the mountains with a new book or two plus several articles (Elkind 1968).

Piaget was honored around the world. He received honorary degrees from Harvard (1936), the Sorbonne (1946), the University of Brussels (1949), the University of Brazil at Rio de Janeiro (1949), and from Columbia (1970). In 1969, he was the first European cited by the American Psychological Association; the citation was for his distinguished contribution to psychology. Before his death, he made several trips to the United States to address American groups concerned with child development and education.

In 1955, with the help of a grant from the Rockefeller Foundation, the International Center for Genetic Epistemology was established in Geneva. Each year, this program permits a number of eminent scholars to visit and do research with the Geneva group that grew up around Piaget; several Americans have studied under the program. Piaget always insisted that knowledge was best pursued from an interdisciplinary perspective. Thus, the scholars working at the center are specialists in several fields: physics, biology, mathematics, and language, as well as psychology and education.

Whether time proves Piaget's basic assumptions to be correct or incorrect, his works have generated more interest and research than those of any other person in psychology in the last 60 years.

Jean Piaget died in Geneva on September 16, 1980. He was 84 years old.

---

[11] *The Language and Thought of the Child* and *Judgment and Reasoning of the Child* (both 1924) were Piaget's first books on psychology, although earlier he had published numerous papers in the field.

THE APPROACH TO RESEARCH

Piaget was a developmental psychologist in that he was concerned with uncovering the ontogenetic[12] changes in cognitive or intellectual functioning from birth through adolescence. His works were slow to gain wide attention in the United States. Aside from the fact that they were written in French, the reasons for this are largely related to the nature of his theory and research methodology. The concepts he used did not gain acceptance easily in America; neither did his "experimental" methodology.

Psychology in the United States has had a strong tradition of behaviorism. Theorists such as Thorndike, Tolman, Watson, Hull, Spence, and Skinner have dominated the scene, each primarily interested in stimulus–response relationships and the concept of reinforcement. Traditionally, American psychologists of the behaviorist school have not inferred the existence of internal mental processes (of thought).

Piagetian concepts such as assimilation were entirely foreign to the behaviorist position. Piaget did not conceptualize behavior exclusively in terms of stimuli and responses, and he did not use the construct of reinforcement to explain everything. Some important Piagetian concepts (explained in Chapter 1) are schemata, assimilation, accommodation, and equilibration. Also, Piaget did infer the existence of internal mental processes. It was difficult for many American psychologists to come to grips with such concepts.

In America, experimental research in psychology typically concerned itself with hypothesis testing, rigorous control of experimental variables, and treatment of data with sophisticated statistical procedures. Most of Piaget's research was not experimental in these ways. He did not typically employ elaborate statistics to test hypotheses or use control groups in his research. From his work in Paris in Binet's clinic, Piaget evolved a clinical-descriptive technique that became a trademark for his work. It essentially involved asking individual children carefully selected questions and noting their responses and their reasoning for those responses. In other cases, data were nothing more than the observation of infant behavior. It was difficult for American psychologists to consider these techniques experimental because Piaget's methodology bore little resemblance to American experimental psychology. Piaget's work was primarily observational, although it was invariably systematic and his analyses were exceedingly detailed; they were designed to detect developmental changes in intellectual functioning.

Piaget often permitted himself to be led by his intuition when interviewing children. In the clinical approach, any two children are not necessarily asked the same questions in the same setting. In effect, no two children ever receive the same experimental treatment. *The Child's Conception of the World* (1929) is an example of Piaget's skillful selection of questions. The book is without statistical tables, and sample sizes are small. The main sources for two of Piaget's books[13] were observations of his own three children, who were born between 1925 and 1931. These meticulous

---

[12] *Ontogenetic* refers to developmental changes that occur in the individual.

[13] *Play, Dreams, and Imitation in Childhood* (1951) and *The Origins of Intelligence in Children* (1952).

observations provided him with an awareness of the relationship between early sensorimotor actions and later intellectual development. From these exceedingly complete and careful descriptions of behavior over a period of years, he drew major conclusions regarding intellectual development from birth to age 2. This type of research was severely criticized because of the small sample size and because it was not considered experimental. The criticisms diminish in importance if one accepts the assumption implicit in Piaget's theory: that the general course of development of intellectual structures is the same in all people. If the purpose of one's research is to reveal what the course of development is like, and if Piaget's assumption is correct, in principle one can accurately determine the course of development by carefully examining (observing) one child over the necessary period of time. Essentially, this is a longitudinal study of one subject. In this view, sample size becomes meaningless.[14] Most agree that there is considerable merit in using the longitudinal approach Piaget used. Although he often observed small numbers of children, his observations of the same subjects on occasion ranged over years.

While much of Piaget's early work can be looked on as intuitive, employing nonexperimental procedures and using small samples of subjects, a large part of his later work was as rigorously experimental as any psychologist might wish. *The Early Growth of Logic in the Child* (1964) and *The Mechanisms of Perception* (1969) carefully report statistical findings and respectable sample sizes. The material reported in *The Growth of Logical Thinking from Childhood to Adolescence* (1958) is based on the testing of over 1,500 subjects.

Many criticisms have been leveled at Piaget's approach to research, but no one has disputed that it is systematic, rigorous, and insightful. Piaget's primary technique was one of systematic observation, description, and analysis of children's behavior. This approach is primarily designed to discover the nature and level of development of the concepts children use, not to produce developmental scales. Piaget defended his approach to research on the basis that it is the most appropriate for the questions he wished to answer. This sounds very reasonable, but it does not always rest well with those who believe American experimental procedures are the only correct ones.

Piaget and Vygotsky

In recent years, Piaget's theory had been criticized for, among other things, not recognizing the significance of social and cultural factors in intellectual development. Many have turned to the work of Russian psychologist Lev Vygotsky (1896–1934) to fill what was perceived as a fatal void in Piaget's work. That Piaget's views were not properly understood in this development is unfortunate but understandable (Zimmerman 1993; Lester 1994). Nonetheless, Vygotsky's work has been brought forward for comparison and Piaget, I am sure, would agree this is healthy and provides

---

[14] Considerable evidence exists that the *course* of cognitive development is basically the same in *all* people, with some variation reflective of culture (see Dasen 1977 for a review of research on this topic).

an opportunity for likely misconstructions of both theories to be modified. Because Piaget and Vygotsky are often contrasted, and often misrepresented, I will highlight my understanding of some of the points of agreement and disagreement between the two and hope to minimize my own misrepresentation. If this book is your first contact with Piaget, you may want to return to the following paragraphs after finishing the rest of the text.

Some of the confusion would certainly have been lessened if the two great minds had had opportunities to exchange ideas. Although they were contemporaries, Vygotsky's relatively early death (1934) precluded exchanges. Differences between the two theorists seem plentiful, but they shared many views. Both saw knowledge as *adaptation* and as individual construction and both believed learning and development were self-regulated. Although they disagreed on the process of construction, both saw the developing/learning child as necessarily active, and that development/learning was not automatic.

Both Piaget and Vygotsky were concerned about intellectual development, but each pursued different problems and questions. Piaget was primarily interested in how knowledge is formed or constructed. His theory is a theory of *invention* or construction, which occurs inside the mind of the individual. Vygotsky was concerned with the question of how social and cultural factors influence intellectual development. Vygotsky's theory is a theory of *transmission* of knowledge from the culture to the child. At its core, it is about how individuals, interacting with more knowledgeable social agents (teachers, peers), *construct* and internalize knowledge the agents have. Piaget, of course, did not believe direct transmission of this sort is possible; he believed children acquire their own version of existing social knowledge through their personal construction of that knowledge. He saw the individual's construction as necessarily unique and different, though usually approximating that of the culture after many episodes of disequilibration and subsequent further construction or reconstruction.

Both Piaget and Vygotsky believed in development and learning, although here, too, their views of the relationship between the two are different. Piaget believed that the level of development placed limits on what could be learned and the level of possible comprehension of that learning. Vygotsky, on the other hand, believed that learning of culturally modeled concepts led to development. Thus, for Vygotsky, learning is the driving force of intellectual development, whereas for Piaget, development is the driving force.

Vygotsky differentiated between what he called the *zone of actual development* and the *zone of proximal development*. The zone of actual development "is the level at which students are capable of solving problems independently. The zone of proximal development is the level at which students can solve problems with support" (Lester 1994, p. 4). That is, with modeling of knowledge by others and social interaction, students can learn things they could not learn on their own. Piaget's theory does not have a zone concept as such.

Piaget's view is that new construction is always built on prior construction and that, with disequilibration, advancing prior constructions is always possible. Both theorists agree that development and learning can be advanced. Their differences appear to be more with *how* learning and development occur rather than what is possible.

For Vygotsky, social factors play a fundamental role in intellectual development. When external knowledge, existing in the culture, is internalized (or constructed) by children, intellectual skills and functions are provoked to develop. Thus, learning leads development. Piaget, in turn, fully recognized the role of social factors in intellectual development. Social interactions were viewed as a source of cognitive conflict, thus disequilibration, and thus development. In addition, social interaction was viewed as necessary for construction of social knowledge.

The sharpest difference between the two is seen in their views of the role of language in intellectual development. For Vygotsky, acquisition of language from the social environment results in qualitatively improved thinking and reasoning, or intellectual development. Piaget viewed spoken language as one manifestation of the *symbolic function* (ability to use symbols to represent), which reflects intellectual development but does not produce it (Fowler 1994). At best, Piaget viewed language as facilitative of, but ultimately not necessary for, intellectual development. "For Piaget, language reflects, but does not produce, intelligence. The only way to advance to a higher intellectual level is not through language, but through action" (Fowler 1994, p. 8).

The implications for education drawn from the two theories are different in certain ways. Although both Piaget and Vygotsky saw knowledge as an individual construction, Vygotsky believed *all* individual construction was *mediated* by social factors. That is, the teacher and instructional program had to model or explain knowledge. The child, then, constructs his or her own internal knowledge from what is modeled. The child does not invent, but very much "copies" what is socially available. This is seen as a process of transmission from the culture (teacher) to the child. Thus, the teacher's job is, among other things, to accurately model knowledge.

Piaget, on the other hand, saw the construction of knowledge as purely the child's. Social factors influence individual disequilibration through cognitive conflict and signal that there is construction to be done. The actual construction of knowledge is not *mediated*, in Vygotsky's sense, by the social environment; it is not copied from a model. Prior knowledge is reconstructed in the face of socially provoked disequilibration. Thus, Piaget's theory is one of individual invention and not transmission. The teacher's role is seen as primarily to encourage, stimulate, and support exploration and invention (construction). Piaget (1973) wrote:

It is obvious that the teacher as organizer remains indispensable in order to create the situations and construct the initial devices which present useful problems to the child. Secondly he is needed to provide counter-examples that compel reflection and reconsideration of overhasty solutions. What is desired is that the teacher cease being a lecturer satisfied with transmitting ready-made solutions; his role should be that of a mentor stimulating initiative and research. (p. 16)

In Piaget's conceptualization, the child can use in construction all sources and forms of information. A child can *actively* listen to a lecture or read a book and use that received information in construction. The process is not one of recreating the model, but of inventing it.

For both Piaget and Vygotsky, the classroom environment requires social interaction, but for different reasons. For Piaget, interaction with peers and adults (particularly peers), and criticism and discussion in its various forms, is a source of necessary disequilibrium. For Vygotsky, the social environment is the source of models of what constructions should look like. It is the source of socially constructed knowledge that models for and mediates the child's constructions. For Vygotsky, learning and thus development is constrained by the models and, of course, the child's motivation.

Although a comparison of Piaget and Vygotsky reveals important differences, their similarities are more striking. Both are clearly constructivists: They both see knowledge as a self-regulated construction. Both see social interactions as having an important role, if for different reasons. In many ways, their work converges.

chapter 1

Intellectual Organization and Adaptation

Piaget's system for conceptualizing intellectual development was greatly influenced by his early training and work as a biologist. Functioning as a biologist, he became vividly aware of, and impressed by, the interaction of mollusks with their environment. Mollusks, like all living organisms, constantly adapt to changes in environmental conditions.

From this early work, Piaget came to believe that biological acts are acts of *adaptation* to the physical environment and help *organize* the environment. He also came to believe that the mind and body do not operate independently of one another and that mental activity is subject to the same laws that biological activity generally is. This led him to conceptualize intellectual development in much the same way as biological development. He saw intellectual acts as acts of *organization* of and *adaptation* to the environment. This does not imply in any sense that mental behavior can be attributed completely to biological functioning, but that the concepts of biological development are useful and valid for looking at intellectual development. Indeed, Piaget asserted that the basic principles of cognitive development are the same as those of biological development. Piaget did not view organization and adaptation as separate processes.

> From the biological point of view organization is inseparable from adaptation: They are two complementary processes of a single mechanism, the first being the internal aspect of the cycle of which adaptation constitutes the external aspect. (Piaget 1952c, p. 7)

For Piaget, intellectual activity could not be separated from the total functioning of the organism. Thus, he considered intellectual functioning a special form of biological activity (1952c, p. 42). Intellectual and biological activity are both part of the overall process by which an organism adapts to the environment and organizes experience.

To begin to understand the process of intellectual organization and adaptation as Piaget saw them, four basic cognitive concepts must be grasped. They are the concepts of *schema, assimilation, accommodation,* and *equilibration.* These concepts are used to explain how and why cognitive development occurs.

SCHEMA

Piaget believed that the mind has structures in much the same way that the body does. All animals have a stomach, a structure that permits eating and digestion. To help explain why people make rather stable responses to stimuli, and to account for many of the phenomena associated with memory, Piaget used the word *schema.* Schemata (the plural of *schema*) are the cognitive or mental structures by which individuals intellectually adapt to and organize the environment. As structures, schemata are the mental counterparts of biological means of adapting. The stomach is a biological structure that animals use to adapt to their environment. In much the same way, schemata are psychological structures or processes that adapt and change with mental development. These structures are inferred to exist. As an organ of the body, a stomach is a real object. Schemata are not physical objects; they are viewed as processes within the nervous system. As such, schemata do not have physical counterparts and are not observable. They are inferred to exist and are properly called hypothetical constructs.[1]

Schemata can be simplistically thought of as concepts or categories. Another analogy might be an index file in which each index card represents a schema. Adults have many cards or schemata. These schemata are used to process and identify or classify incoming stimuli. In this way, the organism is able to differentiate between stimulus events and to generalize. When a child is born, it has few schemata (cards on file). As the child develops, his or her schemata gradually become more generalized, more differentiated, and more "adult."

Schemata never stop changing or becoming more refined. Indeed, the schemata of adulthood have their origins in the schemata of early childhood. Picture, if you will, an index file in a child's head. At birth it contains only a few large cards on which everything is written. As the child develops, more cards are needed to contain the changing classifications. As an illustration, imagine a child walking down a country road with his father. The father looks into a field nearby and sees what adults call a cow, an animal John has never seen before. He says to his son, "John, look at that animal. What is it?" John looks into the field and sees the cow. One can almost see the

---

[1] Constructs are concepts or "things" that are not directly observable but are inferred to exist (such as intelligence, creativity, aptitude, ability, motivation, and instincts). The list of constructs can be endless. A major activity of psychological research is to try to clarify the nature of constructs and verify their existence.

wheels going around in John's head while he is thinking. After a moment of thought, John says, "It's a dog." Assuming John made an honest response, we could infer something like this: John looked out into the field and saw a cow. Presented with this "new" stimulus, he tried to place or classify the stimulus in reference to a card in his card file. In terms of categories in John's "file," the stimulus (cow) most closely approximated John's dog schema, so he identified the object as a dog.

In Piaget's terms, we would say that the child has a number of schemata. These schemata are analogous to concepts, categories, or cards in a file. When confronted with a stimulus, the child tried to fit the stimulus into an available schema. Thus the boy quite logically called the cow a dog because for him, the characteristics of the cow closely approximated the characteristics of a dog. The cow met all the boy's criteria for a dog. The child's structures at this point did not permit him to perceive the differences between a cow and a dog, but he was able to see the similarities.[2]

Schemata are intellectual structures that organize events as they are perceived and classified into groups according to common characteristics. They are repeatable psychological events in the sense that a child repeatedly classifies stimuli in a consistent manner. If a child consistently classifies cows as dogs, we can infer something about the nature of the child's concepts (schemata of cows and dogs). By paying attention to what children say, we can discover what the schemata in their heads look like at a given time.

At birth, schemata are reflexive in nature. That is, they can be inferred from simple reflex motor activities such as sucking and grasping. The sucking reflex illustrates a reflexive schema. At birth, infants typically suck on whatever is put in their mouths—a nipple, a finger—suggesting that there is no differentiation, that only a single, global sucking schema exists. Shortly after birth, infants learn to differentiate; when the infant is hungry, milk-producing stimuli are accepted and non-milk-producing stimuli are rejected. A differentiation exists at this point. In Piaget's words, the infant now has two sucking schemata, one for milk-producing stimuli and one for non-milk-producing stimuli. During the earliest months, schemata are not yet "mental" in the sense in which we usually think of the term. Schemata are reflexive. The infant makes real differentiations within his or her limited environment, but they are made via the reflexive and motor apparatus he or she has available. These differentiations on the most primitive level are the precursors of later "mental" activities.

As a child develops, schemata (cards in the file box) become more differentiated and more numerous; the network they form becomes increasingly complex. During

---

[2] If we are concerned with the accuracy of John's response, we might be tempted to correct John and inform him that the animal is properly called a "cow" and that the response "dog" is incorrect. The result of this may well be confusion for John. John's response, "It's a dog," is a logical response given the configuration of schemata John has available at the time to think about the event. Thus, John's response is not wrong from his perspective—it is wrong only from an adult perspective. In addition, to be told that the proper name for the animal is "cow" may lead John to conclude that the things he calls dogs can be called either dogs or cows. This is a logical inference. These types of "mistakes" can be viewed as a normal part of development and reality testing.

early childhood, an infant has a few reflexive schemata that allow him or her to make a very few differentiations in the environment on a sensory and motor level. An adult has a vast array of comparatively complex schemata that permit a great number of differentiations. The schemata of the adult evolve from the schemata of the child through adaptation and organization. Thus, intellectual development is a constant process of construction and reconstruction.

It is misleading to think that schemata do not change or that the young boy in our example is destined to call cows dogs for the rest of his life. Obviously, this does not happen. As a child becomes better able to generalize across stimuli, schemata become more refined.

At any point, a child's responses are assumed to reflect the nature of the child's concepts or schemata. It is entirely "logical" for the boy described in the example to call a cow a dog when the schemata he has available are considered. Schemata are defined by (or reflected in) the overt behavior of the child. But schemata are more than the behavior; they are the internal structure from which the behavior flows. Behavior patterns that are repeated in the course of cognitive activity are conceptualized as reflecting schemata. A schema subsumes a whole collection of distinct but similar action sequences. "Every schema is . . . coordinated with all other schemata and itself constitutes a totality with differentiated parts" (Piaget 1952c, p. 7).

Because schemata are structures of cognitive development that do change, allowance must be made for their growth and development. Adults' concepts are different from those of children. Concepts—schemata are their structural counterparts—change. The cognitive schemata of the adult are derived from the sensorimotor schemata of the child. The processes responsible for the change are *assimilation* and *accommodation*.

ASSIMILATION

Assimilation is the cognitive process by which a person integrates new perceptual, motor, or conceptual matter into existing schemata or patterns of behavior. One might say that a child has experiences: sees new things (cows) or sees old things in new ways, and hears things. The child tries to fit these new events or stimuli into the schemata he or she has at the time.[3] Suppose, as in the previous example, a boy is walking down a country road with his father and the father points to a cow in the field and says, "What is that?" The child looks at the cow (stimulus) and says, "That's a dog." What has happened? The boy, seeing the object (cow) in the field, sifted through his collection of schemata until he found one that seemed appropriate and that could include the object. To the child, the object (cow) had all the characteristics of a dog—it fit into his dog schema—and so the child concluded that the object was a dog. The stimulus (cow) was assimilated into the dog schema. Thus assimilation can be viewed as the cognitive process of placing (classifying) new stimulus events into existing schemata.

Assimilation occurs all the time. It would be an extreme oversimplification to suggest that a person processes one stimulus at a time. Human beings continually process an increasing number of stimuli.

Assimilation theoretically does not result in a change of schemata, but it does affect the growth of schemata and is thus a part of development. One might compare a schema to a balloon and assimilation to putting more air in the balloon. The balloon gets larger (assimilation growth), but it does not change its shape. Assimilation is a part of the process by which the individual cognitively adapts to and organizes the environment. The process of assimilation allows for the growth of schemata. It does not account for a change of schemata. We know schemata change. Adult schemata are different from those of children. Piaget described and accounted for the change of schemata with *accommodation*.

ACCOMMODATION

When confronted with a new stimulus, a child tries to assimilate it into existing schemata. Sometimes this is not possible. Sometimes a stimulus cannot be assimilated because there are no schemata into which it readily fits. The characteristics of the stimulus do not approximate those required in any of the child's available schemata. What does the child do? Essentially one can do one of two things: One can create a new schema in which to place the stimulus (a new index card in the file) or one can modify an existing schema so that the stimulus fits into it. Both are forms of accommodation and result in change in the configuration of one or more schemata. Thus, accommodation is the creation of new schemata or the modification of old

---

[3] *Assimilation* is a term Piaget borrowed from biology. It is a process analogous to the biological process of eating, wherein food is eaten, digested, and assimilated, or changed into a usable form. Similarly, experience is assimilated or processed.

schemata. Both actions result in a change in, or development of, cognitive structures (schemata).

Once accommodation has taken place, a child can try again to assimilate the stimulus. Because the structure has changed, the stimulus is readily assimilated. Assimilation is always the end product.

The child who is actively assimilating and accommodating is in no way required or expected to evolve schemata that assume a particular form. Implicit in the conceptualizations of schema used here is the idea that schemata are internally constructed with experience over time. Schemata reflect the child's current level of understanding and knowledge of the world. The schemata have been *constructed* by the child. Because they are constructions, schemata are not accurate copies of reality. Their form is determined by the individual's unique pattern of assimilation and accommodation of experience, and over time schemata more closely approach reality in appearance. While the child is an infant, schemata are global and, when compared with adults' schemata, extremely imprecise and often inaccurate. The processes of assimilation and accommodation that convert infants' rather primitive schemata into the more sophisticated adult schemata obviously take years.

No behavior is all assimilation or all accommodation. All behavior reflects both, although some behaviors are more one than the other. For example, what we generally think of as children's play is typically more assimilation than accommodation. On the other hand, children's efforts at imitation of others are usually acts of accommodation more than of assimilation (see Piaget 1962).

During assimilation, a person imposes his or her available structure on the stimuli being processed. That is, the stimuli are forced to fit the person's structure. In accommodation, the reverse is true. The person is forced to change his or her schema to fit the new stimuli, which the person was unable to assimilate. Accommodation accounts for development (a qualitative change) and assimilation accounts for growth (a quantitative change); together these processes account for intellectual adaptation and the development of intellectual structures.

EQUILIBRATION

The processes of assimilation and accommodation are necessary for cognitive growth and development. Of equal importance are the relative amounts of assimilation and accommodation that take place. For example, imagine the outcome in terms of mental development if a person always assimilated stimuli and never accommodated. Such a person would end up with a few very large schemata and would be unable to detect differences in things. Most things would be seen as similar. For John, the cow would forever remain a dog. On the other hand, what would be the result if a person always accommodated and never assimilated? It would result in a person having a great number of very small schemata that had little generality. Most things would be seen as different. The person would be unable to detect similarities. Either of these extremes would result in abnormal intellectual growth. Therefore, a balance between assimilation and accommodation is as necessary as the processes themselves. Piaget called the balance between assimilation and accommodation *equilibrium*. It is the self-regulatory mechanism that ensures the developing child's efficient interaction with the environment.

    Equilibrium is a state of balance between assimilation and accommodation. *Disequilibrium* is a state of imbalance between assimilation and accommodation.[4] *Equilibration* is the process of moving from disequilibrium to equilibrium. This is a self-regulatory process whose tools are assimilation and accommodation. Equilibration allows external experience to be incorporated into internal structures (schemata). When disequilibrium occurs, it motivates[5] the child to seek equilibrium (to further assimilate or accommodate). Disequilibrium activates the process of equilibration and a striving to return to equilibrium. Equilibrium is a necessary condition toward which the organism constantly strives. The organism ultimately assimilates stimuli (or stimulus events) with or without accommodation. This results in equilibrium. Thus, equilibrium can be viewed as a state of cognitive balance that is reached at the point of assimilation. Obviously, the equilibrium related to any particular stimulus may be a very temporary affair, as structures or schemata constantly undergo disequilibrium and change, but it is nonetheless important as development and adaptation inch forward.

---

[4] Disequilibrium can be thought of as a state of cognitive conflict resulting when expectations or predictions are not confirmed by experience. A child expects something to happen in a certain way and it does not. The discrepancy between the expected and what actually occurs is disequilibration and results in disequilibrium.

[5] Motivation can be thought of as that which activates behavior. In Piaget's theory, the major source of motivation in intellectual development is disequilibration. Disequilibrium activates equilibration (assimilation and accommodation).

Everything must be assimilated by a child. The schemata the child uses may not be in harmony with those of adults (as in classifying a cow as a dog), but the child's placement of stimuli into schemata is theoretically always appropriate for his or her level of conceptual development. There is no wrong placement. There are just better and better placements as intellectual development proceeds.

We can say, then, that the child, on experiencing a new stimulus (or an old one again), tries to assimilate the stimulus into an existing schema. If he or she is successful, equilibrium is attained for the moment with respect to the particular stimulus. If the child cannot assimilate the stimulus, he or she attempts to accommodate by modifying a schema or creating a new one. When this is done, assimilation of the stimulus proceeds and equilibrium is reached for the moment.

Conceptually, cognitive growth and development proceed in this way at all levels of development. From birth through adulthood, knowledge is *constructed*[6] by the individual, the schemata of adulthood being built (constructed) from the schemata of childhood. In assimilation, the organism fits stimuli into schemata that exist; in accommodation, the organism changes schemata to fit the stimulus. The process of accommodation results in a qualitative change in intellectual structures (schemata), whereas assimilation only adds to the existing structures—a quantitative change. Thus, assimilation and accommodation—a cumulative coordination, differentiation, integration, and constant construction—account for the growth and development of intellectual structures and knowledge. Equilibration is the internal mechanism that regulates those processes. This is a self-regulatory process. In the same sense that we adapt biologically to the world around us, the development of the mind—intellectual development—is also a process of adaptation.

---

[6] Piaget's assertion that all knowledge is constructed by the individual, a radical view to American psychologists 40 years ago, today is widely accepted. Lauren Resnick writes, "Constructivism, a central tenet of Piagetian theory, in the past sharply divided Piagetians from learning [behavioral] theorists. Today, cognitive scientists generally share the assumption that knowledge is constructed by learners" (1987, p. 19).

chapter **2**

Intellectual Development and Other Factors

CONTENT, FUNCTION, AND STRUCTURE

Piaget viewed cognitive development as having three components: content, function, and structure. *Content* is what children know about. It refers to observable behaviors—sensorimotor and conceptual—that reflect intellectual activity. By its nature, the content of intelligence varies considerably from age to age and from child to child. *Function* refers to the characteristics of intellectual activity—assimilation and accommodation—that are stable and continual throughout cognitive development. *Structure* is the inferred organizational properties (schemata) that explain the occurrence of particular behaviors. For example, if a child is asked to compare a row of nine checkers to a longer row of eight checkers and determine which has more checkers, and she says the row of eight checkers has more even though she counts each row, one can infer that she does not have a complete concept of number. This suggests that her schema for number is not yet fully developed. When confronted with a problem that pits perception against reason, her choice is based on perception. Eventually reason will prevail, but only after the determining structures have developed. These changes in structures are a major aspect of intellectual development. Flavell writes:

> Interposed between function and content, Piaget postulates the existence of cognitive structures. Structure, like content and unlike function, does indeed change with age, and these developmental changes constitute the major object of study for Piaget. What are the structures in Piaget's system? They are the organizational properties of intelligence (schemata), organizations created through function and inferable from the behavioral content whose nature they determine. (Flavell 1963, p. 17)

[handwritten margin notes: "activity can be internal (thoughts?)"]

Piaget concerned himself primarily with the structure of intelligence; he dealt with function and content to a lesser degree. His work involved the careful description and analysis of *qualitative* changes in development of these cognitive structures (schemata). Presumably, qualitative structural changes in cognitive functioning are most clearly changes in intellectual functioning—what is commonly called intelligence.[1]

ACTION AND KNOWLEDGE

Piaget's system requires that a child *act* in the environment if cognitive development is to proceed. The development of cognitive structures is ensured only if the child assimilates and accommodates stimuli in the environment. This can happen only if the child's senses are brought to bear on the environment. When the child is acting in the environment, moving in space, manipulating objects, searching with eyes and ears, or thinking, he or she is taking in the raw ingredients to be assimilated and accommodated. These actions lead to the construction or reconstruction of schemata. An infant cannot learn to differentiate between a nipple and an edge of the blanket unless he or she *acts* on both of them. These actions can be physical actions or mental actions.

As the child becomes older, actions resulting in cognitive change become less overt. For the infant, the instrumental act may be movement of the arm and grasping. For the 9-year-old, the instrumental act may be an internal one, as in thinking while adding a column of numbers. In both cases, the *activity* of the child is essential for development.

Actions necessary for cognitive development to occur are clearly more than just physical movement. Actions are behaviors that stimulate the child's intellectual apparatus and they may or may not be observable. These behaviors produce disequilibrium and allow assimilation and accommodation to occur.

Mental and physical actions in the environment are a necessary but not sufficient condition for cognitive development. That is, the experience alone does not ensure development, but development cannot take place without active experience. Also necessary for development are assimilation and accommodation. Action is one of several interacting determinants of cognitive development.

For Piaget, all knowledge is a *construction* resulting from the child's actions.[2] According to Piaget, there are three kinds of knowledge: physical knowledge, logical-mathematical knowledge, and social knowledge. Each requires the child's actions, but for different reasons.

---

[1] It should be noted that most "intelligence" tests to a large extent sample cognitive content and to a lesser extent cognitive structure. By and large, they are quantitative measures, not qualitative. Piaget's conceptualizations suggest that "intelligence" tests should measure cognitive structures as well as content if intellectual development is to be assessed accurately.

[2] Construction of knowledge occurs when there are physical or mental actions on objects that, when there is disequilibrium, result in assimilation and accommodation of those actions and, thus, construction of schemata or knowledge.

Physical Knowledge: Discovery

Physical knowledge is knowledge of the physical properties of objects and events: size, shape, texture, weight, and so forth. A child acquires physical knowledge about an object while manipulating (acting on) the object with his or her senses. For example, a young boy playing with sand may pour the sand from one container to another, feel it with his hands, or put it into his mouth. Through actions like these, children *discover* and construct their knowledge of sand. Active experiences are assimilated into schemata.

In the acquisition of physical knowledge, the objects themselves (such as sand) "tell" the child what the characteristics of the object are. Feedback or reinforcement is provided by the objects themselves. The child cannot construct an accurate schema of sand unless he acts on sand. Fully accurate knowledge of physical objects cannot be acquired directly from reading, looking at pictures, or listening to what people say—these are all forms of symbolic representation—but only through actions on objects. Objects permit us to construct their properties only to the extent that we *act* on them (Wadsworth 1978).

Logical–Mathematical Knowledge: Invention

Logical-mathematical knowledge is constructed from thinking about experiences with objects and events (Gallagher and Reid 1981).[3] Like physical knowledge, logical-mathematical knowledge can develop only if a child acts (mentally or physically) on objects. But the respective roles of actions and objects in the construction of logical-mathematical knowledge are different. The child *invents* logical-mathematical knowledge; it is not inherent in objects, as physical knowledge is, but is constructed from the *actions* of the child on objects. The objects serve merely as a medium for permitting the construction to occur.

Number concepts are examples of logical-mathematical concepts. We have all observed instances where children have been playing with sets of objects. A little girl may be playing with a set of 11 pennies. She puts them in a row and counts them. There are 11 of them. She puts them in a circle and counts them again. There are still 11 of them. The child stacks the pennies and counts them again. She counts 11 pennies. The child puts the pennies in a box and shakes them up. Removed from the box and counted, the pennies still add up to 11. Through many active experiences like these, children eventually construct the concept or rule that the number of objects in

---

[3] I have chosen to use the term *logical*-mathematical knowledge, whereas Piaget and most of those writing about Piaget's work use the term *logico*-mathematical.

a set remains the same regardless of the arrangement of the individual elements. The sum is independent of the order. This is an invented or constructed rule and an example of logical–mathematical knowledge.

In the development of logical–mathematical knowledge, the nature of the objects is not critical, only that there are groups of objects for the child to manipulate. The concept the girl was developing in the preceding example could have developed as easily using stones, crayons, pots and pans, or flowers. As experiences are repeated over and over in different settings and with different materials and as disequilibration occurs, these concepts become more refined. Like physical knowledge, logical–mathematical knowledge is not directly acquired from reading or listening to people talk. It is constructed from actions on objects.[4]

Social Knowledge

Social knowledge is knowledge on which cultural or social groups come to agree by convention. Examples of social knowledge are rules, laws, morals, values, ethics, and language systems. These types of knowledge evolve within cultures and may be different from group to group. Social knowledge cannot be extracted from actions on objects in the manner of physical and logical–mathematical knowledge. Social knowledge is constructed by children from their actions on (interactions with) other people. As children interact with each other and with adults, they encounter opportunities for the construction of social knowledge.[5]

According to Piagetian theory, all knowledge is physical knowledge, logical–mathematical knowledge, or social knowledge (Wadsworth 1978). Of central importance in the construction of knowledge are the child's mental and physical *actions* on objects and interactions with people. Fully constructed knowledge cannot be derived directly from reading or from listening to people (such as teachers) talk. Before the development of formal operations, fully accurate knowledge can be constructed only from *experience* with relevant objects; it cannot be acquired from representations (such as written or spoken words) of objects and events. Piaget's formulation of what knowledge is has major implications for educational practice.[6]

---

[4] Kamii indicates that all logical–mathematical knowledge involves construction of relationships: "When . . . we are presented with a red chip and a blue one, and note that they are different, the difference is an example of logico-mathematical knowledge. The chips are indeed observable, but the difference between them is not. The difference is a relationship created mentally by the individual who puts the two objects into a relationship" (1982, p. 7).

[5] Chapters 3–6 deal in some depth with the development of moral concepts within the context of affective development. Moral concepts are examples of social knowledge.

[6] If one believes knowledge is a construction in the sense that Piaget conceptualizes it, then one recognizes that knowledge construction is something children do. When confronted with experiences that create disequilibrium, children try to make sense out of this experience (assimilation and accommodation). This active process results in improved schemata (or intelligence). An important educational question is the extent to which activities such as reading (textbooks) and listening (to teachers) can lead to these activities and construction of knowledge. Clearly, Piaget's view is that knowledge fully formed cannot be transmitted directly from a book or teacher to a child in an automatic way. This question is addressed more fully in Chapter 8.

A child is more dependent on physical and sensory experience in the early years of life, when he or she does not possess the power of symbolic representation (language). At this time, interaction with the environment is primarily on a sensory and motor level. The child acts directly on objects in the environment. Development proceeds as the infant explores the environment via his or her reflexes. A variety of objects are placed in the mouth or sucked via the sucking reflex. Objects are grasped. These active reflexive behaviors allow the infant to construct his or her first differentiations within the environment. These actions allow the child to develop internal sensorimotor representations (schemata) of the objects as he or she makes discriminations.

As the typical child develops beyond age 2 or so, he or she becomes increasingly capable of representing action in the mind. The child's actions on the environment are mediated by internalized symbols and language and become less overt. Actions are less sensorimotor and more conceptual. Nonetheless, the active participation of the child remains necessary for development of intelligence.

thus, tv's effect neg,

THE CONTINUUM OF DEVELOPMENT

In the broadest sense, Piaget asserted throughout his work that cognitive and intellectual changes are the result of a developmental process. Piaget's general hypothesis is simply that cognitive development is a coherent process of successive qualitative changes of cognitive structures (schemata), each structure and its concomitant change deriving logically from the preceding one. New schemata do not replace prior ones; as in accommodation, they incorporate them, resulting in a qualitative change. If the young boy who classified a cow as a dog at some later time decides that the cow is no longer a dog but a new object called a cow, he does not *replace* schemata. What he may do is create a new schema (accommodate) for cowlike objects while retaining his old, but now modified, schema for dogs. Thus a change has occurred that results in a qualitatively and quantitatively superior set of schemata, the current schemata incorporating the previous ones.

Piaget conceptualized development as a continuous process along a continuum. Changes in intellectual development are gradual and never abrupt. Schemata are constructed and reconstructed (or modified) gradually. From a Piagetian perspective, development is appropriately viewed as a continuum. For purposes of conceptualizing cognitive growth, intellectual development can be divided into four broad sequential levels.[7]

Piaget has been criticized for using the word *stage* in his theory. Those who objected to his use of stages probably did so out of a misunderstanding. Piaget did not suggest that children move from discrete level to discrete level in development as one moves from one step to another while walking upstairs. Cognitive development flows along, but looking at smaller chunks or parts of the continuum of development is useful in comparing the individual part of the continuum to the whole developmental process. The researcher and theorist can divide the long period of development into bits of shorter length; thus, parts of development can be analyzed and, in some ways, conceptualized more efficiently. This does not in any way deny the continuity of development over its entire course, nor does it mean that the stages are selected without a rationale.[8]

Piaget (1963b) broadly summarized the stages of cognitive development as follows:

1. *The stage of sensorimotor intelligence (0–2 years).* During this stage, behavior is primarily sensory and motor. The child does not yet internally represent events and "think" conceptually, although "cognitive" development is seen as schemata are constructed.
2. *The stage of preoperational thought (2–7 years).* This stage is characterized by the development of language and other forms of representation and rapid conceptual development. Reasoning during this stage is dominated by perception and is thus prelogical or semilogical.
3. *The stage of concrete operations (7–11 years).* During these years, the child develops the ability to apply logical thought to concrete problems in the present.
4. *The stage of formal operations (11–15 years or older).* During this stage, the child's cognitive structures reach their greatest level of development and the child becomes capable of applying logical reasoning to all classes of problems.

---

[7] The number of sequential levels one divides development into is somewhat arbitrary. On different occasions, Piaget divided development into three, four, or six major stages, each time with a number of substages. I have divided the continuum of development into four sequential levels.

[8] I will use the term *stage* where it appears in quotes, but beyond this section I will use the term *level.*

Development is thought to flow along in a cumulative manner, each new step in development built on and becoming integrated with previous steps.

> In a general way, the fact should be emphasized that the behavior patterns characteristic of the different stages do not succeed each other in a linear way (those of a given stage disappearing at the time when those of the following one take form) but in the manner of the layers of a pyramid (upright, or upside down), the new behavior patterns simply being added to the old ones to complete, correct, or combine with them. (Piaget 1952c, p. 329)

The chronological ages during which children can be expected to develop behavior representative of a particular stage are not fixed. The age spans suggested by Piaget are normative and denote the times during which a typical or average child can be expected to display the intellectual behaviors that are characteristic of the particular level. The typical child enters preoperational development around age 2. Although some enter this level earlier—a very small percentage of 1-year-olds enter the preoperational level—other children do not enter the preoperational stage until age 3 or 4. With severely "retarded" or developmentally delayed children, development may be even slower.

The behaviors that are described for each aspect of development are only typical for the age groups. The norms established by Piaget are for samples of children in Geneva and do not necessarily hold rigidly for American or other samples. Piaget assumed that the fixed order of appearance (of structures of behavior) implies nothing concerning the experiential or hereditary basis for the order. The age at which particular developments occur can vary with an individual's experience and his or her hereditary potential (Piaget 1952c). Progress is not automatic (as in maturation theory).

One aspect of Piaget's theory is fixed: Every child *must* pass through the levels of cognitive development in the same order. A child cannot move intellectually from the preoperational level to formal operations without passing through concrete operations.[8]

Nevertheless, the rates at which children develop may not be identical because of experiential or hereditary factors. "Bright" children may develop rapidly; "dull" children may progress more slowly, some never reaching or completely acquiring concrete or formal operations.

Although a concept of levels or stages of intellectual development is used, it should be remembered that the range of intellectual behaviors within a particular level is large. That is, while the child develops the use of language during preoperational development (2-7 years), it is expected that language usage at age 7 will be qualitatively different than at age 2.

---

[8] The concept of a fixed sequence or order of levels or stages is called *ordinality*. Piaget's stages are ordinal stages.

In the early part of the preoperational development, language ability is formed and organized. Thus, the language behaviors of the 3-year-old typically lack the organization and stability of those of the 7-year-old, although they both demonstrate preoperational characteristics. Thus, early in the development of a particular intellectual function, it can be expected to have less stability and to be less sophisticated than behaviors in later periods.

FACTORS IN DEVELOPMENT

We have seen that mental development follows a fixed course along a continuum. From birth through adulthood, the structures of intelligence, schemata, are constantly developing as the child spontaneously acts on the environment and assimilates and accommodates to an increasing array of stimuli in the environment. For purposes of analysis, the continuum of development is divided into the four levels indicated earlier. The roles of active experience and equilibration as agents in development have been discussed in part. Before proceeding to a discussion of each level within the continuum, let us consider in some detail the four factors of development and the relationship of the four factors.

Piaget suggested four broad factors that are related to all cognitive development: maturation, active experience, social interaction, and a general progression of equilibrium (Piaget 1961). He viewed each of these factors and their interaction as necessary conditions for cognitive development, but none alone is sufficient to ensure cognitive development. Movement within and between stages of development is a function of these factors and their interaction.

Maturation and Heredity

Piaget believed that heredity plays a role in cognitive development, although heredity alone cannot account for intellectual development. He asserted that heredity sets broad limits for development at any point in time. Maturation, the (rate of) unfolding of inherited potential, is the mechanism through which these limits are established. Piaget states:

> [M]aturation as regards cognitive functions—knowledge—simply determines the range of possibilities at a specific stage. It does not cause the actualization of the structures. Maturation simply indicates whether or not the construction of specific structures is possible at a specific stage. It does not itself contain a preformed structure, but simply opens up possibilities. The new reality still has to be constructed. (quoted in Green, Ford, and Flamer 1971, p. 193)

Thus, maturation factors (or inherited factors) place *broad* constraints on cognitive development. These constraints change as maturation proceeds. Realization of the potential implied by these constraints at any point in development depends on a child's actions on his or her environment.

Active Experience

Earlier in this chapter we discussed the importance of children's actions on the environment. Active experience is one of the four factors in cognitive development. Each kind of knowledge a child constructs—physical knowledge, logical–mathematical knowledge, and social knowledge—requires him or her to interact with objects or people. Actions may be physical manipulations of objects or events or mental manipulations of objects or events (thinking). Active experiences are those that provoke assimilation and accommodation, resulting in cognitive change (change in structures or schemata).

Social Interaction

Another factor in cognitive development is social interaction. By social interaction, Piaget meant the interchange of ideas among people. This, as we have seen, is particularly important in the development of social knowledge. The concepts or schemata people develop can be classified as those that have sensorially available physical referents (they can be seen, heard, and so on) and those that do not have such referents. The concept *tree* has physical referents; the concept *honesty* does not. A child can develop a socially acceptable concept of *tree* (physical knowledge) relatively independent of others because referents (trees) are usually available. But the same child cannot develop an acceptable concept of *honesty* (social knowledge) independent of others. To the extent that concepts are "arbitrary," or socially defined, the child is dependent on social interaction for the construction and validation of concepts.

Interaction with others can also provoke disequilibration relative to physical and logical–mathematical knowledge. When children are in situations where their thinking conflicts with that of other children (or adults), the conflict can lead them to question their own thinking (disequilibrium). As we shall see later, conflicts in thought can result in disequilibration but do not automatically do so.

Social interaction can be of many kinds. One interacts with peers, parents, and other adults. The events that take place in the schoolroom are most often the interaction of students with other students and with their teachers. There is also the interaction with parents and others in the environment. All forms of social interaction and social experience are important in intellectual development.

Equilibration

Maturation, experience, and social interaction do not sufficiently explain cognitive development. Piaget's remaining factor is *equilibration.*

> It seems to me there are two reasons for having to call in this fourth factor (equilibration). The first is that since we already have three other factors, there must be some kind of coordination among them. This coordination is a kind of equilibration. Secondly, in . . . construction . . . a subject goes through much trial and error and many regulations that in large part involve

self-regulations. Self-regulations are the very nature of equilibration. (Piaget 1977b, p. 10)

In this way, Piaget used the concept of equilibration to explain the coordination of other factors and the regulation of development in general. As children have experiences, construction occurs. Coordination of existing knowledge with the new knowledge occurs (assimilation and accommodation). There is a general internal monitoring and regulating of this system. Equilibration is the regulator that allows new experience to be successfully incorporated into schemata.

The control of development is in large part internal and affective. Piaget viewed this as a self-regulatory process, with equilibration the mechanism for self-regulation.

Four factors are necessary for cognitive development: maturation, active experience, social interaction, and equilibration. Only with the interaction of the four factors are conditions for cognitive development sufficient.

Affective Development

In Piaget's theory, intellectual development is seen as having two components, one cognitive and the other affective.[9] So far, we have discussed primarily the cognitive aspects of development, which deal with how the structures of knowledge (schemata) develop.

Contiguous with cognitive development is affective development. Affect includes feelings, interests, desires, tendencies, values, and emotions in general. Piaget believed that affect develops.

With regard to intellectual development, we are concerned with two aspects of affect. One aspect is the motivation or energizing of intellectual activity. "For a structure of knowledge to function, something must turn it on, determine the effort to be expanded at each point, and turn it off" (Brown and Weiss 1987, p. 63). The second aspect is *selection*. Intellectual activity is always directed at particular objects or events. Why these in particular?

Interest, along with "likes" and "dislikes," is one common and powerful example of affect at work influencing our selection of intellectual activities. Many times when asked why we did a particular thing, the response has to do with interest. I read a book about building timber frame houses, and if I assimilate the content of the book into my schemata (instead of reading a book about the Civil War), I am developing further my schemata with regard to timber frame construction (but not with regard

---

[9] The relations between cognitive and affective development are complex and important and will be expanded on throughout this book. Until recently, psychologists and educators have focused primarily on Piaget's work on cognitive development and overlooked the role of affective development in intellectual growth. There are several reasons for this. One is that Piaget was primarily interested in determining what knowledge is and how it is constructed by children. Piaget focused most of his research, and writing on this question. Thus, many came to Piaget's work believing that the cognitive aspects of intelligence *must* be the most important. Piaget's earliest works speak to the major role of affect in intellectual development. Because this was less emphasized (in a quantitative sense), affect, until recently, has taken a back seat to cognition.

to the Civil War). In Piaget's view, this selection is not provoked by cognitive activities but by affect—in this case, interest.

Although we think about affect as being different from cognition, they are united in intellectual functioning. They are two sides of the same coin, so to speak (Cowan 1981). All behavior has both cognitive and affective elements. Piaget writes:

> It is impossible to find behavior arising from affectivity alone without any cognitive elements. It is equally impossible to find behavior composed only of cognitive elements. . . . [A]lthough cognitive and affective factors are indissociable in an individual behavior, they appear to be different in nature. . . . It is obvious that affective factors are involved even in the most abstract forms of intelligence. For a student to solve an algebra problem or a mathematician to discover a theorem, there must be intrinsic interest, extrinsic interest, or a need at the beginning. While working, states of pleasure, disappointment, eagerness, as well as feelings of fatigue, effort, boredom, etc. come into play. At the end of the work, feelings of success or failure may occur; and finally, the student may experience aesthetic feelings stemming from the coherence of his solution. (1981b, pp. 2–3)

Affect has a profound influence on intellectual development. Affect can speed up or slow down the rate of development. It determines what contents intellectual activity focuses on. Affect is the gatekeeper, so to speak. According to Piaget, affect *cannot* itself modify cognitive structures (schemata) although, as we have seen, it can influence which structure becomes modified. Piaget writes, "even if affectivity can cause behavior, even if it is constantly involved in the functioning of intelligence, and even if it can speed up or slow down intellectual development, it nevertheless does not, itself, generate structures of behavior and does not modify the structures in whose functioning it intervenes" (1981b, p. 6).

Many people believe that the affective aspects of human life arise from some internal source in a more or less predetermined form. Piaget believed that affect is no more preformed than is intelligence itself. In Piaget's view, there are remarkable parallels between the cognitive and affective. First, affect develops in the same sense that cognition or intelligence develops. When we examine children's reasoning about moral questions, one aspect of affective life, we see that children's moral concepts are constructed in the same sense that cognitive concepts are constructed. The preschool or early elementary child who is accidentally bumped by another child usually does not view the incident as an accident, largely because he or she has not yet constructed adequate concepts of intentionality. As the cognitive aspects of intelligence are developing, there is a parallel development of affect. The mechanisms for construction are the same. Children assimilate experience to affective schemata in the same way they assimilate experience to cognitive structures. The outcome is knowledge.

Piaget also argued that *all* behavior has both affective and cognitive aspects. There is no pure cognitive behavior and no pure affective behavior. The child who "likes" mathematics typically makes rapid progress. The child who "dislikes" mathematics typically does not make rapid progress. The cognitive behavior in each case is influenced by affect. "It is impossible to find behavior arising from affectivity alone without any cognitive element. It is equally impossible to find behavior composed only of cognitive elements" (1981b, p. 2).

SUMMARY

Piaget viewed intelligence as having an affective as well as a cognitive aspect. The cognitive aspect has three components: content, function, and structure. Piaget identified three kinds of knowledge: physical knowledge, logical–mathematical knowledge, and social knowledge. Physical knowledge is knowledge of properties of objects and is derived from actions on objects. Logical–mathematical knowledge is knowledge constructed from actions on objects. Social knowledge is knowledge about things created by cultures. Each kind of knowledge depends on actions, physical or mental. Actions instrumental in development are those that generate disequilibration and lead to efforts to establish equilibrium (equilibration). Assimilation and accommodation are the agents of equilibration, the self-regulator of development.

Four factors and their interaction are necessary for development: maturation, active experience, social interaction, and equilibration. Cognitive development, though a continuous process, can be divided into four stages for purposes of analysis and description. Affective development (values, feelings, and interests) evolves in a manner similar to cognitive development. That is, affective structures are constructed as cognitive structures are constructed. Affect is responsible for the activation of intellectual activity and for the selection of which objects or events are acted on. Affect is the gatekeeper.

chapter 3

Sensorimotor Development

$\mathbf{M}$ental development is a process that begins the day an infant is born (and possibly sooner). This does not mean that the child is born thinking (internally representing objects in the mind), but it does mean that the sensory and motor behaviors that occur from birth onward are the earliest aspects of intellectual development and necessary for, and instrumental in, later intellectual development. To look at it another way, intellectual behavior at any age evolves directly from prior levels of behavior. Assimilation and accommodation are fully functional at birth. Infants' adaptation to and organization of the world around them is initially through sensory and motor actions. Thus, the roots of all intellectual development are in early sensorimotor behavior.

In several of his books, Piaget carefully described cognitive and affective development during the first two years of life. From his observation and writings, it is clear that the structures of intelligence and feelings begin to evolve during infancy. At birth, an infant can perform only simple reflex behaviors. Two years after birth, the child is typically beginning to talk (symbolic representation) and has clearly evolved intellectual operations and is beginning to "think." Through internal representation, the 2-year-old typically can mentally "invent" means (behaviors) that permit him or her to do things (attain ends). The child can solve most sensorimotor problems; for example, he or she can get the objects wanted by using one object to retrieve another. At birth and for the first month of life, affect is seen only in undifferentiated reflex activity. Initially there are no true "feelings" or differentiated affective reactions. During sensorimotor development, feelings emerge and soon children's affective feelings can be seen to play a role in the selection of actions.

The 2-year-old is cognitively and affectively different from the newborn infant. At age 2, the typical child has a much larger and more sophisticated array of cognitive and affective schemata. The evolution that occurs is primarily a function of the child's sensorimotor actions on the environment, resulting in ongoing assimilation and

[handwritten margin note: ability to plan actions]

accommodation that in turn result in qualitative and quantitative changes in constructed schemata.

> The period that extends from birth to the acquisition of language is marked by an extraordinary development of the mind. Its importance is sometimes underestimated because it is not accompanied by words that permit a step-by-step pursuit of the progress of intelligence and the emotions, as is the case later on. This early mental development nonetheless determines the entire course of psychological evolution. . . . At the starting point of this development the neonate grasps everything to himself—or, in more precise terms, to his own body—whereas at the termination of the period, i.e., when language and thought begin, he is for all practical purposes but one element or entity among others in a universe that he has gradually constructed himself, and which hereafter he will experience as external to himself. (Piaget 1967, pp. 8–9)

To understand that the development of language in the 2-year-old is related to earlier sensorimotor development, the observer must carefully notice behavior during the first 2 years of life. The evolution that occurs is a remarkably smooth succession of periods, each incorporating the previous period, each marking a new advance as construction of schemata proceeds.

Piaget divided sensorimotor development into six periods in which progressively more complex patterns of intellectual behavior evolve (see Table 3.1). The remainder of this chapter presents aspects of the six periods of sensorimotor development. The general characteristics of each period are discussed. These include the progressive development of a child's *object* concept and his or her concept of *causality,* two of the most important indicators of intellectual and affective development during this stage.

What has previously been said about development applies equally well to the periods of development about to be discussed. As behaviors evolve that represent a more advanced level, the behaviors of previous developments are not totally displaced. Old, less sophisticated behaviors still occur. Regarding new stages, Piaget wrote:

> The new stage would thus be defined by the fact that the child becomes capable of certain behavior patterns of which he was up to then incapable; it is not the fact that he renounces the behavior patterns of the preceding stages, even if they are contrary to the new ones or contradictory to them from the observer's point of view. (Piaget 1964, p. 299)

PERIOD 1 (0–1 MONTH): REFLEX ACTIVITY

Beginning at birth and throughout most of the first period of sensorimotor development, the behavior of a typical infant is largely reflexive and undifferentiated. The basic reflexes that the infant is born with are sucking, grasping, crying, and move-

TABLE 3.1 Characteristics of development during sensorimotor development

Period	General	Object Concept	Space	Causality	Affect
1 Reflex, 0–1mo.	Reflex activity	No differentiation of self from other objects	Egocentric	Egocentric	Instinctual drives and inborn affective reactions
2 First differentiations, 1–4 mos.	Hand-mouth coordination; differentiation via sucking, grasping	No special behavior re vanished objects; no differentiation of movement of self and external objects	Changes in perspective seen as changes in objects	No differentiation of movement of self and external objects	First acquired feelings (joy, sorrow, pleasantness, unpleasantness). Feelings of contentment and disappointment linked to action
3 Reproduction, 4–8 mos.	Eye-hand coordination; reproduction of interesting events	Anticipates positions of moving objects	Space externalized; no spatial relationships of objects	Self seen as cause of all events	
4 Coordination of schemata, 8–12 mos.	Coordination of schemata; application of known means to new problems; anticipation	Object permanence; searches for vanished objects; reverses bottle to get nipple	Perceptual constancy of size and shape of objects	Elementary externalization of causality	Affect involved in activation and retardation or intentional actions. First feelings of success or failure.
5 Experimentation, 12–18 mos.	Discovery of new means through experimentation	Considers sequential displacements while searching for vanished objects	Aware of relationships between objects in space, between objects and self	Self seen as object among objects and self as object of actions	Investment of affection in others
6 Representation, 18–24 mos.	Representation; invention of new means via internal combinations	Images of absent objects, representation of displacements	Aware of movements not perceived; representation of spatial relationships	Representative causality; causes and effects inferred	

SOURCE: Adapted from Wadsworth 1979; Piaget 1981b.

no differentiation

ment of the arms, trunk, and head. When an infant is stimulated, his reflexes respond. Thus, when an object is put in the infant's mouth, he sucks on it, regardless of what it is. When an object contacts the palm of the infant's hand, he grasps it, regardless of what it is. There is no evidence that the infant, behaving so, can differentiate between objects. That is, there is no evidence in behavior that schemata for objects are yet constructed. The infant's reflex responses are more or less the same to all objects. A blanket is sucked on as vigorously as a milk-producing nipple. The hand grasps what comes into it, be it someone's finger or a toy. No distinction is made between stimuli. Thus, during this period, the infant assimilates all stimuli through the reflex systems. At birth, all stimulus events are incorporated (assimilated) into primitive reflexive schemata in an undifferentiated manner.

Within a few weeks of birth, initial accommodations on the part of the child are usually observable. At birth, the infant sucks on what is placed in his mouth. A nipple is sucked on when presented. Soon the infant begins to search for the nipple if he cannot find it—in effect, accommodating to the environment. The infant's searching is a behavior that was not present at birth and cannot be attributed to any reflex system. There is no "searching" reflex; there is only a sucking reflex. Thus, the active searching is a change in reflex behavior on the part of the infant—an accommodation.

The innate, reflex acts observable during the first period undergo modification as a result of their repetitive use and interaction with the environment. Although the young infant seems only to be exercising his reflexes when behaving and no intellectual behaviors are observable, the *use* of the reflexes is essential for development during the stage and for the development of cognitive structures that follow. From the beginning, acts of assimilation and accommodation are present.

Object Concept

One of Piaget's important beliefs was that all concepts, including the object concept, are developed and are not innate. That is, the awareness that objects are more or less permanent and are not destroyed when they disappear is not an inherited or wired-in characteristic. This awareness of objects is developed out of sensorimotor experiences little by little (Piaget 1954). In effect, a child must construct the universe of objects through experiences. At birth, an infant has no awareness of objects other than on a reflexive level. Indeed, the infant is unable to differentiate between the self and the environment. The infant has no concept of objects. Any object presented by the external environment is merely something to suck, to grasp, or to look at—something that evokes an undifferentiated reflexive response.

Concept of Causality

Causality, an awareness of cause-and-effect relationships, is another important concept that emerges during sensorimotor development. At birth, the child is totally egocentric[1] and is not aware of causality at all. Not until later does awareness of causality begin to evolve.

Affect

This first period is one of reflexes and instinctual drives (Piaget 1981b). Newborns seek nourishment and relief from discomfort, with their reflexes determining behavior. They suck and they cry. During this period, there are no "feelings" as such. All affect is associated with reflexes.

PERIOD 2 (1–4 MONTHS): FIRST DIFFERENTIATIONS

The second period of sensorimotor development begins when the reflexive behaviors of the previous period start to be modified. During this period, several new behaviors appear. Thumb-sucking often becomes habitual and reflects the development of some hand–mouth coordination, moving objects are followed with the eyes (eye coordination), and the head is moved in the direction of sounds (eye–ear coordination).

Early in Period 1, an infant's responses to stimuli are purely reflexive. No differentiation is initially made between stimuli. Toward the end of Period 1, an infant begins to distinguish between objects, a behavior not present at birth. For example, the infant actively sucks on a milk-producing nipple (when hungry), but rejects other objects placed in her mouth if she wants milk. A reflex has been modified, indicating that the infant has made an accommodation to the environment. Where a primitive sucking schema that did not permit differentiation existed, a more sophisticated schema permitting differentiation now exists. Changes in behavior such as this are the first observable, if primitive, signs of the internal organization of and adaptation to the environment.

Habitual thumb-sucking is a behavior typically acquired during this period (Piaget 1952c). This new behavior requires hand–mouth coordination, an ability that the infant does not have during the first month. Before this time, thumb-sucking that occurs is usually a random or chance occurrence; the thumb happens to get into the mouth. Habituation of the activity cannot be explained by reflexes alone. It can be explained only by a child's construction of elementary sensorimotor relationships from his or her actions.

Piaget illustrates the transition from random to clearly coordinated thumb-sucking:

---

[1] *Egocentrism* is one of Piaget's most important concepts. In general, it is the cognitive state in which the individual sees the world only from his or her point of view, without being aware that other points of view exist. Thus it is a state that the egocentric cannot be aware of. For the infant, egocentrism means an absence of self-perception, of the self as an object in a world of objects. This is overcome only when the infant's concept of object develops and subsequently permits the development of self-perception.

Observation 19. At 0;1(4)[2] after the 6 PM meal Laurent is wide awake (as was not the case at the preceding meals) and not completely satisfied. First he makes vigorous sucking-like movements, then his right hand may be seen approaching his mouth, touching his lower lip and finally being grasped. But as only the index finger was grasped, the hand fell out again. Shortly afterward it returned. This time the thumb was in the mouth while the index finger was placed between the gums and the upper lip. The hand then moves 5 cm. away from the mouth only to reenter it; now the thumb is grasped and the other fingers remain outside. Laurent then is motionless and sucks vigorously, drooling so much that after a few moments he is removed. A fourth time the hand approaches and three fingers enter the mouth. The hand leaves again and reenters a fifth time. As the thumb has again been grasped, sucking is resumed. I then remove the hand and place it near his waist. Laurent seems to give up sucking and gazes ahead, contented and satisfied. But after a few minutes the lips move and the hand approaches them again. This time there is a series of setbacks; the fingers are placed on the chin and lower lip. The index finger enters the mouth twice (consequently the sixth and seventh time this has succeeded). The eighth time the hand enters the mouth, the thumb alone is retained and sucking continues. I again remove the hand. Again lip movements cease, new attempts ensue, success results for the ninth and tenth time, after which the experiment is interrupted. (1952c, p. 53)

Laurent's thumb-sucking is rapidly becoming habitual. Because it is directed by the child, the behavior is different from all reflex behavior at birth. Such coordination implies an accommodation on the part of the child.

On the matter of thumb-sucking, Piaget wrote:

When the child systematically sucks his thumb, no longer due to chance contacts but through coordination between hand and mouth, this may be called acquired accommodation. Neither the reflexes of the mouth nor of the hand can be provided such coordination by heredity (there is no instinct to suck the thumb!) and experience alone explains its formation. (1952c, p. 48)

During the second period, coordinations develop in the use of the eyes. The child begins to follow moving objects with his or her eyes. Piaget provided an example:

---

[2] "0;1(4)." Designations such as this refer to the age of the child at the time of the observation, with years, months, and days given, in that order. Laurent was 1 month, 4 days old at the time of observation. This quote illustrates Piaget's systematic observational method and the way in which he made sense of his observations.

Observation 28.—Jacqueline at 0;0(16) does not follow with her eyes the flame of a match 20 cm. away. Only her expression changes at the sight of it and then she moves her head as though to find the light again. She does not succeed despite the dim light in the room. At 0;0(24), on the other hand, she follows the match perfectly under the same conditions. The subsequent days her eyes follow the movements of my hand, a moving handkerchief, etc. (1952c, p. 63)

The ability to visually follow moving objects is not present at birth. As can be seen in Jacqueline's case, this ability is acquired.

Coordination between hearing and vision begins to develop at this time. Discriminations between sounds also begin to occur. This is evident when children begin to move their heads in the direction of sounds and when faces of people are clearly associated with sounds by the same person.

Observation 48.—From 0;1(26), on the other hand, Laurent turns to the right direction as soon as he hears my voice (even if he has not seen me just before) and seems satisfied when he has discovered my face even when it is immobile. At 0;1(27) he looks successively at his father, his mother, and again at his father after hearing my voice. It therefore seems that he ascribes this voice to a visually familiar face. At 0;2(14) he observes Jacqueline at 1.90 to 2 meters, at the sound of her voice; same observation at 0;2(21). At 0;3(1) I squat before him while he is in his mother's arms and I make the sound *bzz* (which he likes). He looks to his left, then to his right, then ahead, then below him; then he catches sight of my hair and lowers his eyes until he sees my motionless face. Finally he smiles. This last observation may be considered as definitely indicating identification of the voice and visual image of the person. (1952c, pp. 82–83)

These examples illustrate some of the cognitive differences between a typical child during the first two periods. The younger child makes undifferentiated reflex responses to stimuli. The older child makes primitive sensorimotor differentiations and, we infer, has constructed limited sensorimotor coordinations. This development of schemata comes about as the infant acts using his reflexes, assimilating and accommodating experience.

Object Concept

During the second period of sensorimotor development, the child evokes an awareness of objects that was not present during the first period. The child tries to look at the objects she hears, indicating a coordination between vision and hearing. In addition, the child may continue to follow the path of an object with her eyes after it has disappeared from view. The following example from Piaget illustrates acquired visual following:

Thus, Lucienne, at 0;3(9), sees me at the extreme left of her visual field and smiles vaguely. She looks in different directions, in front of her and to the right, but constantly returns to the place in which she sees me and dwells on it every time for a moment. . . .

At 0;4(26) she takes the breast but turns when I call her and smiles at me. Then she resumes nursing but several times in succession, despite my silence, she turns directly to the position from which she can see me. She does it again after a pause of a few minutes. Then I withdraw; when she turns without finding me her expression is one of mingled disappointment and expectation. (Piaget 1954, pp. 10–11)

Lucienne (one of Piaget's daughters) demonstrates clearly that she has coordination between hearing and vision. She locates visually the source of sounds. In addition, she is able to return and visually locate objects that have left her field of vision.

Intentionality

A number of new sensorimotor coordinations develop in Period 2. An infant's range of responses increases. Although advances have been made, a child's behavior still lacks *intention* in the sense that he or she initiates behaviors directed at certain ends. Behaviors are still primarily reflexive (though modified) and goals are set off only *after* behavior sequences are begun.

As long as action is entirely determined by directly perceived sensorial images, there can be no question of intention. Even when the child grasps an object in order to look at it, one cannot infer that there is a conscious purpose. It is with the appearance of . . . deferred reactions that the purpose of the action, ceasing to be in some way directly perceived, presupposes a continuity in searching, and consequently a beginning of intention. (Piaget 1952c, p. 143)

Intentionality of behavior can be inferred only when the initiation of behaviors is not a reflex act or a simple repetition of preceding behavior.

Thus, the initial steps in intellectual development have begun. The child's actions in the environment, resulting in assimilations and accommodations, have produced initial structural changes permitting simple sensorimotor coordinations. In the next period, these advances are elaborated and surpassed through the same processes.

Affect: Acquired Feelings

According to Piaget, two kinds of feelings make their appearance during this period and the next.

To begin with, *perceptual affects* make their appearance. These are feelings such as pleasure, pain, pleasantness, unpleasantness, etc., that have become attached to perceptions through experience. The second development is the differentiation of needs and interests. This has to do with *feelings* of contentment, disappointment, and all gradations in between that are not just tied to various perceptions but that are *associated with action as a whole.* (Piaget 1981b, p. 21)

General states of global tension and relaxation are observed during these periods.

During the second period of sensorimotor development, affect remains totally invested in one's own activities and body. In Piaget's view, the reason that affect is not yet "transferred" to others is that the infant, at this point in development, has not yet differentiated the self as an object from other objects in the environment. The self and the environment are still one. Thus the infant's body continues to remain the focus of all activity and affect.

PERIOD 3 (4–8 MONTHS): REPRODUCTION OF INTERESTING EVENTS

During Period 3, the child's behaviors become increasingly oriented toward objects and events beyond his or her own body. For example, a child grasps and manipulates objects she can reach, signifying coordination between vision and tactile senses. Before this time, the infant's behavior has been oriented primarily toward herself. She has been unable to effectively distinguish herself from other objects on a sensorimotor level. She has been unable to coordinate the movement of her hands with her eyes.

Another characteristic of the third period is that infants reproduce events that occur that interest them. When interesting experiences occur, they try to repeat them. A cord attached to overhead bells is pulled repeatedly. Grasping and striking acts are repeated intentionally. There are clear attempts to sustain and repeat acts. Piaget referred to these phenomena as *circular reactions*[3] or *reproductive assimilation.* The infant tries to reproduce events that interest him or her. To illustrate:

> Observation 104.—At 0;3(29) Laurent grasps a paper knife which he sees for the first time; he looks at it a moment and then swings it while holding it

---

[3] Piaget used the term *circular reactions* to describe the young child's attempts to repeat interesting events. The repetition of events is felt to be important for several reasons. It is clearly an active attempt to assimilate experience. Circular reactions lead to a greater awareness of objects as objects and to a greater understanding of cause and effect. Three kinds of circular reactions are described by Piaget (1967, 1969). *Primary circular reactions,* appearing in sensorimotor Period 2, involve actions that involve only the infant's body, such as moving a hand from side to side. *Secondary circular reactions* arise in Period 3 and are actions involving objects beyond the infant, such as repeatedly hitting the side of the crib with an object. *Tertiary circular reactions* arise in Period 5 and are characterized by intentional variations in the repetitions to see what effects similar actions have. For example, the infant might hit different parts of the crib with an object.

in his right hand. During these movements the object happens to rub against the wicker of the bassinet. Laurent then waves his arms vigorously and obviously tries to reproduce the sound he has heard, but without understanding the necessity of contact between the paper and the wicker and, consequently, without achieving this contact otherwise than by chance.

At 0;4(3) same reactions, but Laurent looks at the object at the time when it happens to rub against the wicker of the bassinet. The same still occurs at 0;4(5) but there is slight progress towards systemization.

Finally at 0;4(6) the movement becomes intentional; as soon as the child has the object in his hand he rubs it with regularity against the wicker of the bassinet. (Piaget 1952c, pp. 168–69)

When a child successfully repeats previous behaviors, as Laurent did in the example, primitive sensorimotor intentionality is evident. These *circular reactions* are clear examples of active interactions with the environment. They are a form of assimilation that represents an advance over earlier assimilation.

Intentionality

One characteristic of sensorimotor development is the child's progress from nonintentional behavior to a form of intentional behavior. During the second period of sensorimotor development, intentional behavior is not evident. At that time, behavior is elicited by stimulation. Actions are not designed to attain a goal or object. During Period 3, a child begins to engage in the earliest constructed form of goal-directed (intentional) behavior. He or she tries to repeat unusual and interesting events (circular reactions). In Period 3, goals are established only *after* behaviors have begun. The infant's goals become established only during the repetitions of behaviors; consequently, the intentionality (goal direction) is after the fact, so to speak—after behavior has begun. In later sensorimotor periods (Period 4), the infant *initiates* a behavior sequence with a goal to be attained already in mind and selects means he or she thinks will attain the goal. Intentionality is present at the beginning of the sequence, and thus the behavior is not a mere repetition of a previous behavior but, from the beginning, an intentional act. Although behavior in Period 3 is for the first time intentional, it is not intentional until after behavior sequences have begun.

Object Concept

During Period 3, a child begins to anticipate the positions that objects will pass through while they are moving. This indicates development of the child's awareness of the permanence of objects. To illustrate:

Observation 6.—Laurent's reaction to falling objects still seems to be nonexistent at 0;5(24): he does not follow with his eyes any of the objects which I drop in front of him.

[handwritten margin notes: "wants it repeated", "Does something accidentally,"]

At 0;5(30) no reaction to the fall of a box of matches. The same is true at 0;6(0), but when he drops the box himself he searches for it next to him with his eyes (he is lying down).

At 0;6(7) he holds an empty match box in his hand. When it falls his eyes search for it even if they have not followed the beginning of the fall; he turns his head in order to see it on the sheet. Same reaction at 0;6(9) with a rattle.

At 0;7(29) he searches on the floor for everything I drop above him, if he has in the least perceived the beginning of the movement of falling. (Piaget 1954, pp. 14–15)

In the example, by 8 months of age Laurent is looking for objects in places where he predicts they have fallen. He is anticipating the positions falling objects will assume, demonstrating an increasingly sophisticated schema of objects.

Concept of Causality

During Period 3, a child remains egocentric. The child sees himself or herself as the primary cause of all activity. The following example illustrates the child's egocentric awareness of causality during Period 3.

At 0;7(8) Laurent is seated and I place a large cushion within his reach. I scratch the cushion. He laughs. Afterward I move my hand five cm. from the cushion, between it and his own hands, in such a way that if he pushed it slightly it would press against the cushion. As soon as I pause, Laurent strikes the cushion, arches, swings his head, etc. True, subsequently he does sometimes grasp my hand. But it is only in order to strike it, shake it, etc., and he does not once try to move it forward or put it in contact with the cushion.

At a certain moment he scratches my hand; on the other hand, he does not scratch the cushion although this behavior is familiar to him. (1954, p. 245)

Clearly, Laurent believes he alone can cause events. He is not aware that his father's hand is causing the interesting sound when it is in contact with the cushion. He shakes his father's hand to make the sound; he scratches the hand. He acts on the hand and on the cushion, but never on the two together. The child at this period sees himself as the cause of all events.

PERIOD 4 (8–12 MONTHS): COORDINATION OF SCHEMATA

Toward the end of the first year of life, typically, behavior patterns emerge that constitute clear acts of intelligence. The infant begins to use means to attain ends. "The child has the ability to combine behaviors he previously acquired in order to achieve goals" (Piaget 1952c). The child begins to anticipate events, demonstrating rudimentary planning. Objects take on a noticeable measure of permanence for the child. For example, she begins to search for objects that she sees disappear. Also, she comes to see that other objects in the environment can be sources of activity (causality).

Before this period, behavior has always been a direct action of the child on objects. Interesting acts are prolonged or repeated. That is, a single schema had been used to evoke a behavioral response. During Period 4, the child begins to differentiate ends and means and coordinate two familiar schemata in generating a single act; she begins to use means to attain ends that are not immediately attainable in a direct way. Children can be seen to set aside one object (means) to get to another object (end). The child moves a pillow out of the way to reach a toy. There is an *intentional* selection of means before the initiation of behavior. The end is established from the beginning; the means are used precisely in order to reach the end. The following illustrates the means-ends coordination that develops:

> Observation 121.—At 0;8(20) Jacqueline tries to grasp a cigarette case which I present to her. I then slide it between the crossed strings which attach her dolls to the hood (of her bassinet). She tries to reach it directly. Not succeeding, she immediately looks for the strings which are not in her hands and of which she only saw the part in which the cigarette case is entangled. She looks in front of her, grasps the strings, pulls and shakes them, etc. The cigarette case then falls and she grasps it.
>
> Second experiment: same reaction, but without first trying to grasp the object directly. (Piaget 1952c, p. 215)

In the example, Jacqueline pulls the strings (means) to attain the cigarette case (end). Clearly this is an intentional act from the outset. Means and ends (two schemata) are coordinated in one action.

During Period 4, the infant shows clear signs of event anticipation. Certain signs are recognized as being associated with certain actions that follow the signs. These actions illustrate prevision and the meaning of certain events.

> Observation 132.—At 0;8(6) Laurent recognizes by a certain noise caused by air that he is nearing the end of his feeding and, instead of insisting on drinking to the last drop, he rejects his bottle.
>
> Observation 133.—At 0;9(15) Jacqueline wails or cries when she sees the person seated next to her get up or move away a little (giving the impression of leaving).
>
> At 1;1(10) she has a slight scratch which is disinfected with alcohol. She cries, chiefly from fear. Subsequently, as soon as she sees the bottle of alcohol she recommences to cry, knowing what is in store for her. Two days later, same reaction, as soon as she sees the bottle and even before it is opened. (1952c, pp. 248–49)

Such behavior clearly demonstrates anticipation or prevision on the part of the child. An action is anticipated that is independent of the action in progress. During preceding periods, actions of the child were *always* dependent on the immediate actions in the environment. Jacqueline would cry *when* alcohol was put on a cut, not *before* it was put on.

Object Concept

An important construction during this period is the concept of the constancies of shape and size of objects. Piaget and Inhelder comment:

> In fact, the *constancy of shapes* results from their sensorimotor construction at the time of the coordination of perspectives. During the first period [periods 1–3 here] . . . when objects change their perspective such alterations are perceived (by the child) not as changes in the point of view of the subject relative to the object, but as actual transformations of the objects themselves. The baby waggling his head before a hanging object behaves as if he acted upon it by jerking about, and it is not until the age of about 8–9 months that he really explores the perspective effects of actual displacements. Now it is just about this age (8–9 mos.) that he is first able . . . to reverse a feeding bottle presented to him wrong way round. That is, to attribute a fixed shape to a permanent solid.
>
> As for *size constancy* it is linked with the coordination of perceptually controlled movements. All through the first period [periods 1–3 here] the child makes no distinction between movements of the object and those of his body. In the course of the second period [periods 3 and 4 here] the subject begins to distinguish his own movements from those of the object. Here is found the beginning . . . of searching for objects when they disappear. It is in terms of this grouping of movements, and the permanence attributed to the object, that the latter acquires fixed dimensions and its size is estimated more or less correctly, regardless of whether it is near or distant. (Piaget and Inhelder 1956, p. 11)

As with other concepts, those of size and shape develop in the expected manner. To the 4-month-old child, different perspectives on objects appear to change the shape and size of the objects. Not until Period 4 do shape and size of objects begin to be stabilized concepts for the child.

During Period 4, a new dimension in the object concept of the child appears. Until this time, if an object the child has been playing with, such as a rattle, is placed under a blanket while the child is looking on, the child does not search for it. If an object is out of sight, it appears no longer to exist. Between the ages of 8 and 10 months (approximately), the child begins to search for objects that disappear, indicating that the child is aware that the objects exist even when they cannot be seen. The rattle hidden under the blanket is retrieved. The following illustrates this new awareness of object permanence and some of its limitations:

Observation 40.—At 0;10(18) Jacqueline is seated on a mattress without anything to disturb or distract her (no coverlets, etc.). I take her parrot from her hands and hide it twice in succession under the mattress, on her left, in *A*. Both times Jacqueline looks for the object immediately and grabs it. Then I take it from her hands and move it very slowly before her eyes to the corresponding place on her right, under the mattress, in *B* (sequential displacement). Jacqueline watches this movement very attentively, but at the moment when the parrot disappears in *B,* she turns to her left and looks where it was before, in *A*.

During the next four attempts I hide the parrot in *B* every time without having first placed it in *A*. Each time Jacqueline watches me attentively. Nevertheless each time she immediately tries to rediscover the object in *A;* she turns the mattress over and examines it conscientiously. (Piaget 1954, p. 51)

Clearly, Jacqueline searches for objects that disappear. To do this she must have a concept that objects still exist after they disappear from view. But her searches are limited; she searches for objects only where they usually disappear, not always where they are viewed to disappear.

Concept of Causality

During Period 4, the child for the first time shows awareness that objects (besides himself) can cause activity. Until this time, the child typically considered his own actions as the cause of all things. The following illustrates this change in the concept of causality:

At 0;8(7) [Laurent] . . .A moment later I lower my hand very slowly, starting very high up and directing it toward his feet, finally tickling him for a moment. He bursts out laughing. When I stop midway, he grasps my hand or arm and pushes it toward his feet.

At 0;9(0) he grasps my hand and places it against his belly which I have just tickled.

At 0;9(13) Laurent is in his baby swing which I shake three or four times by pulling a cord; he grasps my hand and presses it against the cord. (Piaget 1954, p. 26)

Piaget commented:

[T]he cause of a certain phenomenon is no longer identified by the child with the feeling he has of acting upon this phenomenon. The subject begins to discover that a spatial contact exists between cause and effect and so any object at all can be a source of activity (and not only his own body). (1952c, p. 212)

For the first time, there is an elementary externalization of causality. The child is aware that objects other than the self can be the causes of actions.

Affect

During the second year of life, three affective developments are noteworthy. The first is that feelings begin to play a role in determining means used to achieve goals as well as in selecting goals. Things that are useful in attaining goals come to have value to the child.

Second, children begin to experience "success" and "failure" from an affective point of view. Feelings associated with particular actions or activities are preserved (remembered). Children are attracted to activities at which they are successful.

> In learning to walk, for example, previous success or failure can be seen to influence the interest and endeavor. This clearly indicates that some sort of self-estimation is taking place. (Piaget 1981b, p. 32)

Third, in Periods 5 and 6, children begin to invest affectivity in (transfer affect to) others. Until this time, feelings have revolved around the self. With the cognitive differentiation of the self from other objects (object concept), feelings such as liking and disliking begin to be directed toward other people as objects. The investment of affect in others is the first clear "social" development.

PERIOD 5 (12–18 MONTHS): INVENTION OF NEW MEANS

In previous periods, a child developed coordination between schemata for vision and touch that permitted him or her to prolong and repeat unusual events (Period 3) and subsequently become able to coordinate familiar schemata in solving new problems (Period 4). In Period 5, the child attains a higher level of operation when he or she begins to form new schemata to solve new problems. The child develops new means to ends through experimentation rather than through the application of habitual, previously formed schemata. In this case, both new schemata and new coordinations are present. When confronted with a problem not solvable by the use of available schemata, the child can be seen to experiment and, through a trial-and-error process, to invent new means (schemata). This appears in several examples:

> Observation 167.—At 1;3(12) Jacqueline throws a plush dog outside the bars of her playpen and she tries to catch it. Not succeeding, she then pushes the pen itself in the right direction! By holding onto the frame with one hand while with the other she tried to grasp the dog, she observed that the frame was mobile. She had accordingly, without wishing to do so, moved it away from the dog. She at once tried to correct this movement and thus saw the pen approach its objective. These two fortuitous discover-

ies then led her to utilize movements of the playpen and to push it at first experimentally, then systematically. There was a moment's groping, but it was short.

At 1;3(16), on the other hand, Jacqueline right away pushes her playpen in the direction of the objects to be picked up. (Piaget 1952c, p. 315)

In the example, Jacqueline experiments with playpen moving. The utility of this behavior evolves after much trial-and-error experimentation. With experience, a new schema is developed (playpen moving) and results in the solution of a problem previously unsolvable to the child.

In the first half of the second year, the child spends much time experimenting with objects, as in the example above. In the bathtub, objects are repeatedly pushed under water; things are splashed. The child typically is very intent on seeing how objects behave in new situations. For the first time, the child is able to adapt (accommodate) to unfamiliar situations by finding new means.

In terms of intellectual development, these new behaviors are particularly important. Piaget suggested that behavior becomes intelligent when the child acquires the ability to solve new problems. Problem-solving abilities are clearly adaptive.

[I]t can be said that the mechanism of empirical intelligence has been definitely formed. The child is henceforth capable of resolving new problems, even if no acquired (currently available) schema is directly utilizable for this purpose, and if the solution of these problems has not yet been found by deduction or representation, it is insured in principle in all cases due to the combined working of experimental search and the coordination of schemata. (1952c, p. 265)

The child has reached a significant period in cognitive development when he or she becomes able to solve new sensorimotor problems. It marks the beginning of truly intelligent behavior, the development of which can be traced back to the reflex activities of the young infant.

Object Concept

As we have seen, around age 12 months, a child's behavior indicates an awareness that objects continue to exist even though they cannot be seen. Before Period 4, the child did not search for desired objects that were hidden, even though he or she viewed the disappearance. The rattle hidden under the blanket was not retrieved. In Period 4 (8–12 months), the child searches for objects that are hidden, but not always in the place where they were seen to be hidden. In this case, the child was said to be unable to handle *sequential displacements;* that is, if the rattle that is usually hidden in place *A* now is hidden in place *B*, the child searches for it in place *A*. In Period 5, the child typically accounts for sequential displacements; he or she searches for objects in the position resulting from the last visible displacement, not where it is usually hidden. When the rattle is hidden in *A,* it is searched for in *A;* when it is hidden in *B,* it is searched for in *B.*

Still, the object concept is not yet fully developed. The child during Period 5 typically is able to follow displacements if they are visible, but is unable to follow *invisible displacements.* The following illustrates this case:

> Observation 56.—[A]t 1;6(9), I resume the experiment but with a celluloid fish containing a rattle. I put the fish in the box under the rug. There I shake it and Jacqueline hears the fish in the box. I turn the box upside down and bring it out empty. Jacqueline immediately takes possession of the box, searches for the fish, turns the box over in all directions, looks around her, in particular looks at the rug but does not raise it.
>
> The next attempts yield nothing further. . . .
>
> That evening I repeat the experiment with a little lamb. Jacqueline herself puts the lamb in the box and when the whole thing is under the coverlet she says with me, "Coucou, lamb." When I take out the empty box she says, "Lamb, Lamb," but does not look under the coverlet.
>
> Whenever I leave the whole thing under the coverlet she immediately searches for the box and brings out the lamb. But when I start again, using the first technique, she no longer looks under the coverlet! (Piaget 1954, p. 69)

Although the abilities developed during Period 5 permit Jacqueline to solve problems involving visible sequential displacements, she cannot yet solve those involving invisible displacements. This ability will not come about until she develops mental or internal representation of objects (Period 6).

Concept of Causality

In the previous period, the typical child demonstrated an awareness that other objects beyond the self can be a source of actions (causality). The following illustrates the elaboration of the concept of causality in Period 5.

> At 1;3(30) Jacqueline holds in her right hand a box she cannot open. She holds it out to her mother, who pretends not to notice. Then she transfers the box from her right hand to her left, with her free hand grasps her mother's hand, opens it, and puts the box in it. The whole thing has occurred without a sound. . . .
>
> So also, during the next days, Jacqueline makes the adult intervene in the particulars of her game, whenever an object is too remote, etc.: she calls, cries, points to objects with her fingers, etc. In short, she well knows that she depends on the adult for satisfaction; the person of someone else becomes her best procedure for realization. (1954, p. 275)

Not only does Jacqueline demonstrate an awareness that other people can effect activity, but also that other objects can. The following illustration shows this clearly:

> Observation 175.—At 1;2(30) Jacqueline is standing in a room which is not hers and examines the green wallpaper. Then she touches it gently and at once looks at her fingertips. This is evidently the generalization of schemata . . . touching food (jams, etc.) and looking at her fingers. . . .
>
> At 1;3(12) she is standing in her playpen and I place a clown, which she recently received, on the top of the frame, in different places in sequence. Jacqueline advances laboriously along the frame but, when she arrives in front of the clown, she grasps it very cautiously and delicately, knowing that it will fall at the slightest shake. She behaved in this way ever since the first attempt. . . . Jacqueline foresees certain properties of the object which are independent of its action with respect to herself. The green wallpaper is conceived as though it ought to leave colored traces, . . . and the clown as falling down at the first touch. (Piaget 1952c, pp. 327–28)

In these examples, Jacqueline clearly sees objects (wallpaper, clown) as the causes of possible phenomena that are external to her actions. Prevision is seen that is *not* based on sequences of actions already observed in the same form (the wallpaper and doll are new to Jacqueline). Thus objects beyond the self are for the first time seen as causes of actions.

PERIOD 6 (18–24 MONTHS): REPRESENTATION

During Period 6, a child begins the transition between the sensorimotor level of intelligence to representational intelligence. That is, the child becomes able to internally (mentally) represent objects and events and subsequently becomes able to solve problems through internal representation. In Period 5, new means for solutions to problems were attained through active experimentation. In Period 6, the child develops new means also, but there is not the same reliance on motor and sensory experimentation as in the previous stage. For the first time, invention of means is arrived at by trying out action sequences at the representational level in the head (thinking) rather than in active experimentation. In effect, the experimentation is done in thought (through representation of actions) rather than through physical movement or actions. The following illustrates Period 6 invention of means, through representation and mental activity:

> Observation 181.—At 1;6(23) for the first time Lucienne plays with a doll carriage whose handle comes to the height of her face. She rolls it over the carpet by pushing it. When she comes against a wall, she pulls, walking backward. But as this position is not convenient for her, she pauses and without hesitation, goes to the other side to push the carriage again. She

therefore found the procedure in one attempt, apparently through analogy to other situations but without training, apprenticeship, or chance.

In the same kind of inventions, that is to say, in the realm of kinematic[5] representation, the following fact should be cited. At 1;10(27) Lucienne tries to kneel before a stool, but, by leaning against it, pushes it further away. She then raises herself up, takes it and places it against a sofa. When it is firmly set there she leans against it and kneels without difficulty. (1952c, p. 338)

Lucienne, in these examples, demonstrates the sudden invention of a solution to sensorimotor problems along with an awareness of causality. This kind of invention and the lack of overt experimentation suggests that the solutions are arrived at internally through mental combinations, independent of immediate experiences. Trial and error experimentation is not present.

> [I]nstead of being controlled at each of these stages and *a posteriori* by the facts themselves, the searching is controlled *a priori* by mental combination. Before trying them, the child foresees which maneuvers will fail and which will succeed. . . . Moreover, the procedure conceived as being capable of succeeding is in itself new, that is to say, it results from an original mental combination and not from a combination of movements actually executed at each stage of the operation. (1952c, pp. 340–41)

Thus a child becomes able to construct possible solutions to problems mentally by carrying out action sequences in his or her head (in representations). For about two years, this ability has been gradually evolving from sensorimotor behaviors. At this stage, the child can arrive at solutions to simple motor problems without the aid of sensorimotor experimentation or the assistance of concurrent experiences.

Object Concept

The ability of the Period 6 child to represent events internally is reflected in the child's object concept. Representation allows the child to find objects that are hidden by invisible displacement. That is, not only can the child find objects when they are visibly hidden, but representation of possibilities permits the child to search for and find objects that he or she does not see hidden. This amounts to a measure of liberation from immediate perceptions. The child knows that objects are permanent and that they continue to exist even when they are not visible. The following observation of Jacqueline demonstrates this awareness:

> Observation 64.—At 1;7(20) Jacqueline watches me when I put a coin in my hand, then put my hand under a coverlet. I withdraw my hand closed;

---

5 *Kinematics:* the science of motions considered apart from their causes and as applied to mechanical contrivances.

Jacqueline opens it, then searches under the coverlet until she finds the object. I take back the coin at once, put it in my hand and then slip my closed hand under a cushion situated at the other side (on her left and no longer on her right); Jacqueline immediately searches for the object under the cushion. I repeat the experiment by hiding the coin under a jacket; Jacqueline finds it without hesitation.

II. I complicate the test as follows: I place the coin in my hand, then my hand under the cushion. I bring it forth closed and immediately hide it under the coverlet. Finally I withdraw it and hold it out, closed, to Jacqueline. Jacqueline then pushes my hand aside without opening it (she guesses that there is nothing in it, which is new), she looks under the cushion, then directly under the coverlet where she finds the object. . . .

I then try a series of three displacements: I put the coin in my hand and move my closed hand sequentially from A to B and from B to C; Jacqueline sets my hand aside, then searches in A, in B and finally in C.

Lucienne is successful in the same tests at 1;3(14). (Piaget 1954, p. 79)

The ability of the child to maintain "images" of objects (representation) when they are absent is clearly seen in the above example. The displacement of objects results in a search on the child's part until they are found. There is a logic to the child's search.

Concept of Causality

As with the object concept and other development, a child's awareness of causality is greatly enhanced by his or her new ability to internally represent objects. Through Period 5, the child remains unable to predict true cause–effect relationships in his or her sensorimotor world.

Just as during the sensori-motor development of objects and the spatial field the child becomes capable of evoking absent objects and of representing to himself displacements not given as such in the perceptual field, so also at the sixth stage the child becomes capable of reconstructing causes in the presence of their effects alone, and without having perceived the action of those causes. Inversely, given a certain perceived object as the source of potential actions, he becomes capable of foreseeing and representing to himself its future effects. (1954, p. 293)

The following example demonstrates Laurent's concept of causality at this stage. Clearly through representation, he accurately predicts a cause-and-effect relationship.

At 1;4(4) . . . Laurent tries to open a garden gate but cannot push it forward because it is held back by a piece of furniture. He cannot account either visually or by any sound for the cause that prevents the gate from opening, but after having tried to force it he suddenly seems to understand; he goes around the wall, arrives at the other side of the gate, moves the armchair which holds it firm, and opens it with a triumphant expression. (1954, p. 296)

Again, the rapid invention of solutions to problems is seen. Such solutions were not observed in behaviors before Period 6. From Laurent's actions, we can infer representation of objects, a clear object concept, and a clear understanding of causality in a sensorimotor problem.

In a general way, therefore, at the sixth stage the child is now capable of causal deduction and is no longer restricted to perception of sensori-motor utilization of the relations of cause to effect. (1954, p. 297)

Affect

By the end of the sensorimotor period, young children have typically developed affective feelings and preferences that are distinct from their earlier reflexive responses. Reflexes continue to operate, but behavior is now directed in part by new affective (and cognitive) capabilities. Feelings become factors in deciding what to do and what not to do. Thus the affective world of the 2-year-old is very different from that of the newborn.

The cognitive differentiation of the self as an object and others as objects opens the door for true social interchange. Young children become capable of investing affect in (having feelings for) other people. Likes and dislikes for others are established, and initial interpersonal relationships begin to form. With the child's affective and cognitive capabilities expanded through continuous construction, relationships with others

. . . start to become true exchange relationships between the self and the other person. These exchanges make more important, more structured, and more stable valuations possible. Such valuations indicate the beginning of interpersonal "moral feelings." (Piaget 1981b, p. 41)

Development of Moral Reasoning

Early in his career, Piaget became interested in children's concepts of rules and other moral feelings. His major work in this area was *The Moral Judgment of the Child* (1965), originally published in 1932. Piaget studied the development of children's concepts of game rules. Marbles was one game studied because it has a rule structure and was a favorite game of children at that time.

Piaget discovered, as we see in later chapters, that children's understanding of rules and other moral concepts (cheating, lying, justice, to name a few) develops in a manner essentially the same as cognitive concepts and other affective concepts. Moral concepts are constructed.

As one might suspect, there is no evidence of understanding game rules or other moral concepts during the sensorimotor period. During the first few years of life, which often extend into the preoperational period (years 2–7) of cognitive development, activity games such as marbles are played according to the whim of the child. Children at this level do not understand rules at all. The activity is nonsocial. To the sensorimotor child, marbles are simply objects to be explored and little else, with the child's enjoyment coming from this activity.

Although children at 2 years of age typically have not yet started to construct moral concepts, they clearly have developed affective feelings, preferences, and likes and dislikes, and they are entering the social realm. These experiences are necessary for the development of moral feelings and further affective development. From this point onward, the child's world becomes increasingly influenced by interactions with others.

SUMMARY

The typical child at age 2 is cognitively and affectively different from the infant at birth. This chapter has presented Piaget's conceptualization of how this transformation takes place. At birth, the child's behavior is reflexive. Toward the second month of life, an infant makes primitive differentiation of objects in his or her immediate environment, primarily via the sucking reflex. Between the fourth and eighth months, coordination of vision and touch typically occurs for the first time. The child grasps what he or she sees (Period 3). Toward the end of the first year, the child begins to develop object permanence and an awareness that objects other than himself or herself can cause events. Two (or more) familiar schemata are coordinated to solve new problems (Period 4). Early in the second year, true intelligent behavior typically evolves; the child constructs new means of solving problems through experimentation. Also the child sees himself or herself as an object among objects (Period 5). Toward the end of the second year, the child becomes able to internally represent objects and events. This ability liberates the child from sensorimotor intelligence, permitting the invention of new means of solving problems through mental activity.

Do infants construct knowledge? In Piaget's view, they clearly do. The functioning of assimilation and accommodation is evident shortly after birth. Much of the knowledge constructed during the first two years of life is *physical knowledge,* knowledge about the physical characteristics of objects. An infant discovers properties of objects in his or her environment by manipulating them. Most of the discussion in this chapter has been directed at the child's development of *logical–mathematical knowledge.* Concepts about causality, space, and the object concept are examples of logical–mathematical concepts. Each deals with relationships and is created mentally by the child.

Concurrent with the development of cognitive structures is the development of affective structures. We have seen that at birth an infant's reactions are primarily reflexive (as in crying) and lack differentiation. With initial cognitive differentiations, the first acquired feelings are observed. These are connected with the infant's actions. In the second year of life, likes and dislikes are observed and affect begins to play a role in the selection and avoidance of actions. Throughout most of the first two years of life, affect is invested in the self and in one's own activities, largely because the young infant has not cognitively constructed the notion that the world is composed of many physically independent objects of which the infant (the self) is one. As a result, during the second year of life comes the possibility of investing affect in objects other than the self (in other people). This is when likes and dislikes of others are first expressed.

An infant is born asocial. At the outset, nothing he or she does involves true social interchange. By the end of the second year of life, the typical infant is developmentally at the point where true social interchanges become possible.

The cognitive aspects of sensorimotor development evolve as a child acts on the environment. The child's actions are spontaneous. The motivation for particular actions is internal. The adapting and organizing functions of assimilation and accommodation operate from the beginning, resulting in the continuous qualitative and quantitative change in schemata. The child can be seen as constructing knowledge at a primitive level, trying to make sense of the surrounding world. The process is one of self-regulation.

Each new period is characterized by behaviors reflecting qualitatively superior cognitive and affective structures. In the development of intelligence during the first two years of life, it can be seen that each new period of development incorporates previous periods. The new periods do not displace the old, but improve on them. In the same way, each stage of development helps to explain stages that follow. So it is throughout the course of cognitive development.

As the infant develops cognitively, the changes promoted affect behavior in all areas. Concepts do not develop independent of one another. For example, in Period 4 (8-12 months), the typical child becomes able for the first time to systematically turn a bottle around so that he or she can get the nipple. What does this imply about the child's concepts or schemata? First, the behavior suggests the child is aware of the constancy of shape of objects. Objects do not change in shape when perspectives on them change (object concept). Because all actions occur in space, the child must also have a functional concept of space and the relationships between objects. Also, the behavior of turning the bottle around is clearly an intentional act requiring a measure of hand–eye coordination. Each of these abilities evolves at about the same time. Their paths of development are one. As a child assimilates and accommodates, all of his or her schemata are elaborated. Thus it is that evolving behaviors reflect qualitative changes in many schemata.

It is important to recognize that intellectual development is a self-regulatory process. The processes of assimilation and accommodation are internally controlled, not externally controlled. Affect plays a major role in this control through selection and energizing of behavior. It should also begin to become clear what Piaget meant when he said "all intellectual development is adaptation in the biological sense." In each period of the sensorimotor stage, new and more sophisticated capabilities and increasing self-control emerge. Each bit of progress makes the individual child better equipped to deal with the demands of life. As such, intellectual development is adaptive.

On completing sensorimotor development (it can be before or after age 2), the child has reached a point of conceptual development that is necessary for the development of spoken language and other cognitive and social skills during the next major aspect of development: preoperational thought. From this point on, the child's intellectual development takes place increasingly in the conceptual–symbolic area rather than exclusively in the sensorimotor area. This does not imply that sensorimotor development ends; it means only that intellectual development is to be affected increasingly by representational, symbolic, and social activity rather than motor and sensory activity alone.

chapter 4

The Development of Preoperational Thought

During preoperational development (age 2-7 years on average), a child evolves from one who functions primarily in a sensorimotor mode and whose "thinking" is through actions into one who functions increasingly in a conceptual and representational mode. The child becomes increasingly able to represent events internally (carry out action sequences in representation, or think) and becomes less dependent on his or her current sensorimotor actions for direction of behavior.

Between the ages of 2 and 7, the child's thought is characterized by newly emerging abilities. Several of the most important characteristics of preoperational thought are discussed in this chapter. The development of representational skills and the socialization of behavior are presented first. These are followed by a discussion of characteristics of thought of the preoperational child. These characteristics are egocentrism, centration, a lack of reversibility, and the inability to follow transformations.

REPRESENTATION

The major development during the preoperational stage is the ability to represent objects and events. Several kinds of representation are significant in development. In order of their emergence, they are *deferred imitation, symbolic play, drawing, mental imagery,* and *spoken language.* Each kind of representation begins to emerge around age 2. Each is a form of representation in the sense that something other than objects and events (a signifier) is used to represent objects and events (the signified). Piaget referred to this as the *symbolic function,* or the *semiotic function,* the use of symbols and signs.

Symbols are things that bear some resemblance to what they represent: drawings, silhouettes, and so forth. Signs are arbitrary things that bear no resemblance to what they represent. Written and spoken language and numbers are examples of systems of signs.

Let us consider each of the five forms of representation mentioned above.

Deferred Imitation

As early as the third month of an infant's life, attempts to imitate others who are present can be observed. Not until the second year of life do the first true forms of mental representation occur. Deferred imitation is the imitation of objects and events that have not been present for some time. For example, the child who plays patty-cake by himself, imitating an earlier session with his parents, is engaging in deferred imitation. The significance of deferred imitation is that it implies that the child has developed the ability to mentally represent (remember) the behavior imitated. Without representation, deferred imitation would be impossible. Because the child usually tries to accurately copy a prior behavior, imitation is primarily an accommodation.

Symbolic Play

The second form of representation that preoperational children engage in is symbolic play. One might observe a child with a block of wood, playing with it as if it were a car and giving it all the attributes of a car. This is symbolic play, a game of pretending, a kind of activity not found in sensorimotor development (Wadsworth 1978).

The nature of symbolic play is that it is imitative, but it is also a form of self-expression with only the self as the intended audience. There is no intention of communicating with others. In symbolic play, the child, without constraints, constructs symbols (which may be unique), inventions that represent anything he or she wishes. There is an assimilation of reality to the self rather than an accommodation of the self to reality (as in deferred imitation). As Piaget wrote in 1967: "[Symbolic play's] function is to satisfy the self by transforming what is real into what is desired" (p. 23).

The child's intended meaning in play may or may not be apparent to the viewer. Because there is no accommodating focus in symbolic play, as there is in imitation and drawing, and because symbolic play is not directed at an audience other than the self, what the child is representing in play is often totally unclear to the observer. Although we may recognize the child's play with a block as pretending it to be a car, we may not recognize the child curled up motionless on the floor as pretending to be a sleeping animal.

Children's play may, on the surface, appear to be of little value to the cognitive and affective development of the child. Yet Piaget assures us that the free-ranging nature of symbolic play has an essentially functional value and is not simply a diversion.

> In symbolic play this systematic assimilation takes the form of a particular use of the semiotic (symbolic) function—namely, the creation of symbols at will in order to express everything in the child's life experience that cannot

be formulated and assimilated by means of language alone. (Piaget and Inhelder 1969, p. 61)

Thus, when language is not sufficiently available or is inappropriate in the child's view, symbolic play is a forum for ideas, thoughts, and concerns.

Drawing

The early preoperational child's use of crayon, pencil, and brush initially amounts to scribbling. At first, there is no preconception on the child's part of drawing (representing) something, although sometimes forms emerge during the course of scribbling. Over the course of the preoperational stage, children increasingly attempt to represent things through drawings and their efforts become more realistic.

Young children's drawings are usually realistic in intent, although the drawings are confounded by the fact that up until 8 or 9 years of age children draw what they think rather than what they see—what is visually accurate. Thus, if 5- or 6-year-olds are asked to draw a house and trees on the side of the hill, they draw them perpendicular to the side of the hill (see Figure 4.1.). Not until age 8 or 9 or so are they able to coordinate the hill and the plane of the earth and draw objects perpendicular to the earth.

Mental Images

Mental images are internal representations (symbols) of objects and past perceptual experiences, although they are not accurate copies of those experiences. Images *are not* copies of perceptions stored in the mind. As drawings bear a resemblance to

FIGURE 4.1

what they represent, so too mental images are *imitations* of perceptions and necessarily bear a similarity to the perceptions themselves. In this sense, images are thought to be symbols.

During preoperational development, images are primarily static. According to Piaget and Inhelder (1969), images of movements begin to appear at the concrete operational level. Thus mental images during this time are more like drawings or photographs (static) than like movies.

Spoken Language

The most evident development during preoperational development is that of spoken language, the last form of representation to be discussed. Around 2 years of age (give or take a few months), the typical child begins to use spoken words as symbols in place of objects. A sound (word) comes to represent an object. Initially the child uses one-word sentences, but his or her language facility expands quickly given normal social interaction. By age 4, the typical child has largely mastered (constructed) the use of spoken language. The child can speak and use most grammatical rules and can understand what is heard if it contains familiar vocabulary. Children before this stage of development may use words in a imitative way. They may say "mama" or "dada" during the first year. These early words are usually not used to *represent* objects and are not language in the representational sense.

The rapid development of this form of symbolic representation (spoken language) is instrumental in facilitating the rapid conceptual development that takes place during this stage. Regarding the effects of language on intellectual life, Piaget wrote:

> [Language] has three consequences essential to mental development: (1) the possibility of verbal exchange with other persons, which heralds the onset of the socialization of action; (2) the internalization of words, i.e., the appearance of thought itself, supported by internal language and a system of signs; (3) last and most important, the internalization of action of such which from now on, rather than being purely perceptual and motor as it has been heretofore, can represent itself intuitively by means of pictures and "mental experiments." (1967, p. 17)

THE DEVELOPMENT OF SPOKEN LANGUAGE

Spoken language (and other forms of representation)[1] opens doors to the child that were not open before. The internalization of behavior through representation, facilitated by language, acts to speed up the rate at which experience can take place. During sensorimotor development, "experience" took place only as rapidly as movement could occur. The child, in effect, had to carry out actions in order to "think." (Movement produced "thought.") With the development of representation during the preoperational development, thinking can begin to occur through representations of actions rather than actions alone. Representational thought is carried out more rapidly than thought through movement because the former is not tied to direct experience.

In 1926, Piaget suggested, on the basis of his observations of young children's conversations, that there are essentially two classifications of the preoperational child's speech: egocentric speech and socialized speech. Egocentric speech is characterized by a lack of real communication. From age 2 to age 4 or 5, a child's speech is in part lacking in communicative intent. The child often speaks in the presence of others but without any apparent intention that others should hear the words. Even though the child speaks with others, there is often no communication. Nonconversations of this type Piaget called *collective monologues.* Such speech is clearly egocentric. The following example demonstrates the noncommunicative egocentric speech of the early preoperational child:

Mlle. L. tells a group of children that owls cannot see by day.
LEV: "Well, I know quite that it can't."
LEV: (*at a table where a group is at work*): "I've already done moons so I'll have to change it."
LEV: (*picks up some barley sugar crumbs*): "I say, I've got a lovely pile of eyeglasses."
LEV: "I say, I've got a gun to kill him with. I say, I am the captain on horse back. I say, I've got a horse and a gun as well." (1926, p. 41)

These examples of speech are clearly egocentric. Lev is simply thinking out his actions aloud, with no desire to give anyone any information. He is having a conversation with himself in the presence of others (collective monologue).

By age 6 or 7, language has become intercommunicative. Children's conversations increasingly involve an exchange of ideas. In the following, Lev, now considerably older than in the previous example, communicates with others in his conversations:

PIE (6;5): "Now, you shan't have it [the pencil] because you asked for it.—" HEI (6;0): "Yes I will, because it's mine.—" PIE: "Course it isn't yours. It belongs to everybody, to all the children.—" LEV (6;0): "Yes, it belongs to Mlle. L. and all the children. . . ." PIE: "It belongs to Mlle. L. because she bought it, and it belongs to all the children as well." (1967, p. 88)

Clearly the above illustration involves communication. Lev in the earlier example spoke only to himself. Here he speaks to others and clearly intends them to hear.

---

[1] Other than spoken language, forms of representation that preoperational children use and comprehend include drawings, some symbols, and pictures and their internal "images." The use and comprehension of some written forms of representation, such as letters, written words, and numbers, develop later.

The development of language during the preoperational stage is seen by Piaget as a gradual transition from egocentric speech characterized by *collective monologue* to socialized intercommunicative speech.[2]

How Children Learn Spoken Language

Spoken language is a form of social knowledge. The symbols used in a language are arbitrary and bear no relationship to what they represent. Most children in all cultures begin to master their native language around age 2. Because language learning is so universal, one is tempted to believe that acquisition of spoken language is automatic or innate. Piaget's theory emphatically states that this is not the case and that spoken language is acquired (constructed). Piaget (1963b) wrote:

> It is fundamental that there is hereditary transmission of the mechanism making this acquisition possible. Language itself is, however, learned through external transmission. Ever since humans began speaking, there has never been an example of the hereditary appearance of a ready-made linguistic structure. (p. 4)

Certainly one of the most difficult and complex tasks we face in our lives, considering the level of development when it occurs, is learning to use and understand spoken language. At 2 years of age, children begin to master spoken language, a system of arbitrary signs. Children receive no formal instruction in learning spoken language, although models are absolutely necessary. By and large, children master the use of the language fairly quickly. Is there a learning task of equivalent difficulty with which adults at an advanced level of development are confronted? I think not.

Piaget's theory suggests that the motivation for learning spoken language is the *adaptation value* of doing so. The child who learns one word as representation (such as *drink* or *cookie*) thus is able to communicate more effectively with his or her caretakers and have personal needs met. Thus, language learning has immediate and long-lasting value (adaptation value) to the child.[3]

How do children learn spoken language? Children acquire spoken language the same way they acquire all other knowledge. The child constructs the language. At the outset, the child's task is similar to code breaking. The child figures out (constructs)

---

[2] All children use both egocentric and socialized speech. The point here is that early preoperational children typically use relatively more egocentric speech than older children.

[3] In some cases where children do not learn to speak between the ages of 2 and 4, the reason may be that there was not any adaptation value for them to do so. One example is of a 3 1/2- year-old boy who used little speech and was suspected of being retarded. An investigation determined that the boy's mother was extremely good at anticipating the boy's every need and did so effectively. Every need was met. There was little need for the boy to speak or learn to speak. Other examples can be found in Wadsworth 1978.

the rules of the language from his or her social-language experience.[4] With that experience, children's constructions become refined (the code is more thoroughly broken). Much progress is usually made between ages 2 and 4.

LANGUAGE AND THOUGHT

The relationship between language and thought is important. Piaget's formulation of sensorimotor development demonstrates that the rudiments of intelligent behavior evolve *before* language develops.

> Intelligence actually appears well before language, that is to say, well before internal thought, which presupposes the use of verbal signs (internalized language). It is an entirely practical intelligence based on the manipulation of objects; in place of words and concepts it uses precepts and movements organized into "action schema." For example, to grab a stick in order to draw up a remote object is an act of intelligence (and a fairly late developing one at that: about eighteen months). Here, an instrument, the means to an end, is coordinated with a pre-established goal. . . . Many other examples could be cited. (Piaget 1967, p. 11)

Piaget contended that the emergence of internal representation (of which spoken language is one form) increases the powers of thought in range and speed. He suggested that there are three major differences between representational and sensorimotor behavior. First, the sequence of events in sensorimotor patterns is restricted to the speed of sensorimotor acts, making sensorimotor intelligence relatively slow. On the other hand, actions represented in internalized language can be carried out at the speed of thinking, relatively quickly. Second, sensorimotor adaptations are limited to the immediate actions of the child, whereas language permits thought and adaptation to range beyond present activity. Finally, sensorimotor intelligence proceeds in a one-step-at-a-time fashion, whereas representational thought and language permit the child to simultaneously handle many elements in an organized manner (Piaget and Inhelder 1969).

Thus, because language is a form of representation of objects and events, thought involving language is liberated from the limitations of the direct action of sensorimotor thought. Intellectual activity can proceed rapidly and with a range and speed not previously available.

Another important question is whether language (in a simplistic sense) determines logical thought or whether thought determines language. Every language has a

---

[4] Children raised in bilingual homes learn two languages at the same time without any apparent increase in effort. Until about age 5, children tend to mix the two languages in their talking. They use the words of each interchangeably and have no difficulty understanding either language when it is spoken to them. Sometime around age 5, they realize they are dealing with two different, if parallel, codes and rapidly begin to unmix the two languages in their talking.

logical structure that is a socially elaborated system for relationships, classifications, and so on. The language exists before the child exists. Does this mean that the logic of language is the source of all the logic of the child, or does the child invent and create his or her own logic? In 1969, Piaget and Inhelder cited two kinds of studies that supported their contention that language is neither a necessary nor a sufficient condition to ensure the development of logical thought. Studies of deaf mutes (no spoken language) showed that they develop logical thought in the same sequential steps as normal children, but with a one- to two-year delay in some operations. This suggests that language is not necessary for the development of logical operations, but it clearly acts as a facilitator. Other studies of blind children with normal verbal development demonstrated longer delays, up to four years on the same tasks. Blind children are hindered from birth in the development of sensorimotor schemata, and normal language development does not compensate for this.

> Child B (Betty) hears Child A's (Albert) words. Child B processes the words (symbols) through her schemata to derive their meaning. The meaning resides in the schemata, not in the word. Now it would seem that whether Child B can end up with the *same meaning* that child a wished to communicate depends, in part, on whether they both have schemata that permit this. If their structures are vastly different, then the probability of their "understanding" each other seems low. If they have the "same" or similar structures, then their capacity for meaningful understanding seems considerably greater. (Wadsworth 1978, p. 109)

For Piaget, the development of language is based on the prior development of sensorimotor operations and a normal social environment in which spoken language is used. Thus the development of sensorimotor operations is necessary for language

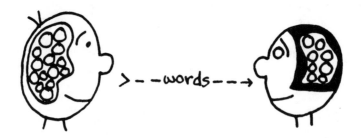

Albert   Betty

> - -words- - →

og = structures, schemata, or concepts

development and not the other way around. Only after achieving the capability to internally represent experience do (can) children begin to construct spoken language. When language develops, there is a parallel development of conceptual abilities that language helps to facilitate, in part because language and representation permit conceptual activity to proceed more rapidly and more broadly than sensorimotor operations do. The development is seen as a facilitator of cognitive development (as in deaf children) but not as a prerequisite for it nor as necessary for it.

The development of physical and logical–mathematical knowledge rests on the activity of the child. Children construct knowledge out of spontaneous actions. Language does not play a direct role in the construction of physical and logical–mathematical knowledge. In the construction of social knowledge, the role of spoken language is primarily one of providing an efficient means of communication between the child and others. This helps to make social experience more accessible to the child. As children's communication skills improve, the opportunities to encounter views of others that conflict with their own also increase. Such social activity is an important general source of disequilibrium.

THE SOCIALIZATION OF BEHAVIOR

Piaget (1963b) wrote: "[T]he individual is not born social, but progressively becomes it" (p. 6). Almost every newborn encounters an environment that acts toward it in a social way. The newborn's responses to the environment are limited essentially to reflexive reactions and are not initially social as such. We have seen that during the first two months of life, the infant begins to make differentiations in the environment (as in the sucking reflex) and active interchanges with parents occur. With the onset of development of spoken language, social exchanges are facilitated.

Although some theorists argue that an inherited "social instinct" exists and that it explains the universality of social development, Piaget believes this is not the case, but that children become increasingly social over time: "[T]he baby's behavior is conditioned from the beginning by social factors" (1963b, p. 6). As with cognitive and affective development, Piaget believes that social development proceeds as the child acts on and interacts with the social environment. As affective development is inseparable from cognitive development, social development is inseparable from cognitive and affective development. We have already seen that egocentric speech prevalent early in the preoperational stage has social aspects. As we shall see later in this chapter, preoperational egocentrism is in large part due to the child's inability to take the perspective of others, a characteristic of and limitation imposed by cognitive development at this time.

A cognitive aspect of social development is the acquisition of social knowledge discussed earlier (Chapter 2). Social knowledge is constructed by each child as he or she interacts with adults and other children. It is clear that in Piaget's view one's level of cognitive development determines the nature of the social knowledge one can construct at any time. Spoken language is not acquired before development of the cognitive capability for internal representation (around age 2).

Similarly, development of affect plays a role in social development. The interconnectedness of social, cognitive, and affective development is clearly seen in the discussions of moral reasoning that occur throughout this book.

CHARACTERISTICS OF PREOPERATIONAL THOUGHT

Piaget suggested that there are three levels of relationship between the actions of a child and his or her thought. The first is the sensorimotor level of direct action on the environment. Between birth and age 2, all schemata are sensorimotor and dependent on the actions of the child. The third level, typically after age 7 or 8, is the level of operations, or logical thought. The child becomes able to reason in a way that is not dependent on immediate perceptual and motor actions (concrete operational thought). Between ages 2 and 7 is the preoperational or prelogical period, which is an advance over sensorimotor intelligence but is not as advanced as the logical operations of later stages. During preoperational development, cognitive behavior is still influenced by perceptual activities. Actions can be internalized via representational functions, but thought is still tied to perception (Piaget and Inhelder 1969).

The following characteristics of preoperational thought are necessary for continuous development. In addition, they act as obstacles to complete logical thought. The obstacles to logical thought presented are egocentrism, transformations, centration, and reversibility.

Egocentrism

Piaget characterized a preoperational child's behavior and thinking as *egocentric.* That is, the child cannot take the role of, or see the viewpoint of, another. He believes that everyone thinks the same way he does and that everyone thinks the same things he does. As a result, the child never questions his own thoughts because they are, as far as he is concerned, the only thoughts possible and consequently must be correct.

The preoperational child does not reflect on or think about his own thoughts. As a result, he is never motivated to question his thinking, even when he is confronted with evidence that is contradictory to his thoughts. Where contradiction is present, the egocentric child is inclined to conclude that the evidence must be wrong because his thoughts are necessarily correct. Thus the child's thinking, from his point of view, is always logical and correct.

This egocentrism of thought is not egocentric by intent. The child remains unaware that he is egocentric and consequently never seeks to resolve it. Egocentrism is manifest in all the behavior of the preoperational child. As stated before, the 2- to 6-year-old's language and social behavior are largely egocentric. The child talks to himself when in the presence of others (in collective monologues) and often does not listen to others. Verbal behavior involves very little communication or exchange of information and thus is nonsocial for the most part.

It is not until around age 6 or 7 that children come to the awareness that their thoughts and those of their peers clearly conflict. With this awareness, children begin to accommodate to others, and egocentric thought begins to give way to social pressure. Peer-group social interaction, the repeated conflict of one's own thoughts with those of others, eventually jars the child to question and seek verification of his thoughts. The very source of conflict, social interaction, becomes the child's source of verification. To be sure, verification of one's thoughts comes about only through comparison with the thoughts of others. Thus, peer-group social interaction is the primary factor that gradually dissolves cognitive egocentrism. This is an important *adaptation* to the social world.

Although egocentrism pervades the behavior of the preoperational child, it should not be thought that egocentric behavior does not occur in other stages of development. Egocentrism of thought is a continuous part of cognitive development. Egocentrism takes different forms at different levels of development but is always characterized by a lack of *differentiation* in thought, which is characteristic of the initial use of each new advance in reasoning. The sensorimotor child is initially egocentric in that he lacks differentiation between the self as an object and other objects. We have seen that the preoperational child initially is unable to differentiate between the thoughts of others and his own thoughts. We will see that during later aspects of development children have difficulty differentiating between perceptual events and mental constructions (concrete operational reasoning) and between an "ideal" constructed world and the "real" world (formal operational reasoning). Thus, egocentrism does not go away but is always an element in the initial use of all new levels of thought, taking a somewhat different form at each new level. The child aged 2-4 is much more consistently egocentric in a preoperational sense than the child aged 6-7. As development proceeds, egocentrism slowly wanes and is revived in a different form when new cognitive structures are attained. Thus, egocentrism is a normal characteristic that pervades thought in some way in all periods of development.

Egocentric thinking, though a necessary characteristic of preoperational thought, in a sense restricts the development of intellectual structures during the preoperational stage. Because the child is never required by his own reasoning to question his thinking or validate his concepts, intellectual development is restricted at that time. Egocentrism can be viewed as acting to inhibit disequilibrium. Egocentrism acts to maintain the structural status quo. Because the child does not question his own thinking, schemata are less likely to change through accommodation. Although egocentrism in one sense limits cognitive development during the preoperational level, it is an essential and natural part of the level and of the initial use of any newly acquired cognitive characteristic. One must be egocentric in ones thinking before one can overcome it.

Transformational Reasoning

Another characteristic of the preoperational child's thinking is her inability to reason successfully about transformations. While observing a sequence of changes or successive states, the child focuses exclusively on the *elements* in the sequence, or the successive states, rather than on the *transformation* by which one state is changed to another. The child does not focus on the process of transformation from an original

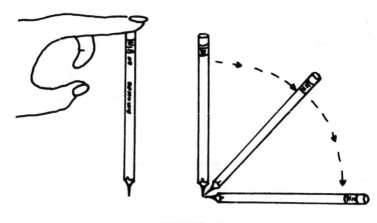

FIGURE 4.2

state to a final state, but restricts her attention to each in-between state when it occurs. The child moves from a particular perceptual event to a particular perceptual event, but cannot integrate a series of events in terms of any beginning-end relationships. Her thought is neither inductive nor deductive; it is transductive.

For example, if a pencil is held upright (Figure 4.2) and is allowed to fall, it passes from an original state (vertical) to a final state (horizontal) and through a continuous series of successive states. Preoperational children, after viewing the pencil fall, typically cannot draw or otherwise reproduce the successive steps. They cannot attend to or reconstruct the transformation. They usually reproduce only the initial and final positions the pencil assumes.

A second example of the transformation problem is seen in a child walking through the woods. At different points along a trail the child sees snails—different snails each time. The child cannot tell whether they are all the same snail or different snails. The child cannot reconstruct the *transformation* from event to event (snail to snail).

The inability of the preoperational child to follow transformations inhibits the development of logic in thought. Because the child is not aware of the relationship between events and all this can mean, comparisons between states of events are always incomplete.

Centration

Another characteristic of preoperational thought is what Piaget called *centration*. A child presented with a visual stimulus tends to center or fix attention on a limited perceptual aspect of the stimulus. The child seems unable to explore all aspects of the stimulus, or *decenter* the visual inspection. As a result, the child, when centering, tends to assimilate only limited aspects of an event; those aspects they center on. Any cognitive activity seems to be dominated by the perceptual aspects. Perceptual evaluations dominate the cognitive evaluation (in the preoperational child) in much the same way as they did in the direct action of the sensorimotor child.

A child of age 4 or 5 who is asked to compare two rows of like objects in which one row contains nine objects and the other, a longer row, contains only eight objects (but spread farther apart) typically selects the perceptually longer row as having "more" objects. This occurs even when the child "knows" cognitively that nine is more than eight. Perceptual evaluation dominates cognitive evaluation. Conflicts between reasoning and perception are resolved in favor of perception. Thought is *preoperational.*

The child tends to center on perceptual aspects of objects. It is only with time and experience that he becomes able to *decenter* and evaluate perceptual events in a coordinated way with cognitions. After age 6 or 7, children reach the point where cognitions begin to assume their proper position with respect to perceptions in thought.

Reversibility

According to Piaget, reversibility is the most clearly defined characteristic of intelligence (1963b, p. 41). If a child's thought is reversible, she can follow the line of reasoning back to where it started. For example, a child without reversible thought is shown two equal-length rows of eight coins each. She agrees that each has the same number of coins. One of the rows is lengthened while the child is watching. She no longer agrees that there are the same number of coins in each row. Part of her problem is that she is not able to mentally *reverse* the act of lengthening. She cannot maintain the equivalence of number in the face of perceptual change in a dimension that is irrelevant to number (length). Only when actions become reversible will she be able to solve such problems. The inability to reverse operations is characteristic of the cognitive activity of the preoperational child.

Preoperational thought retains much of the rigidity of sensorimotor thought, although preoperational reasoning is a clear advance over sensorimotor reasoning. It is relatively inflexible, is dominated by perceptions, and is initially irreversible. The attainment of reversible operations is extremely difficult for a child. This is reasonable if one considers that most sensorimotor operations are irreversible by definition. Once a motor act is committed, it typically cannot be reversed. In much the same way, perceptions cannot be reversed in experience. Thus representational acts, which are based on prior sensorimotor patterns and perceptions, must develop reversibility with few prior patterns to follow.[5]

Sensorimotor and preoperational children construct concepts and knowledge about such things as space and causality from their actions on their environment. The environment contains physical elements and orderings; when these are acted on by

---

[5] Most actions are not fully reversible. Water running out of a faucet cannot be run back into the faucet. A ball thrown cannot return to one's hand in reverse. Some actions are reversible or closely so. A door or gate can be opened and then closed. An object (such as a block) can be turned over and then turned over again. Thus, although many actions children observe and engage in do not have the capacity to illustrate reversibility, some do.

the child, they permit concepts to be constructed or "discovered" (physical knowledge). Certain concepts or knowledge cannot be constructed or discovered directly from examples in the environment but must be invented by the child. This is true of many logical–mathematical concepts. For example, the environment does not contain many physical examples of reversibility a child can use as models for developing reversibility of thought and reasoning. Reversibility must therefore be invented by the child.

Piaget's concepts of egocentrism, centration, transformation, and reversibility are closely related. Early preoperational thought is dominated by the presence or absence of each of them. As cognitive development proceeds, these characteristics gradually subside in unison. A deterioration in egocentrism permits (requires) a child to decenter more and attend to simple transformations. All this in turn helps the child in the construction of reversibility.

CONSERVATION

The characteristics of preoperational thought described above can be viewed as obstacles to logical thought. Nonetheless, they are necessary for the development of logical thought and they occur naturally. They are most clearly seen in what have come to be called conservation problems. The problems described in this section were developed by Piaget and his co-workers to assess children's levels of conceptual development and their level of attainment with respect to the concepts involved.

Conservation is the conceptualization that the amount or quantity of a matter stays the same regardless of any changes in an irrelevant dimension. For example, if we have a row of eight pennies and we move the pennies farther apart in the row, we still have eight pennies. That is, the *number* of pennies does not change when a change is made in a dimension irrelevant to number (in this case, the length of the row or the distance between pennies). An awareness of number invariance would imply the ability to conserve number and that corresponding schemata have developed. Lack of this awareness implies a lack of number conservation and that corresponding schemata (reversibility) have not developed. Level of conservation ability is a measure of the logical–mathematical structure a child has developed. During preoperational development, children typically cannot conserve; that is, they cannot hold one dimension invariant in the face of changes in other dimensions. By the end of the preoperational stage (age 7), some conservation structures (ie., conservation of number) are usually developed.

The development from nonconservation to conservation is a gradual one brought about by active reconstruction of developing schemata. As with all other changes in cognitive structures (schemata), the change is largely a function of the actions (cognitive and sensorimotor) of the child. According to Piaget, conservation structures cannot be induced through direct instruction (teaching) or reinforcement techniques. Active construction is the key. Conservation of number, area, and volume problems are presented next.

Conservation of Number

If a 4- to 5-year-old is presented with a row of checkers or other objects and asked to construct a row that has the same number of checkers, he typically constructs a row of the same length, but his row may not have the same the number of elements as the model. The typical construction proceeds by placing two checkers, one opposite each of the end checkers in the model, and then filling in a number of checkers without one-to-one correspondence. If there is correspondence, it is accidental (Piaget 1967).

The typical 5- to 6-year-old is usually a little more systematic. When she is asked to perform the same conservation of number task, she often uses one-to-one correspondence and makes each row equal in number and length to the model. But if she sees one row lengthened (transformed as in Figure 4.3) without any change in the number of elements, she declares they are no longer equivalent and that the longer one has more. When asked for her *reasoning,* she typically indicates that one row has more because it is longer. This is often true even if she accurately counts the elements in each row. The preoperational child holds that the rows are equivalent in number only as long as there is visual correspondence in the length of arrays (Piaget 1967).

The typical 5-year-old does not conserve number. He cannot yet reason that the number of elements in a series does not change in the face of a perceptual change in a dimension irrelevant to number. According to Piagetian theory, what has happened is that after a transformation (the length of one row), the child makes a perceptual response instead of a cognitive response. This is inferred from the *reasoning* he provides for his answer.[6] In terms of previous notions of *centration,* the child focuses or centers on one aspect of the event—the length of the rows—and ignores another salient aspect of which he is cognitively aware: the number of objects. Also, the child does not focus on the *transformation* of stimulus arrays, but focuses on each successive state as if it were independent of the previous states. Thus the child, because of his inability to decenter and focus on the transformation, typically ends up making a perceptual response. Unable to *reverse* the changes he has seen occur, he resorts to a

---

[6] Piaget developed a procedure for assessing children's construction of knowledge with respect to a particular schema or concept. This is called the clinical interview. In this procedure, a child is presented with a concrete problem or verbal question and asked questions relative to the concept of interest. Children's responses, whether correct or incorrect, are always followed by a request for their reasons for their answers. This may be followed by more questions and requests for reasoning. The examiner's objective is to understand the child's concept (of number) as it exists at that time. Thus, questions are often made up on the spot in response to children's previous answers and reasoning. The clinical interview relative to a particular concept is ended only when the examiner is satisfied that the child's level of understanding of the concept has been established.

In this process, the examiner makes inferences about the child's comprehension from his or her answers and reasoning. The reasoning the child gives is at least as important as the answers. Children can provide correct answers ("both rows have the same number") and have incorrect reasoning ("I guessed" or "I thought you were trying to trick me, so I didn't say what I thought"). Both correct answers and correct reasoning are necessary to conclude that the child has fully constructed the concept.

A more complete discussion of Piaget's clinical method and procedures for assessment can be found in Wadsworth 1978. For Piaget's original discussion of the procedure, see Piaget 1963a.

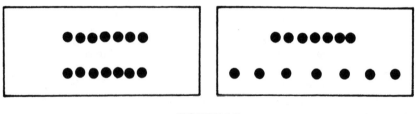

FIGURE 4.3

perceptual response. In this respect, the child is perception-bound. When confronted with a problem where cognitive and perceptual solution conflict in his mind, he makes a decision based on the perceptual cues.

Around age 6 or 7 and when reversibility is firmly in place, the typical child constructs the reasoning necessary to conserve number. Concurrently she *decenters* her perceptions, attends to the *transformations,* and *reverses* operations. She constructs an awareness that a change in the length of a row of elements (an irrelevant dimension) does not change the number of elements in the row.

Conservation of Area

A second kind of conservation problem reflects a child's concept of *area.* This can be demonstrated by the cows-in-the-field problem (Piaget, Inhelder, and Szeminska 1960). Two same-size sheets of green paper are placed before a child and a toy or paper-cutout cow is placed in each field, as in Figure 4.4A. Several blocks of the same size are kept on hand to represent buildings. It is explained to the child that there are two fields of grass and a cow in each field. The child is asked, "Which cow has more grass to eat, or do they both have the same amount?" Typically, the response is that both cows have the same amount of grass to eat. Once visual equivalence of area is established, the child is shown a barn (a block) being placed in each field, and the question is repeated: "Which cow has more grass to eat now, or do they both have the same amount?" Again, the response is typically that they both have the same amount of grass. The child's reasoning for their response is requested and noted. A second block is placed in each field; but in the first field, the second block is placed away from the first, and in the other field the second block is placed adjacent to the first (see Figure 4.4B). The question is repeated: "Which cow has more grass to eat now, or do they both have the same amount?" The child who cannot conserve typically says that the cow in the second field (blocks adjacent) has more grass to eat. The child's reasoning, which is always requested, suggests that the field with two adjacent barns (one set of barns) has more grass area than the field with two separated barns (two sets of barns), even though the barns are seen as the same size. The child who can conserve says that they both have the same amount to eat. The conserver clearly reasons that the placement of barns is irrelevant to area. The important thing is the number of barns. The extension of this problem by more

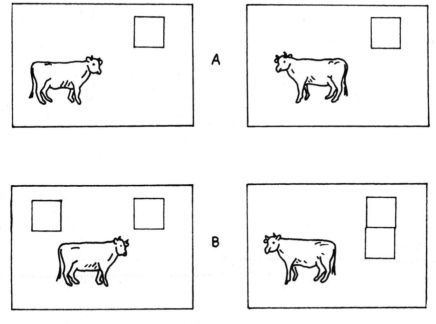

FIGURE 4.4

barn placements can be varied to check the reliability of conservation or nonconservation responses.[7]

Again, the nonconserving preoperational child has made a perceptual response. The second field looks as if it has fewer buildings (because the buildings are attached) than the first field. The child is not able to decenter and attend to all salient aspects of the event, nor does he follow the *transformations* that have taken place. Each new placement is independent of the previous. Thus, as with conservation of number problems, the preoperational child fails to conserve. Not until age 7–8 is the knowledge and reasoning necessary for conservation of area with respect to this kind of problem usually constructed.

Conservation of Liquid

A third conservation ability can be assessed with the conservation of liquid volume problem. The preoperational child's ability or inability to conserve liquid can usually

---

[7] Farm children may answer this question differently based on their experience. For example, some children indicate that the cow in the field with two adjacent barns has more grass to eat than the cow in the field with two separated barns. Their reasoning sometimes is that the area of grass next to barns is usually negligible or unfit to eat, and because the adjacent barns have fewer sides to the field, there is more edible grass in that field. From this reasoning, it cannot be concluded that they do not have the conservation of area concept.

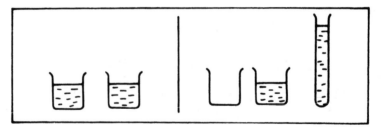

FIGURE 4.5

be shown with the following task: A child is presented with two containers of equal size and shape, as in Figure 4.5. She is asked to compare the amount of liquid in the two containers. A few drops are added to one container, if necessary, to establish visual equivalence of volume. When equivalence is attained, the liquid from one of the glasses is poured into a taller and thinner glass (or shorter and wider glass), and the child is again asked to compare the two containers holding liquid: "Does one container have more water than the other, or do they both have the same amount?" As in the previous problems, an irrelevant dimension (shape of the container) has been changed. The typical preoperational child does not see the two containers as equivalent in volume and declares that one or the other (usually the taller and thinner container) has more liquid. Reasoning is often based on the height of one column of liquid compared with the height of the other. This is clearly a nonconservation response. If the liquid is then poured back into the original container, visual equivalence is usually achieved again for the child and they declare they both have the same amount.

As in the previous conservation problems, the preoperational child typically does not attend to all aspects of *transformation* that she sees. She *centers* on the perceptual aspects of the problem. Because the column of water in the taller cylinder looks higher, it must contain more liquid. Reasoning is not logical. Reversibility is not present. It is not until the stage of concrete operations (age 7–11) that conservation of liquid volume is usually present.[8]

The preceding conservation problems illustrate but do not begin to exhaust the phenomena of conservation. Qualitative differences in the logical thought of a child manifest themselves in *all* aspects of children's thinking. A change along one irrelevant dimension always seems to imply changes in the relevant dimensions for the preoperational child. The reverse is true for older counterparts, who develop schemata that permit conservation.

The picture of conservation presented here is somewhat oversimplified. A child does not develop conservation schemata overnight in an all-or-nothing manner.

---

[8] Liquid problems are usually solved after age 7 or 8. More sophisticated volume conservation problems, such as those requiring the measurement of displaced water when an object is immersed, are not solved until about age 12 (Piaget and Inhelder 1969).

Kamii (1982) identifies three different levels or substages leading up to conservation of number. Conservation concepts are acquired slowly after much experience and subsequent assimilation and accommodation. Qualitatively new patterns of responses are interpreted by Piaget to reflect newly constructed or reconstructed intellectual structures.

The acquisition of schemata that permit conservation does not take place at the same time in all areas. The application of conservation principles to different kinds of problems usually follows a sequence and thus constitutes a scale of development. Conservation of number is always attained before other conservation skills, and conservation of volume is usually attained last. The structures permitting conservation are typically acquired in the following sequence at the following ages on average:

Conservation	*Age*
number	5–6
substance (mass)	7–8
area	7–8
liquid volume	7–8
weight	9–10
volume (solids)	11–12

Such a developmental sequence suggests that the ability to conserve liquid volume implies the ability to conserve area, substance, and number. Each new kind of conservation always implies that previous levels in the sequence have been attained.[9]

Piaget and his collaborators conducted and published research on children's acquisition of conservation concepts almost continuously from 1937 until 1977 (Easley 1978). Many dozens of studies were carried out by Piaget and his collaborators in Geneva to understand more thoroughly the conservation phenomenon and, more generally, children's construction of knowledge. In addition, hundreds of research studies were conducted by scholars in various countries interested in conservation. Not all psychologists agreed with Piaget's interpretation of his research or with the assumptions he made in his theory.

Piaget contended that the reasoning underlying conservation abilities evolves spontaneously out of the assimilation and accommodation of active experiences most children have. This activity is self-regulated. Children tend to develop conserva-

---

[9] Under the guidance of competent and trained people, problems such as conservation problems can be used to assess children's intellectual development from a Piagetian point of view. They can also be used to determine a child's level of development regarding a particular concept. Many professionals feel that a Piagetian methodology provides a substitute for, or a supplement to, conventional intelligence testing because Piagetian methods *clearly* measure reasoning, logical thought, and constructed knowledge. Competency in making valid assessments takes time and training. Those interested in learning more about how to make such assessments can consult works that deal with Piagetian assessment in detail (such as Wadsworth 1978, Piaget 1963a, and Copeland 1974).

tion abilities at about the same age and tend to develop different conservation operations in an invariant sequence. In most cultures, children without formal schooling
attain conservation as readily as children with schooling.[10] Direct teaching of conservation skills to preoperational children is not generally successful.[11]

According to Piagetian theory, the interpretation of these findings is that conservation abilities do not emerge until cognitive structures (schemata) evolve that make
possible the reasoning necessary for true conservation responses. Changes in
schemata come about only after considerable assimilation and accommodation of
experience. A child must attain reversibility, learn to decenter perceptions, and be
able to follow transformations. He or she must become less egocentric and learn to
question his or her thinking. These changes all come about gradually and are prerequisites to the development of the schemata permitting conservation.

Many readers of Piaget's writings have come to regard the sensorimotor and preoperational child as one with serious limits or even incompetent. Part of what defines
them is what they cannot do! It was certainly not Piaget's intent to create such a
view. Piaget saw children's intellectual development as moving forward along a continuum. At any given point in development, one's abilities can be characterized by
what their constructed reasoning permits them to do and what has yet to be accomplished.

Piaget generally used a conservative or strict criterion when inferring competence. Other researchers use less strict criteria and claim to find competence where
Piagetians, using their criterion, do not. Thus there is legitimate and continuing
debate here. In addition, Piaget and those who have done research based on Piaget's
work often focus on the abilities young children *do not have;* for example, the typical 5-year-old cannot conserve number or mass or liquid volume.

This is often interpreted as meaning that certain cognitive capabilities are
absent, which is true only in one sense. What is often overlooked is that when children do not have conservation of number ability according to a strict Piagetian criterion, it does not mean they have no number concepts at all. Gelman (1978) has
shown that some children who do not show an understanding of invariance of number using a Piagetian criterion do show understanding of invariance of number using
a different (less strict) criterion.

It is clear that children's construction of knowledge in all areas is gradual and
not an all-or-nothing affair. Schemata progress from being less accurate to being more
accurate. It is helpful to recall that Piaget viewed development as a continuum and

---

[10] This should not be interpreted to mean that children learn regardless of whether they go to school. It
means only that cognitive structures (schemata) evolve in most cases regardless of whether children
go to school. Chapter 8 deals with this in more detail.

[11] Although the foregoing discussion implies that all children could be classified as nonconservers (of
number, area, etc.) or conservers, there is really a third category to be aware of, called *borderline*
conservers (Wadsworth 1978). Borderline conservers are children whose responses and reasoning
problems are mixed, or inconsistent, but not consistently either conservation or nonconservation
responses and reasoning. Borderline children are developmentally closer than nonconservers to
becoming conservers. Often they can be "provoked" to experience disequilibrium and move quickly
to the conserver level. Nonconservers cannot be so provoked.

has written about the gradualness of concept construction. At every point along the continuum of development, children's thinking has a logic that is consistent within the context of the child's cognitive status at that time.

AFFECTIVE DEVELOPMENT: THE EMERGENCE OF RECIPROCITY AND MORAL FEELINGS

Reciprocity of Feelings

The first fully social feelings arise during preoperational development. Certainly, younger children show affection and have feelings of liking and disliking. Representation and particularly spoken language are instrumental in the development of social feelings. Representation allows for the creation of images of experiences, including affective experiences. Thus, for the first time, feelings can be represented and recalled (remembered).[12] In this way, affective experiences come to have an effect that can last longer than the experiences themselves.

---

[12] According to Piaget, what we can recall or remember is *not* an exact replica of the object or action being remembered. What is remembered is derived from the representation (image) of the object or event that we have. Representations are not mirror images of objects and events. Images are imitations shaped by the cognitive and perceptual capabilities of the individual at the time they are created. What is remembered is reconstructed from the images available. Thus, when we talk of feelings being remembered, we are talking of reconstructions from images of feelings, not the feelings themselves.

> Representation and language allow feelings to acquire a stability and dura-
> tion they have not had before. Affects, by being represented, last beyond
> the presence of the object that excites them. This ability to conserve feel-
> ings makes interpersonal and moral feelings possible. (Piaget 1981b, p. 44)

During the sensorimotor level, past events and experiences cannot be reconstructed or remembered because they are not internally represented by the child.
With the capacity for reconstruction of the cognitive and affective past during preoperational development, behavior can assume an element of consistency that was
not possible before representation. With the reconstructed past an element in current behavior, affect is less tied to immediate experience and perception than it
previously was. Behavior can become a bit more stable and predictable. Feelings
have the potential of becoming longer-lasting and more consistent as preoperational development proceeds. Thus, where the sensorimotor or early preoperational child may like an object or person one day but not the next, the preoperational child typically becomes increasingly capable of showing more consistency in
liking and disliking when the past is remembered and taken into account in the
present.

Piaget contends that the basis for social interchange is a *reciprocity* of attitudes
and values between the young child and others.

> These considerations lead us to see liking other people not so much as the
> consequences of the enrichment that each partner draws from the other
> but as a reciprocity of attitudes and values. (Piaget 1981b, pp. 45–46)

This form of exchange—reciprocity—leads, or can lead, to each party valuing
the other person (mutual respect). Each is appreciated by the other in some way. In
subsequent interactions, the values derived through reciprocal actions are not lost
but are represented and remembered. Because these prior value placements are
retained, as representations, future interchanges are more likely to anticipate positive
(or negative) affective experiences.

First Moral Feelings

Piaget studied the development of moral *reasoning* in children. He viewed the development of moral reasoning as an outgrowth of both cognitive and affective development. Moral feelings, for Piaget, were feelings that have "to do with what is necessary
and not just what is desirable or preferable to do" (Piaget 1981b, p. 55). A voluntary
sense of duty or obligation typifies developed moral feelings.

Piaget suggested that moral norms have three characteristics:

> (a) a moral norm is generalizable to all analogous situations, not just to iden-
> tical ones; (b) a moral norm lasts beyond the situation and conditions that

engender it; and (c) a moral norm is linked to a feeling of autonomy.[13] (1981b, p. 55)

He indicated that moral norms or characteristics of moral reasoning are not fully in place until the concrete operational stage.

> From two to seven years, none of these conditions is met. To begin with, norms are not generalized but are valid only under particular conditions. For example, the child considers it wrong to lie to his parents and other grown-ups but not to his comrades. After the age of eight, however, children understand that it is wrong to lie in any situation, and they argue in a valid way that lying to one's comrades is more serious. Second, instructions remain linked to certain represented situations analogous to perceptual configurations. An instruction, for example, will remain linked to the person who gave it, or children will judge that a lie is "not as naughty" if the person duped is unaware he has been lied to. . . . Finally, there is no autonomy during the preoperational period. "Good" and "bad" are defined as that which conforms or fails to conform to the instructions one has received. (1981b, pp. 55–66)

During preoperational development, moral reasoning is viewed as prenormative.[14] But moral reasoning during this stage is a clear advance over the capabilities of the sensorimotor child. Children's concepts of rules, accidents, lying, and justice are outlined briefly in the pages that follow.

CHILDREN'S CONCEPTS OF RULES

To investigate children's understanding of rules, Piaget (1965) asked children questions about the rules of a child's game. As mentioned earlier, the game was marbles, which requires two or more players. Piaget viewed marbles as an appropriate activity for study because it is a social game with a structure of rules. The rules vary from place to place, but there are always rules. Marbles was, and is, a popular game among children in Geneva.

Piaget interviewed 20 boys and girls, ages 4–13, regarding their understanding of the rules. The questions that Piaget directed to the children were designed to determine whether the rules of the game were externally determined, just, and alterable. Thus, typical questions were "What are the rules of marbles?" "Show me how to play,"

---

13 Autonomy is selecting one's own course of action rather then following a prescribed course. Autonomy is self-regulation. It will be discussed more completely in the next chapter.

14 Normative feelings are feelings that have "to do with what is necessary and not just what is desirable and preferable to do" (Piaget 1981b, p. 55). Normative has to do with one's constructed sense of obligation as contrasted to blind obedience of authority. Prenormative reasoning is based on obedience to authority out of fear rather than mutual respect.

"Can you invent a new rule?" and "Is it a fair rule?" In these interviews, the experimenter functions both as a participant and an observer. The experimenter actually plays the game with the children in order to learn their way of playing (Gruber and Vonèche 1977).

> The experimenter speaks more or less as follows. "Here are some marbles. . . . You must show me how to play. When I was little I used to play a lot, but now I've quite forgotten how to. I'd like to play again. Let's play together. You'll teach me the rules and I'll play with you." . . . You must avoid making any sort of suggestions. All you need do is to appear completely ignorant [about the game of marbles] and even make intentional mistakes so that the child may each time point out clearly what the rule is. Naturally, you must take the whole thing very seriously, all through the game. Then you ask who has won, and why, and if everything is not quite clear, you begin a new set. (Piaget 1965, p. 24)

In addition to questions about the rules, as in previous interviews, Piaget asked children to give the reasoning behind their answers. As we have seen, it is children's reasoning rather than their answers per se that usually provides the most information about their knowledge and concepts.

Piaget found that there were four broad levels in the development of children's knowledge of the rules of marbles. These levels parallel Piaget's four levels of cognitive development:

1. ***Motor.*** In Piaget's first level of comprehension of rules, a child is not aware of any rules. During the first few years of life and often extending into preoperational development, marbles are played with according to habit and in any way the child wants. At this time, children play with marbles by themselves. The activity is nonsocial. Marbles are primarily objects to be explored (physical knowledge). A child's enjoyment seems to come largely from the motor or muscular manipulation of the marbles. There is no evidence of any awareness of a game in the social sense.

2. ***Egocentric.*** Usually between age 2 and age 5, children become aware of the existence of rules and begin to want to play the game with other, usually older, children. Young children begin by imitating older children's play, but the cognitively egocentric child continues to play *by himself or herself,* without trying to win. In the same way, children's early preoperational use of spoken language is characterized by asocial collective monologues (egocentric); their play in groups is characterized by a lack of any social interaction or true cooperation. Piaget's observation helps illustrate the point.

   > Loeff (5) often pretends to be playing with Mae [another boy] . . . he immediately begins to "fire" at the marbles assembled in a heap and plays without either stopping or paying any attention to us.

"Have you won?—*I don't know, I think I have.*—Why?—*Yes,
because I threw the mibs* [marbles]—and I?—*Yes, because you
threw the mibs.*" (1965, p. 38)

At this level of reasoning about rules, children believe everyone can
win. Rules are viewed as fixed and respect for them is unilateral.

What seems to be asocial behavior, egocentrism, and isolated play is
actually an advance over the behavior of the previous stage from a social
point of view. The child wants to play with other children. Still, the egocentric child typically lacks any appreciation or knowledge of the game from a
social point of view. Such children imitate what they see but do not yet reason like their older playmates. Thus their play does not involve cooperation. There is no autonomy of reasoning. But because adaptations are
attempted, their behavior represents an advance over the behavior of the
earlier level.

3. ***Cooperation*** It is usually not until age 7 or 8 that children begin to cooperate socially in playing games. Around this time, there is usually a clearer
   understanding of the rules of the game. The object of the game for children
   becomes to win.

4. ***Codification of rules*** Around 11 or 12 years of age, most children come
   to understand that rules are, or can be, made by the group; the group can
   change rules; and rules are necessary for fair play. Further understanding of
   rules are dealt with in detail in Chapters 5 and 6.

Concepts of Accidents and Clumsiness

Parents and teachers of preschool and early elementary school children know that
children often have difficulty viewing other children's accidents as accidents. For
example, one child may accidentally bump into another. The child who has been
bumped typically views the act as intentional and worthy of appropriate retribution.
Endless physical and verbal classroom scuffles are initiated by such accidents or
clumsiness. Young children are often unable to appreciate other children's *intentions*
or to see another child's point of view (egocentrism) and parents and teachers are
frustrated in their attempts to explain to young children that accidents and clumsiness on the part of others do not deserve punishment. The problem is that young
children typically have not yet *constructed concepts of intentionality.* They firmly
believe in the moral credo "an eye for an eye, and a tooth for a tooth" and in its application in all cases. Piaget's work suggests that until children construct a concept of
intentionality, reasoning alone cannot dissuade them from believing retributive acts
are just. They are simply not capable of understanding intentionality.

Piaget interviewed children to discover their concepts and beliefs about clumsiness and accidents. He used pairs of stories that contrasted children's intentions
against the quantitative results of their accidents. Children were asked to compare
the accidents in two stories to decide which was worse and then to explain their
selection. One pair of stories follows:

A. A little boy who is called John is in his room. He is called to dinner. He goes into the dining room. But behind the door there was a chair, and on the chair was a tray with fifteen cups on it. John couldn't have known that there was all this behind the door. He goes in, the door knocks against the tray, bang go the fifteen cups and they all get broken!

B. Once there was a little boy whose name was Henry. One day when his mother was out he tried to get some jam out of the cupboard. He climbed up on a chair and stretched out his arms. But the jam was too high up and he couldn't reach it and have any. But while he was trying to get it he knocked over a cup. The cup fell down and broke. (1965, p. 122)

Piaget found that among children younger than age 7 or 8, the boy in the first story, John, is usually viewed as having committed a worse act. John's actions are typically viewed as worse than Henry's because John broke *15 cups* whereas Henry broke only *1 cup.* The children's judgments are based on the concrete or quantitative results of the actions. John broke more cups, and that's that! There is no appreciation yet of *intention* in judging actions. Motives are not considered.

Around age 8 or 9 (concrete operational level) with the construction of concepts related to intentionality, children typically *begin* to be able to consider events from someone else's point of view. This parallels a reduction in egocentric thought. Children begin to see that motives and intentions are *as important* as the results of actions. Piaget recorded the following responses and reasoning of a 9-year-old to the above stories.

> CORM (9): *"Well, the one who broke them as he was coming isn't naughty, 'cos he didn't know there was any cups. The other one wanted to take the jam and caught his arm on a cup*—Which one is naughtiest?—*The one who wanted to take the jam.*—How many cups did he break?—*One.*—And the other boy?—*Fifteen.*—Which one would you punish most?—*The boy who wanted to take the jam. He knew, he did it on purpose."* (1965, p. 129)

Increasingly, intentions become more important to the child than the consequences of a particular action. This comes about only when children are able to view actions from the point of view of others. Children become aware of the inner states of others and they are viewed as having different thoughts from oneself. Similarly, there is a recognition that others have affective states that are not always the same as one's own. Children increasingly become capable of taking into consideration the affective and cognitive states of others.[15]

---

[15] Children early on recognize and become aware of the affective states of others only by observing overt behavior such as crying and facial expressions. Later, children begin to consider possible affective feelings of others in their own thoughts without behavioral prompts.

Children and Lying

Another interesting social and moral topic Piaget investigated is the development of children's concepts about lying. Parents and teachers often observe a great deal of what they would call lying among young children. Understandably, this can be a source of great concern to adults. Many parents ask themselves if they are rearing a "liar." What Piaget learned about children's concepts of lying may help us understand these behaviors. In this research, Piaget asked children questions to determine their definition of a lie and why one should not lie.

What Is a Lie?   Before age 6 or 7, most children view a lie as something that is "naughty." In addition, young children usually consider involuntary errors to be lies.

> Nus (6): "What is a lie?—*It's when you say naughty words.*—Do you know any naughty words?—*Yes.*—Tell me one.—*Charogne* [Corpse].—Is it a lie?—*Yes.*—Why?—*Because you mustn't say naughty words.*—When I say 'Fool!' is it a lie?—*Yes.*" ...
>
> Rad (6): "*A lie is words you mustn't say, naughty words.*" . . .
>
> Web (6): "Once there was a boy who didn't know where the Rue des Acacias was [the street where Web lives]. A gentleman asked him where it was. The boy answered 'I think it's over there, but I'm not sure.' And it wasn't over there! Did he make a mistake, or did he tell a lie?—*It was a lie.*—Did he make a mistake?—*He made a mistake.*—Then it wasn't a lie?—*He made a mistake and it was a lie.*" (1965, pp. 143-44)

Between age 6 or 7 and age 10 or so, a lie is typically viewed as something that is *not true.* A false statement is viewed as a lie regardless of the intent. If it is not true, then it is a lie.

CHAP (7): "What is a lie?—*What isn't true, what they say that they haven't done.*—Guess how old I am.—*Twenty.*—No, I'm thirty. Was it a lie what you told me?—*I didn't do it on purpose.*—I know. But is it a lie all the same, or not?—*Yes, it is all the same, because I didn't say how old you really were.*—Is it a lie?—*Yes, because I didn't speak the truth.*—Ought you to be punished?—*No.*—Was it naughty or not naughty?—*Not so naughty.*—Why?—*Because I spoke the truth afterwards!"* (1965, p. 144)

It is as if young children usually define a lie as a moral fault. Only after age 10 or 11 do children begin to recognize intentions in relation to lying. At this level of reasoning, a lie is defined as something that is *intentionally false.* As we have seen with the previous moral concepts, an appreciation of intentions is not attained in most children until the development of formal operations.

Why One Should Not Lie.   Piaget reported that when children under age 7 or so were questioned about why one should not lie, the reason typically given was, "You get punished." A typical child's report follows:

ZAMB (6): "Why must we not tell lies?—*Because God punishes them.*—And if God didn't punish them?—*Then we could tell them.*" (1965, p. 168)

Punishment is the criterion used to determine whether a lie is permissible or not. According to young children, one does not tell a lie because of the punishment lying can bring. But if there is no punishment, it is perfectly acceptable to tell lies.

For the older child, after age 9 or so, there is a separation of the concept of lie from punishment. At this point in development, children typically believe that a lie is wrong even if it goes unpunished.

GIRL (9): "Why is it naughty [a lie]?—*Because we get punished.*—If you didn't know you had told a lie, would it be naughty too?—*It would be naughty, but less naughty.*—Why would it be naughty?—*Because it is a lie all the same.*" (1965, p. 169)

Here the rule is viewed by the child as obligatory and independent of punishment. There is clearly an element of cooperation in the child's reasoning, although rules are still seen as imposed by authorities on children rather than as an integral part of cooperation.

Piaget observed that a maturing of children's concepts about lying generally occurs around age 10–12. Intentions become the major criterion used to evaluate lying. The older child also recognizes that *not lying* is necessary for social cooperation. Children come to oppose lying because truthfulness is necessary for cooperation. Once again, there is a shift from a morality of constraint to a morality of cooperation.

In the first stage, a lie is wrong because it is an object of punishment; if the punishment were removed, it would be allowed. Then a lie becomes something that is wrong in itself and would remain so even if the punishment were removed. Finally, a lie is wrong because it is in conflict with mutual trust and affection. Thus the consciousness of lying gradually becomes interiorized and the hypothesis may be hazarded that it does so under the influence of cooperation. (1965, p. 171)

Young children's "lies" are often spontaneous and not designed to deceive.

[T]he tendency [in young children] to tell lies is a natural tendency, so spontaneous and universal that we can take it as an essential part of the child's egocentric thought. In the child, therefore, the problem of lies is the clash of the egocentric attitude with the moral constraint of the adult. (1965, p. 139)

The egocentric child often alters the truth according to his or her desires. Lying is viewed as "bad" by the young child *if it is punished by adults.* On the other hand, the child who has some expectation that lying will go unpunished sees nothing morally wrong with lying.

Punishment and Justice

In Piaget's research on the development of children's concepts of justice, and more specifically on their concepts of punishment, two distinct kinds of punishment emerge. The concept of punishment Piaget observed in young children he called *expiatory* punishment. Expiatory punishment is strong punishment administered to children by parents or other adult authorities for breaking rules. The general reasoning children use to support the use of expiatory punishment as just is that painful punishment will deter further rule breaking. Expiatory punishment is *arbitrary* in character because it does not bear any relationship to the offense. For example, a boy who did not clean up his room after being told to do so is punished by not being allowed to go to a movie. Or a child is sent on an important errand by the parent but does not carry out the request. The child is punished by not being allowed to play in the next school baseball game. In both cases, the punishments are not related to the *content* of the rule broken. Had the first boy been deprived of the use of everything in the room he did not clean up, the punishment would not be arbitrary (regarding the content). Expiatory punishment is always handed out by authorities, always involves constraint, and usually is arbitrary with respect to rules broken.

The second major type of punishment sanctioned by older children Piaget called *reciprocity.* Punishment by reciprocity assumes there is no need for painful punishment to gain adherence to rules. The person who breaks the rules must simply be made aware that breaking rules destroys the social relationship and the basic social contract of cooperation. This awareness, in itself, is believed to generate sufficient grief to restore and ensure cooperation. If material or social punishment is necessary, the punishment is not arbitrary. Punishment on the basis of reciprocity is *always* related in some way to the content of the rule broken. For example, the boy who did not clean up his room after being told to do so may be deprived of the objects (toys, clothes, books, and the like) he did not clean up. The child who did not perform a requested errand is denied similar help by his parents when the child requests it. These punishments are "natural consequences" of rule breaking and presumably help to point out to children the consequences of their actions. Although there can be a strong element of coercion in punishment by reciprocity, the emphasis is on persuasion and prevention rather than on arbitrary punishment or punishment for its own sake. Punishment by reciprocity is guided by principles of cooperation and equality rather than adult authority and constraint.

Piaget investigated children's concepts of justice by telling them stories about children who did things they were not supposed to do and asking which forms of punishment were most appropriate or just. Here is one of the stories:

> A little boy is playing in his room. His mother asks him to go and fetch some bread for dinner because there is none left in the house. But instead of going immediately the boy says that he can't be bothered, that he'll go in a minute, etc. An hour later he has not gone. Finally, dinner time comes, and there is no bread on the table. The father is not pleased and he wonders which would be the fairest way of punishing the boy. He thinks of three punishments. The first would be to forbid the boy to go to the Roundabouts [fair] the next day. . . . The second punishment the father thought of was not to let the boy have any bread to eat. (There was a little bread left from the previous days.) . . . The third punishment the father thinks of is to do to the boy the same thing as he had done. The father would say to him, "You wouldn't help your mother. Well, I am not going to punish you, but the next time you ask me to do anything for you, I shall not do it, and you will see how annoying it is when people do not help each other." (The little boy thinks this would be all right, but a few days later his father would not help him reach a toy he could not get by himself. The father reminded him of his promise.) . . . Which of these three punishments was the fairest? (1965, p. 202)

Children between 6 and 12 years of age were told four such stories and asked to judge which punishments were fairest and to give their reasoning for their judgments. Children were also asked to rate the punishments according to their severity. The responses children gave to the stories were classified as punishment by either reciprocity or expiation and the frequencies for different ages were determined. Piaget found a distinct increase in children's preference for punishment by reciprocity with increase in age and development (see Table 4.1). Although some children at all ages recommended expiatory punishment as most appropriate and some recommended punishment by reciprocity, a clear trend is evident. Younger children favor expiatory punishment; older children favor punishment by reciprocity.

> ANG (6) repeats story . . . correctly: "How should he be punished?—*Shut him up in a room.*—What will that do to him?—*He'd cry.*—Would that be fair?—*Yes.*" He is then told of the three possible punishments: "Which is the fairest?—*I'd not have given him his toy.*—Why?—*He's been naughty.*—Is

TABLE 4.1   Age and preferred punishment

Age	Percent of Children Preferring Punishment by Reciprocity
6–7	28
8–10	49
11–12	82

that the best of the three punishments?—*Yes.*—Why?—*Because he was very fond of his toy.*—Is that the fairest?—*Yes.*"Thus it is not the principle of reciprocity that carries the day, it is the idea of the severest punishment. . . .

ZIM (6): Zim does not think much of the last two punishments. The third "*is not hard.*—Why?—*On the little boy.*—Why is it not hard on him?—*It isn't much.*—The second is also '*not much.*'"The fairest therefore is the first "*because he's not on the Roundabouts* [at the fair]." (1965, p. 211)

Among younger children, the harshest punishment is usually judged as the fairest; the punishments selected are arbitrary relative to the behavior punished. It is clear that younger children believe in the need for severe punishment. As children develop, Piaget found that their concepts of justice change gradually. About half the children Piaget interviewed between the ages of 8 and 10 made judgments based on reciprocity and abandoned a criterion based on severity of punishment (expiatory punishment).

BAUM (9):"*The last [punishment] is the best. Since the boy won't help, well, his mother won't help him either.*—And which is the fairest of the other two punishments?—*Not to give him any bread, then he'd have nothing to eat at supper, because he wouldn't help his mother.*—And the first?—*That*

was the one he deserved least. He wouldn't have minded. He'd still have been able to play with his toys and he would have had bread in the evening." . . .

Nus (11): *"I'd have given him a smacking.*—The father thought of three punishments." (I tell them to him.) "Which do you think is the fairest?—*Not to give him any help.*—Do you think it is fairer than smacking him?—*Fairer.*—Why?—(He hesitates.) . . . *Because it's doing about the same thing to him as he had done.*—And of the other two, which is the fairest?—*Not to let him have any bread.*—Why?—*Because he didn't fetch any."* (1965, pp. 215-16)

These interviews demonstrate that the older children Piaget interviewed view neither severe nor arbitrary punishment as the most appropriate. For these children, punishment based on reciprocity is more just than punishment based on expiation. The emphasis is clearly on punishment that fits the crime and helps the child realize the social consequences of his or her actions. Older children's judgments as to which punishments are most appropriate seem to focus more on prevention and less on retaliation than do the judgments of younger children.

During preoperational development, moral concepts begin to develop. Children begin to be aware that some things are necessary to do even if they are not desirable to do. Children become aware of rules during this stage. Initially they view rules as fixed and unchangeable and as having been passed down by some authority.

Preoperational children do not have concepts of intentionality and fail to take the intentions of others into account. Thus, the accidents of other children are rarely viewed as accidents.

For preoperational children, justice tends to be equated with punishment and whatever adults say is right must be right. Again, lacking concepts of intentionality, children judge lies to be what authority says lies are.

SUMMARY

Qualitatively, the thought of the preoperational child is an advance over that of the sensorimotor child. Preoperational thought is no longer restricted to immediate perceptual and motor events. Thought can proceed at the level of representation and behavior sequences can be played out in the head rather than only in real physical events. Even so, perception still dominates reasoning. When conflicts arise between perception and thought, as in conservation problems, children using preoperational reasoning make judgments based on perception.

The preoperational stage is marked by some dramatic attainments. Language is constructed very rapidly between ages 2 and 4. Behavior in the early part of the period is largely egocentric and nonsocial. These characteristics become less dominant as the stage proceeds and, by age 6 or 7, children's conversations become largely communicative and social.

Although preoperational thought is an advance over sensorimotor thought, it is not yet fully logical; it is prelogical. At the outset, the child is unable to reverse operations and cannot follow transformations, perceptions tend to be centered, and the child is egocentric. These characteristics make for relatively slow, concrete, and restricted thought. During this stage, thought is still largely under the control of the immediate and the perceptual, as can be seen in the typical preoperational child's inability to solve conservation problems. As cognitive development proceeds, so too does affective development.

As the child continues to assimilate and accommodate experience into cognitive schemes, so too are affective and social schemata under constant construction and reconstruction. The 2-year-old is egocentric in his or her view of the world and use of spoken language. Under the press of social interaction with others (particularly peers), the child by age 7 or so comes to understand that others' points of view may differ from his or her own. Affective experiences, such as feeling, are represented and remembered, changing forever the nature of affective thoughts. As cognitive reasoning during the preoperational stage is semilogical, so too are preoperational children's understandings of rules, justice, and other elements of moral reasoning semilogical.

Cognitive development and affective development are not arrested from age 2 to age 7. Rather, they move steadily along, assimilation and accommodation resulting in the constant construction of new and improved cognitive machinery (schemata). The preoperational child's behavior is initially like that of the sensorimotor child. By age 7, there is little resemblance.

chapter **5**

The Development of Concrete Operations

Whether one conceives of development as proceeding along a straight-line continuum or in a spiraling continuum (Gallagher and Reid 1981), the important point is that progress between stages is continuous, as are changes within stages. There are no abrupt changes.[1]

During the development of concrete operations (ages 7–11), a child's reasoning processes become logical. He or she develops what Piaget called *logical operations.*[2] Piaget said that an intellectual (logical) operation "is an internalized system of actions that is fully reversible" (1981a, p. 59). During the concrete operational stage, the child evolves logical thought processes (operations) that can be applied to problems that exist (are concrete). Unlike the child who is preoperational, the child at the stage of concrete operations has no trouble solving conservation problems and providing correct reasoning for his or her answers. When faced with a discrepancy between thought and perception, as in conservation problems, the concrete operational child makes reasoning-based decisions, as opposed to perceptual decisions. The child is no longer perception-bound and becomes able, typically between the ages of 7 and 11, to solve most of the cognitive problems (such as the conservation problems) that the preoperational child could not solve. The concrete operational child decenters his or

---

[1] Some readers of Piaget conclude that Piaget's "stages" or levels are discrete and separate, as if a child goes to bed one night being preoperational and wakes up the next morning concrete operational. Nothing could be further from the truth. The progress is gradual, and over the years children develop from reasoning that is typical of the preoperational child to reasoning that is typical of the concrete operational child.

[2] An *operation* is "an action that can be internalized or thought about and this is mentally reversible—namely, that it can take place in one direction or in the opposite direction. An operation always implies conservation and the relation to a system of operations, or a total structure. For Piaget, operations are the *result,* not the *source,* of growth in intelligence" (Gallagher and Reid 1981, p. 234).

her perceptions and attends to *transformations.* Most important, the concrete operational child attains *reversibility* of mental operations.

In addition, the concrete operational child is increasingly more social and less egocentric (in use of language) than the preoperational child. Language is used primarily for communication. For the first time, the child becomes a truly social being.[3]

The quality of concrete operational thought surpasses that of preoperational thought. Schemata for the logical operations of seriation and classification appear. Improved concepts of causality, space, time, and speed evolve. In essence, the concrete operational child attains a level of intellectual activity superior in all respects to that of the preoperational child.

Although a concrete operational child evolves a functional use of logical reasoning not evidenced in the behavior of younger children, he or she does not attain the highest level of use of logical operations. Here the term *concrete* (as in concrete operations) is significant. Although the child clearly evolves logical operations, these operations (reversibility, classification, and so on) are useful only in solving problems involving concrete (real, observable) objects and events in the immediate present (Piaget 1972a). For the most part, concrete operational children cannot yet apply logic to problems that are hypothetical, purely verbal, or abstract. In addition, they cannot correctly reason about concrete problems that involve many variables. If concrete operational children are presented with a purely verbal problem, they are usually unable to solve it correctly. If the same problem is presented in terms of real objects, they can apply logical operations and solve the problem if there are not multiple variables involved. Thus, the concrete operational stage can be viewed as a transition between prelogical (preoperational) thought and the capability for completely logical thought of older children who have attained formal operations.

HOW CONCRETE OPERATIONAL THOUGHT DIFFERS FROM PREOPERATIONAL THOUGHT

The preoperational child's thought is characterized by the dominance of perception over reasoning and by egocentrism, centration, an inability to follow transformations, and an inability to reverse operations. These obstacles to logical thought are reflected in the preoperational child's inability to solve conservation problems. In contrast, concrete operational thought eventually becomes free of all the characteristics that

---

[3] Again, Piaget uses a strict criterion for what is social.

[4] The transformation from the latter part of preoperational thought to early concrete operational thought is not an abrupt one. The characteristics of preoperational reasoning are gradually modified throughout the latter part of the preoperational stage and the early part of the concrete operational stages.

Children typically construct and can use reversibility with regard to conservation of number problems by age 6 or so. The successful application of reversibility to liquid volume problems is not attained until about age 7. Piaget called this apparent "unevenness" in development of reasoning *décalage.*

Translators T. Brown and K. Thampy note that "décalage has been variously translated or left untranslated in English versions of Piaget's works. There being no standard translation, . . . "phase differences" . . . seems to most adequately express its meaning" (Brown 1985, p. 8).

dominated preoperational thought.[4] The typical concrete operational child can solve conservation problems. His thought is less egocentric; he can decenter his perceptions; he can follow transformations; and most important, he can reverse operations. When conflicts arise between perception and reasoning, the concrete operational child makes judgments based on reasoning. These characteristics are discussed in the pages that follow.

Egocentrism and Socialization

The preoperational child's thinking was dominated by egocentrism, an inability to assume the viewpoint of others, and the lack of a need to seek validation of her own thoughts. The concrete operational child's thinking is not egocentric in this respect. She constructs the understanding that others can come to conclusions that are different from hers, and as a consequence she is able to see a need for validation of her thoughts. In this respect, the concrete operational child is liberated from the intellectual egocentrism of the previous period.

According to Piaget, liberation from egocentrism comes about primarily through social interaction with peers,[5] as the child is compelled to seek verification of ideas.

> What then gives rise to the need for verification? Surely it must be the shock of our thoughts coming into contact with that of others, which produces doubt and the desire to prove. . . . The social need to share the thoughts of others and to communicate our own with success is at the root of our need for verification. Proof is the outcome of argument. . . . Argument is, therefore, the backbone of verification. (Piaget 1928, p. 204)

The concrete operational child does not display the egocentrism of thought characteristic of the preoperational child. During concrete operations, the use of language becomes more fully communicative in function. Concepts are verified or denied through "arguments" with others in social interaction. As said previously, the socialization of behavior is a continuous process that begins in early childhood with simple imitations. Social interaction involving dialogue and argument over ideas, by its very nature, is an important source of disequilibrium. Coming to look at something from another's viewpoint, questioning one's reasoning, and seeking validation from others are all essentially acts of accommodation.

With the development of concrete operations, language becomes less egocentric. Collective monologues, characteristic of children's speech before age 6 or 7, are largely absent. Children exchange information with one another in their conversations and learn to view events from the position of others.

---

[5] Piaget identified social interaction as one of the major variables that facilitate cognitive development. His writings suggest that social interactions are any behaviors (conversations, play, games, and so forth) that involve a real interchange between two or more people. Thus, when language becomes functionally communicative, it is a form of social interaction.

Centration

The preoperational child's thinking is characterized by centration. Perceptions of events tend to center on single or limited perceptual aspects of a stimulus and do not take into account all the salient features of the stimulus. Thus, as we saw in the conservation of number problems, preoperational children tend to center on the length of stimulus configurations. The concrete operational child's thinking is not characterized by centering. Concrete thought becomes decentered. Decentering, using all salient perceptual features, is one of the abilities found in concrete thought that permits more fully logical solutions to concrete problems.

Transformation

The preoperational child was unable to focus and coordinate on successive steps in a transformation. Each step in a transformation was viewed as independent of each successive step. There was no awareness or attention paid to the sequence or transformation involved.

The concrete operational child constructs a functional understanding of transformations. He or she can solve problems involving concrete transformations and is aware of, and understands, the relationship between successive steps. Transformational reasoning becomes apparent in reasoning about affect as well. For example, concrete operational children develop the ability to understand the reasons for changes or transformations in states of feeling of others, say, from happy to sad.

Reversibility

Preoperational thought lacks reversibility. Concrete operational thought is reversible. The difference between the two levels of thought can be seen in the following illustration of *inversion* (Piaget 1967). A child is shown three balls of the same size but each of a different color, marked *A, B, C* (see Figure 5.1). The balls are placed in a cylinder in the order *C, B, A*. The preoperational child correctly predicts that the balls will exit from the bottom of the cylinder in the same order: *C, B, A*. Once more, the balls are put in the cylinder in the same order. Then the cylinder is rotated 180 degrees. A preoperational child, lacking reversibility, continues to predict that the balls will exit from the bottom of the tube in the same order as before: *C, B, A*. He or she is surprised when they exit in the order *A, B, C*. This is an example of the inability of preoperational thought to mentally reverse operations and use the form of reversibility called *inversion*. A concrete operational child who has constructed reversibility has no trouble with the above problem.[6] He or she can invert the change and make the appropriate deduction. Inversion is one of two primary forms of reversibility.

---

[6] The rotation of balls problem demonstrates simple reversibility. Heard and Wadsworth (1977) found this form of reversibility to be attained, on average, late in the sixth year.

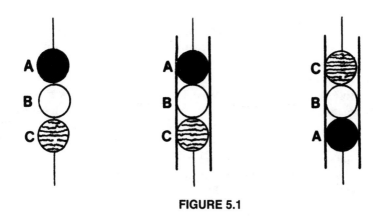

FIGURE 5.1

The second kind of reversibility that concrete operational children use is *reciprocity*. In response to the conservation of liquid problem (see Chapter 4), some concrete operational children argue that when liquid is poured into a taller but thinner container, the quantity of liquid does not change because the increased height is compensated for by the narrowness of the container (width compensates height). This is reasoning with *reciprocity*, or by compensation, and is the second form of reversibility found in concrete operational reasoning.[7]

Conservation

A hallmark of preoperational thought is the child's inability to conserve. With the attainment of concrete operations, the ability to reason logically about and solve conservation problems emerges. The related abilities to decenter, to follow transformations, and to reverse operations by inversion and reciprocity are all instrumental in developing conservation skills and advancing reasoning. A child becomes able to solve conservation of number problems around age 6 or 7. Conservation of area and mass problems are usually solved by age 7 or 8. Conservation of volume problems (measurement of displaced water when an object is immersed) are not solved correctly until age 11 or 12.

LOGICAL OPERATIONS

Cognitively, the most important development of the concrete operational stage is the attainment (construction) of logical operations. Logical operations are internalized cognitive actions that permit a child to arrive at conclusions that are "logical." These

---

[7] The argument by inversion for the conservation of liquid problem would be that if the liquid were poured back into its original container—from the tall, thin container—there would be the same amount of liquid.

actions are directed by cognitive activity rather than dominated by perceptions, as was the case with preoperational thought. Logical operations are constructed, as are all cognitive structures, out of prior structures as a function of assimilation and accommodation. Logical operations are means of organizing experience (schemata) that are superior to prior organization.

According to Piaget, an operation always has four characteristics: It is an action that can be internalized or carried out in thought as well as materially, it is reversible, it always supposes some conservation and some invariance, and it never exists alone but is always related to a system of operations (Piaget 1970a). Operations become truly logical during the concrete operational stage. Previous operations (at the preoperational stage) were prelogical, never meeting all the above criteria. One logical operation, already discussed, is reversibility. Two other structures central to concrete operations are *seriation* and *classification* (Piaget 1977b). Seriation and classification are basic to the child's understanding of number concepts (Wadsworth 1978; Gallagher and Reid 1981).

Seriation: Ordering Objects According to Differences

Seriation is the ability to mentally arrange a set of elements accurately along a dimension such as size, weight, or volume. The ability to seriate *length* develops throughout the preoperational and concrete operational development. The task originally used by Piaget to assess knowledge of seriation of length is a simple one. A child is presented with a set of approximately 10 sticks varying in length by small but perceptible differences (1/4 inch). The child is asked to order the sticks from the smallest to the largest. The examiner may show a properly arranged construction before asking the child to make his or her construction. Piaget's research discerns five levels in development of seriation of length knowledge.

At the first level, age 4 or earlier, children typically place some of the sticks in a construction, with no order discernible (see Figure 5.2). At Level 2, children construct pairs made up of a small stick and a large stick, but their constructions show no relationship between pairs. Any stick can be placed in relation to any other stick but is not simultaneously related to 2 sticks. Four- and five-year-olds eventually begin to form groups of 3 sticks, but without any order between groups of sticks.

At the next level, which is transitional (between Level 2 and Level 3), advances are made and several partial coordinations are seen. Children aged 5–7 years often align the tops of the sticks (as in Figure 5.2) while paying no attention to the alignment of the bottoms of the sticks. Some children successfully order 4 or 5 sticks in a set, but usually no more.

At Levels 3 and 4, children aged 7–8 successfully order the set of 10 sticks (as in the model), but there are qualitative differences in methods between the two levels. Level 3 children typically use a trial-and-error approach.

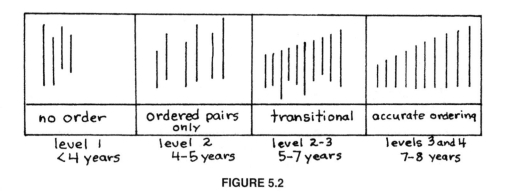

no order	ordered pairs only	transitional	accurate ordering
level I < 4 years	level 2 4–5 years	level 2–3 5–7 years	levels 3 and 4 7–8 years

FIGURE 5.2

The entire series is finally ordered but by an empirical grouping method, that is, with local errors and corrections afterwards. On the other hand, the subject has not mastered the transitivity problem. (Piaget 1977a, p. 131)

At Level 3, the child is unable to order 3 or more sticks in order mentally, demonstrating a lack of *transitivity*.[8] If it is unclear whether a child can order the series mentally, he or she can be asked to place the sticks successively in order behind a visual screen. This requires a mental ordering of the series for successful construction.

At Level 4, children have no difficulty with the seriation task. The 10 sticks are ordered accurately without trial and error. Children use strategies such as searching for the smallest stick, then the next smallest, and so on.

This strategy implies both transitivity and the reversibility inherent in an operational structure: any stick is longer than all the preceding ones and also shorter than all those that follow it in the series. (Gallagher and Reid 1981, p. 97)

Children at this level also have no difficulty making their construction behind a visual screen. They are confident that their constructions are correct, even when they cannot see them.

---

[8] Understanding *transitivity* is understanding that if A is less than B and B is less than C, then A is necessarily less than C. Comprehension of transitivity is usually determined by using a problem similar to the following one: A child is presented with two sticks. One stick (A) is slightly shorter than the other stick (B). The child is asked to compare the two sticks and determine which stick is longer. The child is then shown stick B and a third stick (C), which is slightly longer. Stick A is hidden from the child during the new comparison. The child is asked to compare sticks B and C. These first two comparisons are almost always accurate. With stick A still hidden, the child is asked to compare sticks A and C. To solve this problem, the child must be able to mentally order the three sticks A, B, and C. Children typically develop transitive reasoning of this kind around age 7.

Children's knowledge about seriation is constructed over a period of years. Each advance is a new equilibrium in the child's reasoning. Seriation of length is generally attained around age 7 or 8.[9]

Classification: Mentally Grouping Objects According to Similarities

In Piaget's traditional classification studies, children are presented with sets of objects (such as geometric shapes varying in size and color) and are asked to put the objects that are alike together (Piaget and Inhelder 1969; Piaget 1972b). Three levels of development emerge from these studies.

Level 1.   Children 4 or 5 years old typically proceed by selecting objects to go together based on similarities. But the criterion they use is what is similar between two objects at a time. Thus, a child may put together a black circle and a white circle (both circles), then may add a white triangle to the white circle (both white), then may place a gray triangle with the white triangle (both triangles), insisting that they all go together (Figure 5.3). Objects are assimilated to similarities between individual pairs of objects only. Differences between objects in the set are ignored. There is no plan for the total set.

FIGURE 5.3

<hr />

[9] Different kinds of seriation learning, like different kinds of conservation learning, occur at different ages in an invariant sequence. Seriation of length is mastered usually at age 7 or 8 years. Seriation of weight (objects of the same size but different weights) is usually attained around age 9. Seriation of volume is not attained until age 12 or so (Piaget 1967).

The seriation task described has been used in studies on children's memory with interesting results (Piaget and Inhelder 1969). The 10-stick seriation task is presented and constructions noted. After a period of time (a week or more), the same children are asked to order the sticks again as they were asked to on the prior occasion. Again, performance is noted. Piaget and Inhelder found that many of the children's performance improved between the two occasions with improvement in their levels of development. They interpreted these results as indicating that "memory causes the schemes corresponding to the child's level to predominate: the image-memory relates to this scheme rather than the perceptual model" (Piaget and Inhelder 1969, p. 82). The conclusion was that children remember what they understand rather than strictly what they see, and that memory (what they understand) will improve over time if understanding improves.

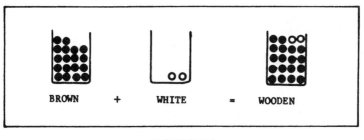

FIGURE 5.4

Level 2. Through age 7, children typically form collections of like objects along one dimension. That is, circles are put together, triangles are put together, and so on, when children are classifying by shape. If children are classifying by color, they put black circles and black triangles together. Missing at this level of reasoning is any awareness of the *relationships between* collections or subcollections. Children at this level do not understand the logical relationship between a class and a subclass—or *class inclusion.*

In the typical class inclusion task, a child is presented with 20 brown wooden beads and 2 white wooden beads (Figure 5.4). After the child agrees that the beads are all wooden and 20 are brown and 2 are white, the following kind of question is asked: "Are there more wooden beads or more brown beads?" (Piaget 1952a).

Level 2 children typically respond that there are more brown beads than wooden beads because they compare the classes of brown and white and are unable to compare the subclass of brown beads to the larger class of wooden beads. These children do not understand class inclusion.

Level 3. Around age 8, children typically demonstrate an understanding of the class inclusion principle. Their reasoning on the class inclusion problem indicates that they understand that the class of brown beads must be smaller than the class of wooden beads. They consider *differences* (non-brown beads) as well as similarities in classification and are able to reason about the *relationships* between classes and subclasses.

Children's number concepts result from a synthesis of the logical operations of seriation and inclusion (Piaget and Inhelder 1969). Number concepts involve both order (seriation) and group membership (inclusion). The number concept "8" is a place in a series, and it is part of a set that includes 1, 2, 3, 4, 5, 6, 7, and 8.[10]

By now it should be clear to the reader that Piaget conceptualized cognitive development as occurring not in isolation but in all areas at the same time. A cognitive advance in one area affects other areas. With this in mind, consider the concrete operational child's concepts of causality, time, and speed.

---

[10] For more on number concepts, see Wadsworth 1978; Kamii 1982; Copeland 1974.

Causality

Children's concepts of causality develop in the same manner that other concepts do. Development of causal concepts during the sensorimotor period was illustrated in Chapter 3. Piaget and Inhelder (1969) investigated children's concepts of causality in the following problem situation:

> [W]e once asked children from five to twelve what happens after lumps of sugar are dissolved in a glass of water. For children up to about seven, the dissolved sugar disappears and its taste vanishes like a mere odor; for children seven to eight its substance is retained without either its weight or its volume. After nine or ten, conservation of weight is present, and after eleven or twelve, there is also conservation of volume (recognizable in the fact that the level of water, which is slightly raised when the sugar is added, does not return to its initial level after the sugar is dissolved). (p. 112)

As the above illustrates, children's causal concepts develop during the concrete operational stage. Qualitative changes in structures (schemata) are reflected in the development.

Time and Speed

Piaget and Inhelder contended that children typically do not understand the relationship between time and speed (velocity = speed/time) until age 10 or 11 (1969). Before this age, an object is considered to travel faster than another object only if it overtakes it while moving. When comparing the speeds of two objects, the preoperational child usually considers only the points of arrival and does not consider starting points and subsequent velocity or paths followed. Consider the following: Two cars leave point A in Figure 5.5 at the same time. They both arrive at B at the same time, but they traverse different routes (1 and 2). After viewing this problem, observing the movement of the cars, the preoperational child reports that both cars traveled at the same speed. Not until age 8 or so does a ratio concept of speed in terms of the relationship between time and distance traveled begin to evolve.

The concrete operational child's concepts of time and speed are superior to those of the preoperational child. Not until the stage of concrete operations do accurate concepts appear.

AFFECTIVE DEVELOPMENT: COOPERATION

Cognitive development, affective development, and social development are inseparable. Thus, when social, cognitive, and affective development are conceptualized independently, it is no surprise that there are clear parallels between them.

Piaget (1963b) attached clear importance to the social relations among children for intellectual and affective development. Because children's relations are among

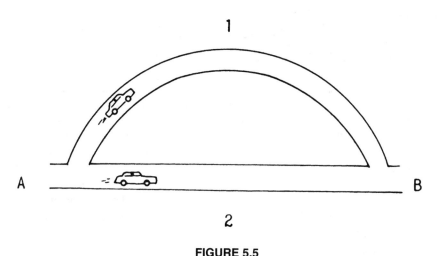

FIGURE 5.5

equals, cooperation becomes a real possibility. Although partially socialized behavior is evident from the time of spoken language, Piaget asserts that it is around 7 or 8 (the emergence of cognitive operations), with preoperational egocentrism well in retreat, that there is usually systematic progress in cooperation. This is seen clearly in children's understanding of rules in games. Youniss and Damon (1992) write:

> Piaget depicted children's relationships with peers as the ideal context for cooperation. His reasoning was that peers would, on the average, have to cooperate to get along since their relationship was based on symmetrical reciprocity. (273)

Children have the potential to interact socially with one another as equals, but typically they interact with adults as if they (the children) are inferiors (unilateral respect). Conflicts between children are overcome only through genuine cooperation. Youniss and Damon continue:

> Piaget . . . argued strongly that in the process of discovering and practicing procedures that mediate peer cooperation, children form a common sense of social solidarity. There . . . is reliance on processes that require the cooperation of others . . . and is based in mutual understanding that results from children's communicative exchanges of ideas. (273)

Thus Piaget viewed the preoperational child as developing two streams of interpersonal moral reasoning concurrently. In general, interactions with adults are based on unilateral respect whereas interactions with peers, where peer problems are worked out, come increasingly to be based on mutual respect (cooperation). Thus, the ways in which children interact differently with peers and adults have different outcomes for development.

In concrete operations, reasoning and thought acquire greater stability than prevails in preoperational thought. The capability for reasoning becomes increasingly logical and less subject to influence by apparent perceptual contradictions. Reversibility of thought and decentering help bring consistency and conservation to the concrete operational child's reasoning.

These factors influence not only cognitive reasoning but also affective reasoning. During concrete operations, affect acquires a measure of stability and consistency that was not present earlier.

During the development of concrete operations, internalized *reversible* operations (reversibility) appear in the child's affective reasoning. The origins of reversibility in affective life were seen in the preoperational thought. At that time, feelings were not fully "conserved" and affect was prenormative; but because day-to-day feelings could be represented and remembered, feelings were no longer unrelated to prior feelings.[11]

Around age 7 or 8, there emerges *conservation of feelings* and values. Children become able to coordinate their affective thoughts from one event to another. What is preserved or conserved, over time, are aspects of past feelings. Affective thought is now reversible. The past can be made a part of reasoning in the present through the ability to reverse and conserve.

Piaget suggested that social interaction during the preoperational stage encourages the development of conservation of feelings.

> [S]ocial life requires thought to acquire a certain permanence. For this to occur, mental activity can no longer be represented in terms of personal symbols such as playful fantasies [symbolic play] but will have to be expressed in universal signifiers such as linguistic signs [language]. The uniformity and consistency of expression enforced by social life plays a large part, therefore, in the development of intellectual structures with their conservations and invariants; and it will lead to analogous transformations in the domain of feelings. In effect, the permanence obviously lacking from spontaneous feelings will appear with social and, especially, moral feelings. . . .
>
> [L]iking another person is a feeling that varies as long as it is spontaneous and linked to particular situations. It becomes lasting and reliable when feelings of *semi-obligation* are added. [italics added] (Piaget 1981b, p. 60)

We noted in the last chapter that preoperational affect was prenormative. That is, preoperational children typically have not developed a sense of obligation (what is necessary) as opposed to a sense of obedience. Although behavior occasionally

---

[11] Prenormative behavior is behavior that is not regulated by norms or values constructed by the individual.

seems to reflect a sense of obligation during preoperational development, such is not the dominant pattern. Affect does not meet fully any of the three criteria for being normative: being generalizable, lasting beyond the moment, and being linked to autonomy. During the concrete operational stage, these criteria are normally met as children's affective reasoning capabilities become operational. In the same way that the construction of reversibility leads to a logic of thought, reversibility leads to a logic of affect.[12] Internalized reversible operations appear in the affective domain.

To better understand Piaget's beliefs about affective development during the concrete operational stage, it is important to understand his conceptualization of *the will* and *autonomy.*

The Will

There are situations where one is confronted with a choice between what one wants to do (desire) and what one "should" do or feels obligated to do morally. For example, you have two free hours and you can either go see the movie you're dying to see (desire) or visit your invalid uncle in a nursing home (obligation). One chooses to visit the invalid uncle and forgoes the anticipated pleasure of seeing the movie. Such choices are social and interpersonal, and imply a sense of obligation and values. The capability for reasoning and behavior of this sort emerge during Piaget's concrete operational period. Piaget attributes the capability of this form of decision making to the emergence of what he calls the will, "an instrument for conserving values" (p. 61).

Piaget (1981) says:

> [I]n order to speak of *will,* a conflict between two impulses or tendencies must be present. Second, the impulse that is initially weaker must become the stronger of the two in the course of an act of will. (p. 61)

Thus it is when the original stronger impulse, the desire to see the movie, is replaced by the weaker impulse to visit the uncle in the nursing home. For Piaget, *will* is the affective analogue of cognitive operations—part of the logic of feelings. "The act of will corresponds. . . to the conservation of values; it consists of subordinating a given situation to a permanent scale of values" (p. 65).

Thus, Piaget viewed the will as a permanent *scale of values* constructed by the individual to which he or she feels obliged to adhere. The will assumes the role of reg-

---

[12] Logic of affectivity may sound like a contradiction in terms. Piaget suggested that feelings are variable, and thus the behavior activated by feelings may be variable. When feelings begin to be conserved, that is, to last from one situation to the next, a permanence underlying variable feelings emerges (Piaget 1981b). A contradiction exists only if one asserts that feelings may not vary if they are to be logical: "[S]ome people will say that moral feelings, however normative they may be, remain less universal, less stable, and less coercive than operational rules. This objection, in our opinion, is unfounded. If, in fact, some differences between logical and moral norms were to be found, it would be one of degree, not one of nature. On the whole, we believe this difference to be weaker than is ordinarily imagined. Common thought is at least as far removed from operational norms as everyday behavior is from moral norms" (p. 61).

ulator (self-regulation) of affect and is the mechanism by which *values* are conserved. In cognitive activity, conflicts between perceptual experience and logical reasoning are regulated through conservation—the ability to maintain constancy in the face of logically irrelevant change. Similarly, conflicts between affective impulses are regulated by the will, once the will is developed. Once values are reasonably stable and the will is in place, values can be asserted over conflicting impulses, even though the impulse may have been stronger at one point than the values and the will. The key idea here is that feelings, conserved as values, engender a *sense of obligation* to act on those values. To act contrary to one's constructed values is to act in contradiction to one's self. Values can change over time through further construction.

According to Piaget, a number of factors prompt the gradual development of the will. One factor, already mentioned, is the demand of social experience, which encourages cooperation and a consistency in affective life. Behavior that has continuity is reinforced by others more than inconsistent behavior. In addition, affective experiences and feelings are now conserved. At any given moment, the affective past—now represented in memory and the present—is a part of affective reasoning. The affective experiences of the past can no longer be disregarded. An awareness of past and present feelings, now instituted as values, can lead to different affective decisions than an awareness of only present feelings.[13]

Autonomy

A second major developmental advance in affectivity during the concrete operational period is the emergence of autonomous feelings and their eventual products, mutual respect relations with adults. Piaget (1981b) writes:

> The notion of *autonomous* . . . means that it is possible for the [child] . . . to elaborate his [or her] . . . own norms, at least in part. [p. 66] After seven or eight years of age, the child becomes capable of making his own moral evaluations, performs freely decided acts of *will,* and exhibits moral feelings, which in certain cases, conflict with feelings seen in the heteronomous morality of obedience [unilateral respect]. (p. 65)

Autonomy of reasoning is reasoning according to one's own constructed set of norms. It evaluates rather than automatically accepts the preformed values of others. In addition, autonomous reasoning considers others as well as the self. Autonomy is *self-regulation.*[14]

---

[13] The existence of will does not mean that behavior is never impulsive. The presence of the will merely indicates that one has the *capability* to reason about affective issues from a coordinated, reversible perspective. Many factors besides reasoning influence behavior. Thus, it is not necessarily inconsistent to observe what seems to be impulsive behavior after the will is present. On the other hand, to act in opposition to one's will is a contradiction of sorts likely to engender guilt.

[14] Autonomy is discussed here in relation to affective development. The relevance of autonomy for cognitive development is further elaborated in Chapter 8.

During the preoperational stage, children view and accept rules as handed down from some higher authority—parents, God, or the government. Justice is viewed in the light of living up to those rules. The child's morality at the preoperational level is one of obedience, what Piaget called *unilateral respect*. Preoperational children do not reason about what is right or wrong. For them, what is right or wrong is predetermined (by authority) and not subject to their own evaluation. There is little cooperation in the social sense—there is only obedience, or unilateral respect.

Around age 7 or 8, children *begin* to be capable of making their own moral evaluations and thus begin to elaborate their own norms. That is, they begin to reason about the correctness or incorrectness of actions and the effects of actions on others. This, of course, does not mean that their evaluations are necessarily correct; it means only that they begin to shift from a heteronomous morality of obedience to performed values (unilateral respect) to a morality of cooperation and evaluation.

Mutual respect is an agent in the development of autonomous thought that appears during this stage. Until around age 7 or 8, children regard adults with unilateral respect (respect for authority). Children's morality is primarily one of obedience. Mutual respect is respect between "equals." Children can develop mutual respect only after they become able to see someone else's point of view.

One might suspect that mutual respect arises out of social pressures and experience. Piaget suggested that this is not the case, that social experience does not sufficiently explain this development. If anything, adult society usually encourages children to internalize unilateral respect for adult authority.[15]

Piaget (1963b) writes,

[T]he specific source of morality among children is the affective and cognitive reciprocity or "mutual respect" that disengages itself slowly from unilateral respect. This starts as early as the level of concrete intellectual operation and cooperation.

Mutual respect grows out of exchanges between individuals considered as equals. It presupposes, first of all, an acceptance of common values, particularly with respect to the exchanges themselves. Each partner evaluates others from the point of view of these values and is subject to the other's evaluation in such a way that one again finds in mutual respect the combination of sympathy and fear belonging to all respect. In this case, however, fear is not fear of a superior power [as with unilateral respect], but becomes fear of losing the esteem of those who the subject, himself, esteems. . . .

---

[15] One objective often voiced by parents and educators is the development of "self-discipline." Self-discipline presumably is the control of one's behavior *by the self*. If Piaget is correct, self-discipline can most effectively be established through encouraging the development of cognitive and affective autonomy and mutual respect relations. Indeed, it is questionable whether schools and parents functioning exclusively on a morality of unilateral respect can be a source of self-discipline. Autonomy arises only out of environments where children are able to establish mutual respect relationships.

obedience [as in unilateral respect] is, in fact, replaced by the autonomous observation of norms. (pp. 46–47)

Parents and teachers see early indicators of developing autonomy when children begin to come into conflict with adults over what is just and right. The 7-year-old who complains—claiming a lack of justice—that an older sibling got a bigger piece of cake or got to stay up an hour longer is often exhibiting autonomy of reasoning.

Cognitive and affective autonomy grow out of children's efforts toward self-regulation. The act of constructing knowledge—assimilation and accommodation—is self-regulation and is autonomy in action. From birth, children strive to make sense of their experiences, to assimilate the world around them, and to be autonomous in their construction of cognitive and affective knowledge. Thus autonomy can be viewed as a *habit* of action that children can begin to develop early on.

A key period in the continuous development of affective autonomy is during the concrete operational stage, when children normally move from a view of moral reasoning based on unilateral respect to a view based on mutual respect. Cooperative social relations with adults (parents and teachers) and peers where children are respected and treated as equals are necessary.

With the development of the will and autonomy, clear shifts become evident in children's concepts of rules, accidents, lying, justice, and moral reasoning.

Rules

During sensorimotor development, children do not have concepts of rules for games. During preoperational development, children become aware of rules and demand of others a rigid adherence to rules. They view rules as fixed and permanent, and when they play games, they play to win.

Usually around age 7 or 8 (the beginning of the concrete operational stage of reasoning), children begin to grasp the significance of rules for proper game playing. *Cooperation* in a social sense begins to emerge. Rules are no longer seen as absolute and unchangeable. Children typically develop the notion that the rules of the game can be changed if all agree to the change. Children begin to try to win (a social act) while conforming to the rules of the game.

In seeking to win the child is trying above all to contend with his partners *while observing common rules.* The specific pleasure of the game ceases to be muscular [Stage 1] and egocentric [Stage 2] and becomes social. (Piaget 1965, p. 42)

For the child who is beginning to demonstrate cooperation, the aim of the game is no longer to knock the marbles out of the circle or square but to win (in a competitive sense).

Although cooperation is evident in Stage 3 children, they typically do not know (have not constructed) the rules of the game in detail, and many discrepancies are apparent in children's reports of what rules are. This lack of agreement about the rules and the emphasis on winning can be observed in practically any group of young children engaged in a game. If permitted, they will spend more time arguing about what the rules are, in an effort to win, than they will spend actually playing the game.

Accidents and Clumsiness

Earlier it was noted that preoperational children are unable to consider the intention of others in their judgments about accidents. Thus, the preoperational child who is accidentally bumped by another typically views the bumping as intentional rather than possibly accidental. Similarly, the child who breaks 15 cups is naughtier than the child who breaks a single cup, regardless of either child's intentions. Fifteen broken cups are worse than one.

Around age 8 or 9, the typical child who is developing concrete operations begins to develop the ability to consider others' points of view. With this ability, intentions begin to be understood and considered when making judgments. Retribution is no longer automatically sought in the case of accidents. Intentions become more important than the consequences of actions. The boy who broke 15 cups by accident is no longer viewed as worse than the boy who broke a single cup doing something he was told not to do.

Unfortunately, Piaget's view of children's understanding of accidents does not offer any hope that young children can be taught to understand other children's intentions. The understanding of intentions cannot be taught to young children through verbal methods. According to Piaget, each child must *construct* the concept out of his or her active interactions with others. Peers are particularly important in this process. Until a child becomes capable of taking the viewpoint of others, he or she, in theory, cannot construct a concept of intentionality. Piaget's findings help us to understand young children's responses to the accidents and clumsiness of others, but they do not solve the problem of what to do about such behavior.[16]

Lying

We have seen that well into concrete operational development, children view a lie as something that is not true. It is not until around age 10 or 11 that children begin to consider intentions when judging whether an act is a lie. At this level, untruths that are not intended to deceive are not automatically judged to be lies.

---

[16] The obvious implication in this situation is to realize that all children cannot understand intentions and consequently cannot respond to reasoning about intentions. This does not mean you have to excuse a child who hits another child who accidentally bumped into him. What it means is that you cannot expect the child to understand an argument that involves intentions. The only solution is to forbid children to hit other children and to punish them when they do and reward them when they do not. On the other hand, some accidents and their retributions may be necessary in order for children to be prompted to construct the concepts involved. Young children typically understand that they themselves have accidents before they appreciate the accidents of others. Certainly the ability to take the view of another requires interactions.

The "adult" concept of a lie is very different from that of the typical preoperational or early concrete operational child. Implicit in this difference is that most children cannot understand the adult conception of a lie before developing middle concrete operational thought. Even if they wish to, younger children cannot make adultlike judgments about lying.

> The child . . . is told not to lie long before he understands the social value of this order (for lack of sufficient socialization) and sometimes before he is able to distinguish intentional deception from the distortions of reality that are due to symbolic play or to simple desire. As a result, veracity (truth) is external to the personality of the subject and gives rise to moral realism and objective responsibility whereby a lie appears to be serious not to the degree that it corresponds to intent to deceive, but to the degree that it differs materially from the objective truth. (Piaget and Inhelder 1969, p. 126)

Justice

Piaget's research revealed that children's concepts of justice change as they develop. Preoperational children consider rules as fixed and unchangeable. "Just" punishments are harsh and often arbitrary (expiatory punishment). During concrete operational development, children construct a better, though not complete, understanding of laws and rules. They begin to consider the role of intentions in deciding what is just. In addition, concrete operational children increasingly come to regard punishment by reciprocity as more appropriate than expiatory punishment.

Such is the case when a young girl is denied the use of objects scattered around her room after being instructed to clean them up and not doing so. The punishment in this instance is not arbitrary; it bears some relation to the punishable behavior.

As children develop affectively, parallel changes can be observed in their moral reasoning. The development of normative affect, the will, and autonomous reasoning influence the moral and affective life of the concrete operational child. Children develop the capacity to see the view of others, consider intentions, and better adapt to the social world.

SUMMARY

Concrete operational development is a transitional period between preoperational thought and formal (logical) thought. During concrete operational development, a child attains the use of fully logical operations for the first time. Thought is no longer dominated by perceptions and the child is able to solve problems that exist or have existed (are concrete) in his or her experience.

The concrete operational child is not egocentric in thought in the way that preoperational children are. The child at the stage of concrete operations can assume the viewpoint of others and spoken language is social and communicative. Such children can decenter perception and attend to transformations. Reversibility of thought is developed. Two important intellectual operations that develop are seriation and classification, which form the basis of number concepts.

Parallels can be observed between cognitive development and affective development during this stage. The development of the *will*, which engenders a sense of obligation to one's norms or values, allows for the regulation of affective reasoning. Autonomy of reasoning and affect continues to develop in social relations that encourage mutual respect. The child increasingly is capable of evaluating arguments rather than simply accepting preformed unilateral ideas. This is accompanied by an understanding of intentionality and an increased capability of considering motives when making judgments. Growth can be seen in children's moral concepts, such as their understanding of rules, lying, accidents, and justice.

chapter 6

The Development of Formal Operations

During the development of formal operations, which typically begins around age 11 or 12, a child constructs the reasoning and logic to solve all classes of problems. There is a freeing of thought from direct experience. The child's cognitive structures reach maturity during this stage. That is, his or her potential quality of reasoning or thought (compared with the potential of "adult" thought) is at its maximum when formal operations are fully developed. After this stage, there are no further structural improvements in the quality of reasoning. The adolescent with fully developed formal operations typically has the cognitive *structural* equipment to think "as well as" adults. This does not mean that the thinking of the adolescent with formal reasoning is necessarily "as good as" adult thought in a particular instance, although it may be as logical or well-reasoned; it means only that the potential has been achieved. Both adults and adolescents with formal operations reason using the same logical processes.

Assimilation and accommodation, prompted by disequilibrium, continue throughout life to produce changes in schemata. After the complete development of formal operations, changes in reasoning abilities are quantitative and no longer qualitative with respect to logical operations and *structure*. That is, the *structures* of reasoning are complete. The quality of reasoning one is capable of does not improve after this aspect of development. The *content* and *function* of intelligence can be expected to improve. This does not mean that the use of thought cannot or does not improve after adolescence. The content and function of thought are free to vary and improve after this stage, which in part helps explain some of the classical differences between adolescent thought and adult thought.

One should not assume that all adolescents and adults fully develop formal operations. Several studies concluded that no more than half the American population develops all the possibilities of formal operations (Elkind 1962; Kohlberg and Mayer

1972; Schwebel 1975; and Kuhn et al. 1977). Certainly a substantial proportion of the American adult population never advances much beyond concrete operational reasoning even though most have every potential for acquiring formal operations.

HOW FORMAL OPERATIONS DIFFER FROM CONCRETE OPERATIONS

Functionally, formal thought and concrete thought are similar. They both employ logical operations. The major difference between the two kinds of thought is the much greater range of application and type of logical operations available to the child with formal thought. Concrete thought is limited to solving tangible concrete problems known in the present. Concrete operational children have difficulty reasoning about complex verbal problems involving propositions, hypothetical problems, or the future. The reasoning of concrete operational children is content-bound—tied to available experience. To this extent, a concrete operational child is not completely free of past and present perceptions. In contrast, a child with fully developed formal operations can deal with all classes of problems. He or she can reason effectively about the present, past, and future, the hypothetical, and verbal propositional problems. During this phase, the child becomes capable of introspection and is able to think about his or her own thoughts and feelings as if they were objects. Thus the child with fully developed formal operations is capable of reasoning in a manner that is more fully independent of past and current experiences.

A concrete operational child must deal with each problem in isolation; reasoning operations are not coordinated. The child cannot integrate his or her solutions by means of general theories. A person with formal operations has the ability to use theories and hypotheses in the solution of problems. Several intellectual operations can be brought to bear simultaneously and systematically on a problem.

In addition, formal operations are characterized by scientific reasoning and hypothesis building (and testing), and reflect a highly developed understanding of causation. For the first time, the child can operate on the logic of an argument (problem) independent of its content. He or she is aware that logically derived conclusions have a validity independent of factual truth. Although concrete thought and formal thought are both logical, they are clearly different. The concrete operational child lacks the range, power, and depth of reasoning of his or her more developed counterpart.

Formal cognitive thought and reasoning arise out of concrete operations in the same way that each new level of thought incorporates and modifies prior thought. Formal thought has the structural properties of being hypothetical–deductive, scientific–inductive, and reflective–abstractive. In addition, formal thought operates on *contents* that Piaget called *propositional*, or *combinatorial*, and *formal operational schemes*. These structural properties and contents are illustrated in this chapter by a series of problems from Piaget's work. The examples are taken primarily from Inhelder and Piaget 1958 and Piaget 1972a, the two most important works by Piaget on cognitive development during adolescence.

STRUCTURES DEVELOPED IN THE FORMAL OPERATIONAL STAGE

Hypothetical–Deductive Reasoning

Hypothetical reasoning "goes beyond the confines of everyday experience to things of which we have no experience" (Brainerd 1978, p. 205). It is reasoning that transcends perception and memory and deals with things we have not directly known, things that are hypothetical.

Deductive reasoning is reasoning from premises to conclusion or from the general to the specific. Inferences or conclusions based on deductive reasoning are necessarily true only if the premises they are derived from are true. Reasoning can be applied to arguments that have false premises, however, and logical conclusions can be derived.

Hypothetical-deductive reasoning is reasoning that "involves deducing conclusions from premises which are *hypotheses* rather than from facts that the subject has actually verified" (Brainerd 1978, p. 205). In this manner, the possible (hypothetical) becomes an arena in which reasoning can be used effectively.

People with formal operations can reason about hypothetical problems entirely symbolically (in their minds) and can deduce logical conclusions. Thus, when they are presented with a problem in a form "*A* is less than *B* and *B* is less than *C;* is *A* less than *C?*" they can reason appropriately from the premise ($A < B$ and $B < C$) and deduce that *A* is less than *C* ($A < C$). When given the verbal problem "Bob is left of Sam and Sam is left of Bill; is Bob left of Bill?" those with formal operations can make the correct deduction from the hypothesis or premises. Concrete operational children, lacking fully developed deductive reasoning about hypothetical situations, cannot solve problems in this form.

Another feature of hypothetical–deductive reasoning during formal operations is the ability to reason about hypotheses believed to be untrue (false premises) and still come to logical conclusions that can be inferred from the hypotheses. If a logical argument is prefixed by the statement "Suppose coal is white," the concrete operational child, when asked to solve the logical problem, declares that coal is black and that the question cannot be answered. The child with formal operations readily accepts the assumption that the coal is white and proceeds to reason about the logic of the argument. The older child can submit to logical analysis the *structure* of the argument independent of the truth or falseness of its content.

Scientific–Inductive Reasoning

Inductive reasoning is reasoning from specific facts to general conclusions. It is the main reasoning process used by scientists to arrive at generalizations or scientific laws.

Inhelder and Piaget (1958) concluded that when confronted with problems, children with formal operations are capable of reasoning much as scientists do. They form hypotheses, control variables experiment, record effects, and from their results draw conclusions in a systematic manner. Two examples from this work are presented in this section to illustrate scientific–inductive reasoning in formal thought.

One of the characteristics of scientific reasoning is the ability to think about a number of variables at the same time. Those with formal reasoning accomplish this in a coordinated manner and can determine the effect of one, all, or some combination of a set of variables. Piaget referred to this as *combinatorial reasoning.* Combinatorial reasoning, or reasoning about a number of variables at one time, is not something a concrete operational child can do reliably. Concrete operational children typically can reason successfully only when there is a single variable and when causes can be determined directly from observation. Formal reasoning goes beyond observation. The *relationships* between variables must be *constructed* through reasoning and verified through systematic experimentation.

The Colorless Chemical Liquid Problem.   In the colorless chemical liquid problem, a child is presented with five glasses or jars, each containing a different colorless liquid (see Figure 6.1). Four of the five containers look exactly the same. The fifth container contains an eyedropper as well as a clear liquid (potassium iodide, labeled *g*). Water oxidizes potassium iodide in an acid mixture, turning the mixture yellow. Water (2) is neutral and thiosulfate (4) is a bleach. The child is given two glasses, one containing water (2) and the other containing sulfuric acid and oxygenated water (1 + 3). The experimenter puts several drops of potassium iodide (*g*) in each of the two glasses, and reactions are noted. The child is asked to reproduce the yellow color by using the five original containers in any way he wishes. If the yellow color is produced, the child is asked to explain how this was accomplished. The only combinations that will produce the yellow color are 1 + 3 + *g* or 1 + 3 + *g* + 2; the former is the simpler solution. There are 25 possible combinations of two or more of the liquids. The solution to the problem cannot be determined from observation alone.

At the preoperational level, children do little more than try different combinations of two liquids at a time in an unsystematic manner. At the concrete operational level, efforts are more systematic but not fully so. Combinations of three and four liquids are often tried, but concrete methods are primarily trial and error. Occasionally these methods produce the yellow-colored combination, but concrete operational children cannot reliably repeat the process or explain how they got it.

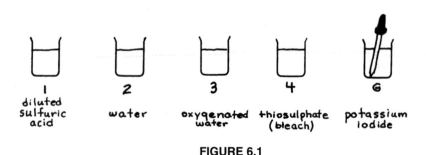

FIGURE 6.1

Kis (9;6) begins with $(3 \times g) + (1 \times g) + (2 \times g) + (4 \times g)$, after which he spontaneously mixes the contents of the four glasses in another glass; but there are no further results. "*O.K., we start over again.*" This time he mixes $4 \times g$ first, then $1 \times g$: "*No result.*" Then he adds $2 \times g$, looks and finally puts in $3 \times g$. "*Another try* $(1 \times g$, then $2 \times g$, then $3 \times g)$. *Ah!* (yellow appeared, but he added $4 \times g$). *Oh! So that! So that's* (4) *what takes away the color. 3 gives the best color.*" "Can you make the color with fewer bottles?"— "*No.*"—"Try." (He undertakes several 2 by 2 combinations, but at random.) (Inhelder and Piaget 1958)

Kis, who is concrete operational, tries different two-by-two combinations. He mixes different combinations and succeeds in getting the yellow color and then losing it. He is unable to repeat his success. All possible combinations are not tried in a controlled manner. Kis's approach is largely one of trial and error.

At the level of formal operations, children understand that the yellow color is the result of a combination. Systematic combinatorial methods are used in their reasoning and in their experimental work.

Sar (12;3) . . . "*I'd better write it down to remind myself: 1 × 4 is done; 4 × 3 is done; and 2 × 3. Several more that I haven't done* (he finds all six, then adds the drops and finds yellow from $1 \times 3 \times g$). *Ah! it's turning yellow. You need 1, 3, and the drops.*"—"Where is the yellow?" . . . "*In there?*" (g)—"*No, they go together.*"—"And 2?"—"*I don't think it has any effect, it's water.*"—"And 4?"—"*It doesn't do anything either, it's water too. But I want to try again; you can't ever be too sure.* . . . (he puts together $1 \times 3 \times 2 \times g$, then $1 \times 3 \times 4 \times g$) "*Ah! There it is! That one* (4) *keeps it from coloring.*"—"And that?" (2).—"*It's water.*" (Inhelder and Piaget 1958, pp. 116–17)

Sar quickly realizes that a systematic combinatorial approach is called for and he proceeds to sort out the combinations of variables. Each combination is tested for the effect. For children with formal operations, combinatorial reasoning is an instrument for conclusive deduction. The solution to this kind of problem cannot be derived from observation alone.

The Pendulum Problem.   In the colorless liquid problem, children had to search out the set of variables that would produce an effect. The pendulum problem (Figure 6.2) also requires combinatorial reasoning, but to a different end. Solving the pendulum problem requires one to *exclude* rather than include variables.

A weight suspended on the end of a piece of string and then set in motion acts as a pendulum. Children provided with strings of varying lengths and different weights are asked to determine and explain what controls the pendulum's rate of movement and oscillation. The factors usually considered by children are the length of the string, the weight at the end of the string, the height from which the weight is dropped to start the motion, and the force or push in starting the pendulum in motion.

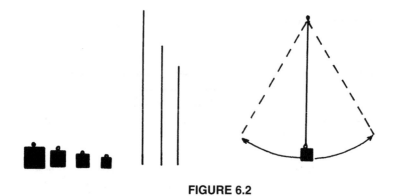

FIGURE 6.2

The single factor that controls the rate of oscillation or movement of the pendulum is the length of the string. Thus, "the problem is to isolate it (length of the string) from the other three and to exclude them. Only in this way can the subject explain and vary the frequency of oscillations and solve the problem" (Inhelder and Piaget 1958, p. 69).

At the preoperational level, most children believe that the pendulum's rate of movement is dependent on their push of it.

> One can see . . . that because of the lack of serial ordering and exact correspondences the subject cannot either give an objective account of the experiment or even give consistent explanations which are not mutually contradictory. It is especially obvious that the child constantly interferes with the pendulum's motion without being able to dissociate the impetus which he gives it from the motion which is independent of his action. (Inhelder and Piaget 1958, p. 69)

At the level of concrete operations, children typically discover the relation between the length of the pendulum's string and its rate of movement. Even so, they are unable to separate the variables and attribute the movement exclusively to the length of the string. They are convinced that weight and "push" have something to do with the oscillation.

> JAC (8;0) after several trials in which he has varied the length of string: "*The less high it is* (the shorter the string), *the faster it goes.*" The suspended weight, on the other hand, gives rise to incoherent relationships: "*With the big ones* (the heavy ones) *it falls better, it goes faster,* for example, *It's not that one* (500 grams), *it's this one* (100 grams) *that goes slower.*" But after a new trial, he says in reference to the 100-gram weight: "*It goes faster*"— "What do you have to do for it to go faster?"—"*Put on two weights.*"—"Or else?"—"*Don't put on any: it goes faster when it's lighter.*" As for the dropping point. "*If you let go very low down, it goes very fast,*" and "*It goes*

faster if you let go high up," but in the second case Jac has also shortened the string. (Inhelder and Piaget 1958, p. 70)

Typical concrete operational children are able to correctly order the effects of altering one variable (the length of string). They are unable to conclude that one factor alone controls the rate of movement of the pendulum. They cannot exclude from causality the other factors. According to Inhelder and Piaget, children at the level of formal operations "are able to isolate all of the variables present by varying a single factor while holding all the other things equal" (1958, p. 75):

> EME (15;1) after having selected 100 grams with a long string and medium length string, the 20 grams with a long and short string, and finally 200 grams with a long and short, concludes: "It's the length of the string that makes it go faster or slower; the weight doesn't play any role." She discounts likewise the height of the drop and the force of the push. (1958, p. 75)

The older child's experimentation and reasoning are systematic. One variable or factor is altered at a time while all others remain constant. All possibilities are explored. The child with formal operations can apply combinatorial reasoning and can exclude variables that do not have any effect.

It is interesting to note that the two problems just presented are concrete problems. Concrete operational children cannot reason successfully about these problems, although they can reason successfully about other concrete problems, such as most conservation problems. Although both kinds of problems are concrete problems, the colorless liquid problem and the pendulum problem require more than observation in order to be solved. In most conservation problems (those discussed earlier), all the necessary information needed to solve the problems is supplied and observable by the child. Either reversibility by inversion or reciprocity is sufficient to ensure understanding. In the colorless liquid problem and the pendulum problem, all the relevant information *is not* given. In each case, the relationships between the variables must be constructed through inductive (scientific) reasoning and verified by experimentation. Reversibility and concrete thought alone do not permit the concrete operational child to do this.

Reflective Abstraction

Reflective abstraction is one of the mechanisms of mental activity by which cognitive construction takes place. In our earlier discussion of knowledge, physical knowledge and logical–mathematical knowledge were differentiated. Physical knowledge is knowledge of the physical properties of objects derived by the manipulation of objects. Logical–mathematical knowledge is knowledge constructed from physical or mental actions on objects. The mechanisms through which logical–mathematical knowledge is derived is called reflective abstraction.

Reflective abstraction (as in the construction of logical–mathematical knowledge) always goes beyond the observable and results in mental reorganization.

Reflective abstraction always involves an abstraction from a lower level to a higher level. The major mechanism present in the construction of all logical-mathematical knowledge is reflective abstraction.

Reflective abstraction is internal thought or reflection based on available knowledge. At the formal operational level, internal reflection can result in new knowledge—new construction. Concrete operational children cannot construct new knowledge from internal reflection alone (Brainerd 1978).

Analogies.   In a study of reflective abstraction published in 1977, Piaget examined children's understanding of analogies (Gallagher and Reid 1981). Analogies are of interest because they require a construction and comparison of relationships between the members that make up the analogy. According to Piaget, these relationships can come about only through reflective abstraction. The relationships in analogies cannot be deduced directly from experience. For example, consider this analogy: Dog is to hair as bird is to feathers. The four members of the analogy—dog, bird, hair, and feathers—are all common objects known to most people through experience. The heart of the analogy is the relationship between dog hair and bird feathers. The relationship is not observable and comes about through reflection (reflective abstraction).

Children between age 5 and age 13 were asked to pair and arrange in a two-by-two matrix the pictures in Figure 6.3. A child who had difficulty establishing pairs or arranging the pairs in a matrix was asked questions such as, "What does a vacuum cleaner run on?" "What does a car run on?" All children were asked for the reasons why they thought particular items went together.

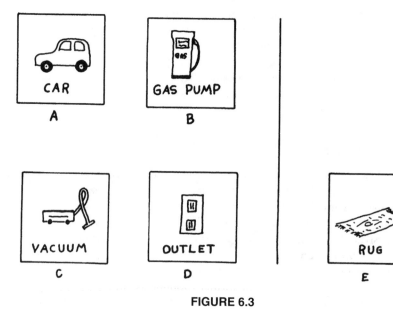

FIGURE 6.3

When analogical sets were established correctly in a matrix, countersuggestions were provided, such as, "Does the rug (*E*) go as well here as the electric outlet (*D*)?" Countersuggestions were used to determine whether the child was reasoning with analogy and how resistant to suggestion this reasoning was.

Gallagher and Reid report that Piaget's research led to the identification of three distinct levels of understanding and reasoning about analogies.

> The younger children at stage 1 (ages 5 and 6) were more likely to arrange pairs but ignore the complete analogical form. For example, they stated that the dog needs hair to keep warm and the bird needs feathers to fly. The relationship between dog and hair (*A* is to *B*) was not compared to the relationship between bird and feathers (*C* is to *D*). For Piaget this is an example of empirical abstraction—attending to the observable characteristics— which prevents true solution according to the analogical form of *A:B* as *C:D*. . . .
>
> Children at stage 2 (approximately ages 8 to 11) were able to complete the matrices. But when countersuggestions were made, the analogical form proved to be weak and the answers were changed. However, according to Piaget, the ability to complete the matrices demonstrated reflexive abstraction—the projection to a higher level of that which is drawn from a lower level. . . .
>
> At stage 3 (approximately age 11 and older) the children were able to resist countersuggestions. The form *A:B* as *C:D* is stabilized, and it is possible for the subjects to *reflect* on their answers by consciously explaining the hierarchical relation obtained from consideration of both parts of the analogy. (1981, pp. 117–18)

Children in Stage 1 may group correctly, but they reason typically that "auto fits with gas pump, and vacuum cleaner fits with electric outlet" without any awareness of the relation between the two pairs. It is the exploration of the children's reasoning, not merely their answers, that reveals their level of understanding. Not until the stage of formal operations are children able to use analogical rules and articulate the form of the analogy.

Analogical reasoning is an example of reasoning constructed almost exclusively independent of content. The central characteristic of analogy is the comparison of relations between the pairs. This clearly goes beyond what is observable.

CONTENT OF FORMAL THOUGHT

The primary structural characteristics of formal thought that differentiate it from concrete thought have been noted. About what kind of *contents*, then, are those with formal operations able to reason and those with concrete operations not able to reason? Piaget identified the contents of formal thought as *propositional operations* and *formal operational schemes*.

Propositional, or Combinatorial, Operations

Inhelder and Piaget (1958) set forth Piaget's belief that reasoning during the stage of formal operations is similar in many respects to the propositional logic used by logicians. Such thought is logical, abstract, and systematic. An understanding of symbolic logic is required to fully appreciate Piaget's perspective.

I will leave the task of explaining propositional logic and the details of Piaget's view to others (see Brainerd 1981; Ginsburg and Opper 1978) and instead look at the kind of reasoning used by formal operational children that bears a resemblance to propositional logic.

One task used by Piaget and Inhelder to examine the use of propositional reasoning was the pendulum problem described earlier in this chapter. It was suggested that only at the level of formal operations do children reason systematically about the causes of the pendulum's oscillation. They go through several steps including generating hypotheses, designing and carrying out experiments, observing results, and drawing conclusions from their results.

In the pendulum problem, the factors of length of the pendulum string, the pendulum's weight, height of release, and push at release could all be hypothesized, either alone or in combination, as responsible for the oscillation.

The design of an experiment typically takes two of these factors and combines them in all possible combinations. Length of string and weight of pendulum could be tried in four possible combinations, and the rate of oscillation observed for each combination. Table 6.1 shows these four combinations and the observed results on oscillation.

Looking at the results regarding the weight factor, it is clear that there is no relation between weight and oscillation. Both heavy weights and light weights have slow and fast oscillations. Weight by itself can thus be eliminated as a causal factor. Looking at the results for length of the pendulum string, one observes a consistent pattern. When the string is long, regardless of the weight, the oscillation of the pendulum is *always* slow. When the string is short, the oscillation is *always* fast. It is clear that the length of the pendulum string *does* play a role in determining the rate of oscillation and that the weight of the pendulum does *not* play a role. Length of pendulum implies oscillation; weight of pendulum does not.

The above experiment combined two of the four factors in all four possible

TABLE 6.1   The pendulum problem: four combinations

	Factors		Results
	Length	*Weight*	*Oscillation*
1.	long	light	slow
2.	short	light	fast
3.	long	heavy	slow
4.	short	heavy	fast

combinations. Similar experiments can be carried out to determine the roles, if any, of the other two factors, height of release and push of pendulum, in combination with each other, and each in the various possible combinations of the other three. Children with formal operations do not always structure their investigations or experiments as formally as suggested in Table 6.1, but they are capable of using the kind of reasoning shown. Combinatorial procedures like these permit adolescents with formal operations to arrive at conclusions that are certain.[1]

Formal Operational Schemes

Formal operational schemes are less abstract than propositional schemes and bear a closer likeness to scientific reasoning than propositional operations do. Two examples of formal operational schemes, *proportion* and *probability,* are examined next.

The development of children's concepts of proportion can be seen in their actions with a seesaw balance, such as the one shown in Figure 6.4. Before age 7, children have difficulty equalizing weights on a balance. They are aware that a balance is possible, but their attempts to attain it are always trial-and-error corrections. Compensation on the balance is never systematic. After age 7 (the age of concrete operations), children discover that a small weight placed farther from the fulcrum can balance a larger weight placed closer to it. They learn to equalize weight and length in a systematic manner. But they do not coordinate the two functions of weight and length as a proportion.

Around age 13, comprehension of the proportion principle ($W/L = 2W/2L$) occurs when the child becomes aware that an increase in weight on one side of the fulcrum can be compensated by an increase in distance from the fulcrum on the other side (Inhelder and Piaget 1958). Thus, the development of a child's conception of proportion is consistent with his or her general conceptual development. Qualitative differences in schemata of proportion are found at different stages.

Probability

Probability is a concept based on understanding chance and proportion. Probability is not constructed before the stage of formal operations.

> [T]he child must be capable of at least two operations characteristic of this level. He must be able to apply a combinatorial system that enables him to

---

[1] In Chapter 5 it was mentioned that concrete operational children use the two reversibilities—inversion and reciprocity—in solving conservation problems. They can mentally reverse by inversion or reciprocity (compensation), although they cannot coordinate the use of inversion and reciprocity. In formal operational thought, children learn to coordinate the two reversibilities. In the balance problem that follows, inversion and reciprocity are seen when a child understands that equal weights at equal distance from the fulcrum effectively cancel each other, or establish balance. In addition, children use reciprocity when they recognize that a small weight placed farther from the fulcrum compensates for a larger weight placed closer. Thus, where the two reversibility operations were previously used independently, in formal thought they function together in a coordinated manner.

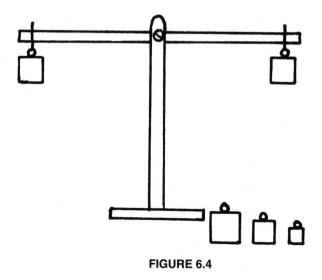

FIGURE 6.4

take into consideration all the possible combinations of the given elements; and he must be able to calculate proportions, however elementary, so that he can grasp the fact (which eludes subjects on the previous levels) that probabilities like 3/9 and 2/6, etc., are equivalent. It is not until the age of eleven or twelve that the child understands combinatorial probabilities. (Piaget and Inhelder 1969, p. 144)

Children's development of the probability concept can be assessed with the following procedure: A set of 96 one-inch wooden blocks of four different colors is placed on a table where they can be seen by the child. The distribution of the blocks by color is 36, 36, 20, and 4. The blocks are separated into groups by color, then each group is halved. Half the blocks of each color (18, 18, 10, 2) are set to one side as a reference set. The remaining blocks, which the child must acknowledge as identical to the reference set, are placed in a bag or box and hidden from view (see Figure 6.5).

The blocks in the bag are thoroughly mixed up. The child is told that the examiner is going to pull two blocks from the bag without looking into the bag. The child is asked to predict what colors the two blocks will be. When the child responds, he or she is asked to explain the response. The blocks are drawn from the bag and placed on the table. The draws are repeated until the examiner is sure of the child's level of understanding of this kind of probability.

Until age 11 or 12, children generally make predictions on some basis other than probability, or with limited conviction in probability. Preoperational children rarely use a strategy based on reasoning. They often predict the next colors to be drawn as the same as the previous block drawn, or they predict their favorite color. Most often, they just guess. Concrete operational children often use a strategy, although they do not adhere to a probability strategy.

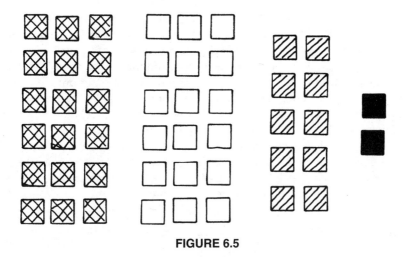

FIGURE 6.5

Children with formal operations typically respond to this kind of problem with responses based on probability. Their responses are always determined by the number of blocks of each color remaining in the bag. Research by Heard and Wadsworth (1977) found children understanding this problem, on the average, at age 12.

The concepts of proportion and probability developed during the stage of formal operations are examples of formal operational schemes. Such schemes are less abstract than propositional schemes because their functioning does not rely on deduction to the extent that propositional operations do.

AFFECTIVE DEVELOPMENT AND ADOLESCENCE

The development of affect during the stage of formal operations flows from the same source as the development of cognitive structures. As we have seen throughout the course of development, cognitive development and affective development bear a common stamp.

During adolescence, affective development is characterized by two major factors: the development of *idealistic feelings* and the continued formation of the *personality.*

Idealistic Feelings

With the development of formal operations comes the emergence of abilities to reason about and to think about the hypothetical—the future—and to reflect on one's own thinking—to think about thinking. "Henceforth intelligence will be able to operate not only on objects and situations but also on hypotheses and, therefore, on the possible as well as the real" (Piaget 1981b, p. 69).

If motivated to do so, and if in possession of the necessary content, adolescents with formal reasoning can reason as logically as adults. The tools for an evaluation of intellectual arguments are formed and fully functional. One of the major affective differences between the thought of the adolescent and that of the adult is that, initially in their use of formal operations, adolescents apply a criterion of pure logic in evaluating reasoning about human events. If it is logical it is good, right, and so on. This is the nature of their egocentrism. Adolescents lack a full appreciation of the way in which the world is ordered. With the capability for generating endless hypotheses, an adolescent believes that what is best is what is logical. He or she does not yet differentiate between the logical world as she thinks it to be and the "real" world. The significance of adolescent idealistic feelings for adolescent behavior are explored later in this chapter in the discussion of adolescent egocentrism.

The Formation of Personality

Although the infant at birth typically can interact with the mother and others, the interactions are initially presocial rather than fully social. The young child's initial sensorimotor interaction with those in the environment is as if they are objects. The early exchanges are not true social exchanges involving communication or relational feelings, but these early exchanges and the cognitive and affective development they assist are nonetheless instrumental in social development. Indeed, one thread in development can be seen as a process of moving from being nonsocial at birth to having the capacity for fully social behavior. Social development is completely meshed with and dependent on cognitive and affective development. What it means to be social is a *construction.* One must learn to be social. It is not automatic; indeed, *well-adapted* cognitive and affective social knowledge is not ensured.

Feelings of affection toward others emerge during sensorimotor development. At the next level, feelings are conserved and a new stability of social relations becomes possible. Children's interactions with peers, engendering the earliest mutual respect relations, become important in developing an understanding of and valuing of cooperation. The development of the will and autonomy assist in the establishment of feelings of necessity and a sense of obligation to those who are valued.

During the course of development of formal operations in adolescence, the social aspects of development continue. It is during this time, Piaget tells us, that there is the completion of what he calls the personality (Piaget, 1981b, 1963b). Piaget distinguished between what he called the personality and the self. The self, beginning its development in the first year of life, is oriented toward the individual. The self "is activity that is centered on the self" (Piaget, 1981b, p. 71). *The self* refers to self-interest and implies no overriding obligation at the moment for others beyond the self. The self is, in this sense, hedonistic.

According to Piaget, the formation of personality in more or less permanent form occurs after formal operations are developed and the adolescent (or adult) seeks to adapt to society and eventually to the world of real work; that is, to take his or her place as a contributing member of society. For Piaget, this is the "final" (but certainly not last) adaptation and is necessarily a freely chosen or autonomous submission of the self to some form of discipline. Thus, unlike the self that is directed at the self, the personality is directed at society and at becoming a part of that society. It is "linked to the role the individual plays in society or to the role he [or she] assigns himself and that he [or she] desires to play" (Piaget, 1963b, p. 45). Personality is "a matter of the fusion of one's work with one's individuality" (Piaget, 1981b, p. 71).

Personality, then, is a product of the desire and active effort to become an adult while still maintaining autonomy and values.

> Personality implies cooperation and personal autonomy. It is opposed both to . . . the complete absence of rules, and to complete heteronomy, abject submission to the constraints imposed from without. (Piaget, 1967, p. 65)

For Piaget, the final aspects of personality at once build on and supersede the will as a means of conserving one's own constructed values while seeking (valuing) an authentic role in society. In many ways, the formation of personality and all it implies can be viewed as the final aspect of social and affective development. Of course, nothing about this is automatic. Many pitfalls can occur (and too often do) in one's development of social knowledge and how one feels about others.

Moral Development During Adolescence

The development of moral reasoning begins with sensorimotor development and reaches its highest levels when formal operations and affective development are fully developed (see Table 6.2).

Codification of Rules.   Around the beginning of formal operations, at age 11 or 12, most children construct a relatively sophisticated understanding of rules. The rules of the game are seen as fixed at any point in time by mutual agreement and changeable through mutual agreement. The earlier belief that rules are permanent and externally imposed by an authority is no longer present. At this stage, the rules in use are known to all, and all agree on what the rules are. Adolescents recognize fully that rules are necessary in order to cooperate and play the game effectively. There also seems to be an interest in rules for their own sake.

Lying.   We have seen that preoperational children generally view a lie as something "naughty." Errors that are involuntary are still considered lies. Transgressions that do not result in punishment are not viewed as lies. Between age 7 and age 10, the criterion for whether a statement is a lie or not is whether the statement is true or false. All false statements are considered lies.

After age 10 or 11, children typically begin to recognize *in their reasoning* the role of intentions in lying and what constitutes a lie. At this level of reasoning, a lie is defined as something that is *intentionally* false. A full appreciation of intentions in moral judgments begins to develop around the transition from concrete to formal operations.

It was noted earlier that through age 7 or so, children view the avoidance of punishment as the reason for not lying. Indeed, the young child typically views an unpun-

TABLE 6.2 Relationship between children's cognitive development and the development of concepts of rules, accidents, lying, and justice

Cognitive Development	Rules	Accidents	Lying	Justice
Sensori motor (0–2 years)	Motor state. Rules not observed			
Preoperational (2–7 years)	Egocentric stage. Games played in isolation; no cooperation or social interaction	Intentions not considered. Children do not take the view of others. Judgments based on quantitative effects of actions	Punishment the criterion for lie. No punishment = no lie. Lying is like being "naughty"	Submission to adult authority. Arbitrary, expiatory punishments considered just
Concrete operations (7–11 years)	Incipient cooperation. Rules observed, though little agreement as to what the rules are	Intentions begin to be considered. Children begin to take the view of others	Lie = not true. Unpunished untruths are lies	Justice based on reciprocity. Equality more important than authority
Formal operations (after 11–12 years)	Codification of rules. Rules known to all; agreement as to what the rules are; rules can be changed by consensus; rules of interest for their own sake		Intentions decide whether a false statement is not a lie. Truthfulness viewed as necessary for cooperation	Equality with equity. Reciprocity considers intent and circumstances

ished act as necessarily not a lie. After age 9 or so, there is a separation of the concept of lie from punishment. The concrete operational child typically believes that a lie is wrong even if it goes unpunished.

Piaget observed that a maturing of children's concepts about lying generally occurs between age 10 and 12. Intentions become the major criterion used to evaluate lying. The older child (with formal operations) also recognizes that *not lying* is necessary for cooperation. This is all part of a long shift from a morality of constraint to a morality of cooperation.

> In the first place a lie is wrong because it is an object of punishment; if the punishment were removed, it would be allowed. Then a lie becomes something that is wrong in itself and would remain so even if the punishment were removed. Finally, a lie is wrong because it is in conflict with mutual trust and affection. Thus the consciousness of lying gradually becomes interiorized and the hypothesis may be hazarded that it does so under the influence of cooperation. (Piaget 1965, p. 171)

Justice. Piaget suggested that the concept of just punishment begins to be constructed by children only after a comprehension of rules emerges, generally around age 7 or 8. Concepts of rules are developed as children interact with other children. All this is concurrent with a decline in intellectual egocentrism and an increased ability to see the viewpoint of others. In moral judgment, we see an evolution from asocial judgments (expiatory punishment) to social judgments (reciprocity).

> [I]n every domain we have studied up till now, respect for the adult—or at any rate a certain way of respecting the adult—diminishes in favor of the relations of equality and reciprocity between children . . . it is perfectly normal that in the domain of retribution [punishment] the effects of unilateral respect [egocentrism] should tend to diminish with age. . . . What remains of the idea of retribution is the notion, not that one must compensate for the offence by a proportional suffering, but that one must make the offender realize, by means of measures appropriate to the fault itself, in what way he has broken the bond of solidarity. . . . the idea of reciprocity, often taken at first as a sort of legalized vengeance or law of retaliation . . . tends of itself towards a morality of forgiveness and understanding . . . the time comes when the child realizes that there can be reciprocity only in well-doing. . . . The law of reciprocity implies certain positive obligations in virtue of its very form. And this is why the child, once he has admitted the principle of punishment by reciprocity in the sphere of justice, often comes to feel that any punitive element is unnecessary, even if it is "motivated," the essential thing being to make the offender realize that his action was wrong, in so far as it was contrary to the rules of cooperation. (Piaget 1965, p. 232)

Piaget concluded that three major periods exist in the development of children's concepts of justice. The first period lasts until age 7 or 8. In this period, justice is subordinated to adult authority. The child accepts as just whatever adults (authorities) say is right. There is no distinction between the notion of just and unjust and the notion of duty and disobedience (Gruber and Vonèche 1977). The child considers punishment to be the essence of justice.

The second period, between age 8 and age 11, evolves around concepts of cooperation. Reciprocity is viewed as the appropriate basis for punishment. A major emphasis is placed on "equality" of punishment, that laws are interpreted equally for all and that all should receive the same (equal) punishment for the same offense regardless of the circumstance. Equality is viewed as more important than punishment. Expiatory punishment is no longer viewed as just.

In the third period, usually beginning around age 11 or 12, reciprocity remains the basis for children's judgments about punishment, but children now consider intentions and situational variables (extenuating circumstances) when formulating judgments. Piaget called this *equity*. Punishment need no longer be dispensed "equally" in a quantitative sense. For example, young children are held less liable than older children. At this level of development, judgments based on equity may be considered by the reader to be a more effective implementation of equality.

INTELLECTUAL DEVELOPMENT AND ADOLESCENCE

Adolescent behavior has always been a matter of concern to parents, educators, and psychologists.[2] Many theorists since G. Stanley Hall (1908) have tried to account for the unique characteristics of the adolescent period. Psychoanalytic theory (Freud 1946; Erikson 1950) offers a rationale for affective and social aspects of adolescent behavior, although there has been little supporting research for this position. Behaviorists, by and large, have avoided the topic of adolescence. Although adolescence has received considerable attention in educational and psychological literature, little of this attention has been concerned with the intellectual development of the older child and the possible effects of the unique cognitive and affective characteristics of adolescent reasoning on adolescent behavior.

Piaget recognized the roles that maturation and sexual awareness play during the adolescent years, but he suggested that these facts are inadequate to explain adolescence.

> But these well known facts, made banal by certain psychological writings, far from exhaust the analysis of adolescence. Indeed, pubertal changes would play only a very secondary role if the thinking and emotions characteristic of adolescence were accorded their true significance. (Piaget 1967, p. 60)

> From the point of view of integration into society (whose psychosociological importance much predominates over its biological importance) ado-

---

[2] For our purposes in this section, adolescence is thought of as roughly from age 15 to age 18 and the adolescent is assumed to have developed formal operations.

lescence is essentially characterized by the fact that the individual no longer considers himself a child. He ceases to see himself as inferior to adults and starts to feel he is equal to the latter; he envisions becoming a member of society, playing a role, and making a career. Now it is readily apparent that adolescence conceived in this way does not correspond with puberty. Its average age will essentially depend on the ambient social structure. In gerontocratic societies where young adults are submissive to the elders, like children, infantile mentality endures much longer and the process of adolescence is strongly blurred.

The crisis of adolescence, as do all developmental phenomena, includes factors at once intellectual and affective. Intellectually, it is the advent of formal . . . operations that permits the individual to detach himself from the present . . . and the local perceptual situation to which the child is more or less confined and permits him to move into what is possible and does not yet exist. . . . Affectively, the construction of a scale of values allows him both to go beyond the restricted circle of his immediate environment and to constitute the central axis of his "personality." . . . Thanks to these two instruments, i.e., the formal operations and a "personal" hierarchy of values, the adolescent plays a fundamental role in our society of liberating the new generation from the older one. This leads the individual to further enhance what he has acquired in his childhood development that is new while partly freeing him from the obstacles issuing from adult constraints. (Piaget 1963b, pp. 20–21)

Thus, for Piaget, the important factors that shape the adolescent are the cognitive and affective development that occurs during those years.

One characteristic of adolescents is their ability to catch adults using illogical reasoning. Every teacher and parent has experienced this persistent and sometimes frustrating characteristic, which is found less often in younger children. It occurs in children with formal operations because they have developed reasoning and logical abilities that are in some ways equal to those of adults. Like adults with formal reasoning, adolescents with formal reasoning do not always use it, but once the reasoning is developed, adolescents have the same capabilities for reasoning as adults do.

A major difference between adult and adolescent reasoning capabilities is the sheer number of schemata, or structures. The development of new schemata or new areas of knowledge does not stop with the attainment of formal operations. As people continue to have new experiences, they continue to develop new schemata and concepts. The adult's range of experiences typically is much greater than the adolescent's. Thus, the typical adult possesses more structures, or content, to which he or she can apply reasoning powers than does the typical adolescent.

The aspect of Piaget's work that has probably been most neglected is that which attempts to account for the uniqueness of adolescent thought and behavior. Although Piaget did not attempt to explain all adolescent behavior, he did provide an important link between cognitive development, affective development, and general behavior. It is unfortunate that Piaget's thoughts on this topic have not attracted more interest and attention, particularly among parents and teachers of adolescents.

Piaget's explanation of adolescent behavior is consistent with the rest of his theory. He saw the unique characteristics of adolescent thought and personality as a normal outgrowth of development. That is, much of adolescent thought and behavior can be explained by prior development. In this respect, the development of cognitive and affective structures before and during adolescence helps account for the characteristics of behavior during the period.

The adolescent is typically one who has entered the stage of formal operations and is developing, or has developed, the cognitive skills and affective reasoning characteristic of that stage. Logical operations permit the child to reason logically about a wide range of logical problems. At this point, the qualitative development of cognitive structures is presumed complete. The typical adolescent has the mental apparatus required to solve problems logically as well as adults can. Why, then, does the typical adolescent think differently from the adult?

Piaget believed that the characteristics of adolescent thought that make the adolescent unique are in part due to the child's level of cognitive and affective development and his or her accompanying egocentrism of thought.

Adolescent Egocentrism

Egocentrism is a constant companion of cognitive development. At each new stage of mental growth, a child's inability to differentiate assumes a different form and is expressed in a novel set of behaviors. Thus one of the characteristics of thought associated with *all* newly acquired cognitive structures is egocentrism. This is a byproduct of mental development that, in a sense, distorts the initial use of newly acquired cognitive structures. Each period of development finds egocentrism manifest in a unique form.

During the sensorimotor period (0–2 years), a child is egocentric in the sense that he cannot differentiate between other objects and himself as an object, or between objects and his sensory impressions. He is the center of his world. With development during the period, this egocentrism subsides. By the time the child becomes able to internally represent objects and events, this form of egocentrism is diminished. The egocentrism of the preoperational period (2–7 years) is seen in the inability of children to differentiate between their thoughts and those of others. They believe their thoughts are always correct. As social interaction with others (particularly peers) increases, this form of egocentrism subsides. Elkind suggests that the preoperational child is also egocentric in being unable to differentiate between symbols (words) and their referents. The child in this stage is seen to give incomplete verbal descriptions to others, believing that words carry more information than they really do (Elkind 1967).

During concrete operations (7–11 years), a child becomes able to apply logical operations to concrete problems. Egocentrism takes the form of an inability to differentiate between perceptual events and mental constructions. The child cannot "think" independently of her perceptions. She is not aware of what are thoughts and what are perceptions. Hypotheses requiring perceptually untrue assumptions ("coal is white") cannot be pursued. With the attainment of formal operations and the ability to reflect on one's own thought, this form of egocentrism diminishes.

As each new plane of cognitive functioning is initially characterized by a form of egocentrism, so too are formal operations and adolescence. The adolescent, in a sense, is possessed by his or her new-found powers of logical thought. In adolescent thought, the criterion for making judgments in reasoning becomes what is logical to the adolescent, as if what is logical in the eyes of the adolescent is *always* right and what is illogical is *always* wrong. The egocentrism of adolescence is the inability to differentiate between the adolescent's world and the "real" world. The adolescent is emboldened with an egocentric belief in the omnipotence of logical thought. Because the adolescent can think logically about the future and about hypothetical people and events, he feels that the world should submit itself to logical schemes rather than to systems of reality. He does not understand that the world is not always logically or rationally ordered, as he thinks it should be.

> [W]hen the cognitive field is again enlarged by the structuring of formal thought, a . . . form of egocentrism comes into view. This egocentrism is one of the most enduring features of adolescence . . . the adolescent not only tries to adapt his ego to the social environment but, just as emphatically, tries to adjust the environment to his ego. . . . The result is a relative failure to distinguish between his point of view . . . and the point of view of the group which he hopes to reform. . . . But we believe that, in the egocentrism found in the adolescent, there is more than a simple desire to deviate; rather, it is a manifestation of the phenomenon of lack of differentiation . . . the adolescent goes through a phase in which he attributes an unlimited power to his own thoughts so that the dreams of a glorious future of transforming the world through ideas . . . seems to be not only fantasy but also an effective action which in itself modifies the empirical world. (Inhelder and Piaget 1958, pp. 343–46)

To some extent the differences between the thought of adolescents and that of adults are a function of the normal course of cognitive development.

> We have seen that the principal intellectual characteristics of adolescence stem directly or indirectly from the development of formal structures. Thus, the latter is the most important event in the thinking found in this period. (Inhelder and Piaget 1958, p. 347)
>
> The adolescent . . . thanks to his budding personality, sees himself as equal to elders, yet different from them. . . . He wants to surpass and astound them by transforming the world. That is why the adolescent's systems or life plans are at the same time filled with generous sentiments and altruistic or mystically fervent projects and with disquieting megalomania and conscious egocentricity. (Piaget 1967, p. 66)

Adolescents are often involved in idealistic crises. They have the powers of formal reasoning but they cannot distinguish between the new powers and their application to real problems. It might seem that adolescents are doomed forever to be idealistic social critics. But as the egocentrism of other periods gradually diminished, so does the egocentrism of adolescence with continued development. Egocentrism subsides when the adolescent learns to use logic effectively in relation to the reality of life and recognizes that all human and worldly events cannot be judged strictly against a criteria of what is logical.

> [T]he focal point of the decentering process is the entrance into the occupational world or the beginning of serious professional training. The adolescent becomes an adult when he undertakes a real job. It is then that he is transformed from an idealistic reformer into an achiever. In other words, the job leads thinking away from the dangers of formalism back into reality. (Inhelder and Piaget 1958, p. 346)

Thus, in Piaget's view, when (and if) adolescents attempt to become a part of the world of work and achievement, as well as "reform" that world, they are compelled to further adapt their reasoning and intelligence to the world as it is rather than as they think it should be.

Idealism

The reasoning of adolescents who have developed formal operations invariably seems to be idealistic. This idealism can be viewed as "false," or incomplete, idealism. What looks like idealism often, in reality, is reasoning based on an egocentric use of formal thought. When a typical adolescent with formal operations makes judgments based on reasoning, his or her conclusions seem to be idealistic because they are "logical." But the adolescent's logic and reasoning often do not, and initially cannot, take into account realities of human behavior that have nothing to do with logic.

Society confirms the biblical dictate "Thou shalt not kill," yet, historically, societies have sanctioned wars, the death penalty for certain crimes, and other killings. From an adolescent's egocentric–logical point of view, these behaviors are illogical and thus wrong. The adolescent does not (cannot) take into account the many *real* causes of human and societal behaviors. Similarly, parents instruct their children not to smoke or drink, yet the parents may engage in those activities themselves. To the adolescent, this seems illogical. The adolescent may argue logically that if my parents (and peers) can smoke and drink, so can I.

The adolescent must learn to assume adult (realistic) roles in the real world. This involves not only cognitive development but also a parallel affective development and adaptation to the adult life. The dilemma of human behavior is more than a logical problem, and it is this perspective that adolescents typically do not appreciate until they have encountered reality in a *serious* way and have adapted to the "real" world. When the world is encountered as it really is, not merely as the adolescent thinks it should or could be, adaptations can be made that permit a shift from a logical-egocentric perspective to a logical–realistic perspective. With egocentrism adapted to reality, the capability for a nonegocentric form of idealism occurs, an idealism that is able to appreciate the logical *and* nonlogical complexities of problems.

American society has greatly extended the length of time that adolescents and young adults spend in the period of false idealism. Many people do not begin a "real job" until after college graduation or even later. For them, the adaptation of logical reasoning to reality may be postponed.[3]

The Reformer

One manifestation of adolescent egocentrism is seen in adolescents' desire to reform society. In their discussions about society, adolescents are often severe critics of society and its institutions. This behavior is often viewed and labeled by adults as antisocial, rebellious, unthoughtful, ungrateful, and generally wrong and inappropriate. Piaget argued that this is not always the case. In Piaget's view, the adolescent's desire to reform society is normal and can be attributed in large part to his or her intellectual capabilities for reasoning about the way things could be (hypothetically and logically) and to adolescent egocentrism.

> [T]he adolescent frequently appears asocial and practically asociable. Nothing, however, could be less true, since he is constantly meditating about society. The society that interests him is the society he wants to reform; he has nothing but disdain or disinterest for the real society he condemns. Furthermore, adolescent sociability develops through the young person's interaction with other adolescents. . . . Adolescents' social interaction . . . is aimed primarily at discussion. Whether in twosomes or in small coteries, the world is reconstructed in common, and the adolescent loses himself in endless discussion as a means of combating the real world. (Piaget 1967, p. 68)
>
> We see, then, how the adolescent goes about injecting himself into adult society. He does so by means of projects, life plans, theoretical systems, and ideals of political or social reform. In short, he does so by means of thinking, and almost, one might say, by imagination—so far does this hypothetico-deductive thinking sometimes depart from reality. (Piaget 1967, p. 67)

Piaget believed that, in part, adolescents' thought and reasoning are necessarily those of a dreamer of better (more logical) worlds. Some of this thought spills over into adolescent behavior, and we often see the adolescent in the role of reformer. Piaget made clear that such reasoning, though egocentric, is a natural and normal phase in the development and refining of adolescent intelligence. The idealistic

---

[3] Piaget writes that "where young adults are submissive to the elders, like children, infantile mentality endures much longer and the process of adolescence is strongly blurred" (Piaget 1963b, p. 20). He points to cultures, such as Samoa, where Margaret Mead found that there was little real adolescence. In Piaget's formulation, the best development in adolescence (and before) occurs when intellectual and affective autonomy is encouraged, that is, where mutual respect relationships predominate. Unilateral respect relationships in adolescence can postpone adaptation to the real world and integration into society. This has educational and potential clinical implications.

reformer phase can be viewed as necessary for eventual equilibration at a higher level.

What, then, moves the adolescent beyond the reformer stage? What provides the disequilibrium necessary for further development?

> True adaptation to society comes automatically when the adolescent reformer attempts to put his ideas to work. Just as experience reconciles formal thought with the reality of things, so does effective and enduring work, undertaken in concrete and well-defined situations, cure all dreams. (Piaget 1967, p. 69)

Thus, when adolescents attempt to implement their theories, dreams, and hypotheses in the real world, the world provides disequilibrium and provokes adjustments in hypotheses. The striving to become an effective member of society is part of the motivation that activates development of the personality.

The mental and affective developments of adolescence are essential to the subsequent development of adult thought, but they do not ensure realistic adult thought. The implementation of formal thought in adolescence is initially egocentric. The adolescent does not differentiate at first between many possible perspectives. Adolescent thought initially is idealistic–logical, and often it is manifest in criticism of society and an elaboration of ideal worlds. Objectivity of thought with respect to conflicting issues is attained and egocentrism is diminished when the adolescent assumes an adult role in the world and can differentiate the many possible points of view (Inhelder and Piaget 1958, p. 345).

SUMMARY

The stage of formal operations, which usually begins around age 12 and can be complete at age 16 or later, builds on, incorporates, and extends the development of concrete operations. Whereas concrete operational thought is logical thought, it is restricted to the concrete world. Not until the development of formal operations does reasoning become content-free or concrete-free. Formal reasoning can deal with the *possible* as well as with the *real.*

Concrete operational thought is reversible thought. Inversion and reciprocity are used independently, and the two reversibilities become coordinated in formal thought.

Several structures emerge during the construction of formal operations. *Hypothetical-deductive* reasoning is the ability to reason about the hypothetical as well as the real and the ability to deduce conclusions from hypothetical premises. *Scientific-inductive* thought is reasoning from the specific to the general; it is the kind of thought typical of the scientist. Those with formal reasoning can explore all possible relations in concrete or hypothetical problems. *Reflective abstraction* is the abstraction of new knowledge from existing knowledge gained by reflection or thought. Reflective abstraction always goes beyond the observable and is the primary mechanism of logical–mathematical knowing.

Two major cognitive contents develop during formal operations: *propositional* or *combinatorial* operations and *formal operational schemes.* Propositional reasoning is similar to propositional or symbolic logic in capability. It is abstract and systematic. Formal operational schemes, such as proportion and probability, bear a closer likeness to scientific reasoning. They are less abstract than propositional reasoning.

The cognitive capabilities of the adolescent with fully developed formal operations are qualitatitively equal to those of the adult. Adolescents can reason as logically as adults with formal operations can, although adults, by virtue of their greater experience, may be able to reason about more things than adolescents can. Not all adolescents and adults develop formal operations fully, but according to Piaget, all normal people have the potential to do so (Gallagher and Reid 1981).

Affective development is not independent of cognitive development. As cognitive development reaches an upper limit with full attainment of formal operations, so too does affective development. The major affective constructions during the stage of formal operations build on those of the concrete operational stage. The development of normative feelings, autonomy, and will during concrete operations leads to the construction of idealistic feelings and the further development of personality during formal operations. Personality formation has its roots in the child's organization of autonomously constructed rules and values. Personality reflects the individual's efforts to adapt to the social world of adulthood as well as change it. It is, in part, a submission of the self to discipline.

Moral reasoning similarly reaches full development with the attainment of formal operations. Rules are understood as necessary for cooperation. Lying is viewed as wrong because it breaks trust. Justice comes to be understood in relation to intentions. Proper punishments for social transgressions are viewed as those based on equity.

Piaget suggested that the normal and necessary cognitive and affective developments during adolescence are useful in understanding many aspects of adolescent behavior heretofore often attributed to puberty and sexual awakening. Adolescent egocentrism is characterized by applying a criterion of what is logical to human and societal actions with insufficient understanding that the world is not always ordered logically and its citizens are not always logical. The adolescent, necessarily an idealist of sorts, explores, in thought and conversation, ways to reform society. These developments, in Piaget's view, are brought on not by puberty, but by the normal and necessary intellectual and affective developments that take place during the acquisition of formal operations.

A final equilibrium is attained only when the adolescent strives to enter the adult world and works at a "real" job. This effort necessarily generates disequilibrium as the logical adolescent is confronted with the views of others who have adapted their reasoning to a world that is not always ordered as simply as adolescents think it must be.

chapter 7

Further Aspects of Piaget's Theory

Earlier chapters have presented an introduction to Piaget's theory of cognitive and affective development. The basic elements of Piaget's work have been discussed. A complete evaluation of Piaget's theory cannot be based solely on the material in this book.

The development of the cognitive and affective structures of intelligence from birth through adulthood have been outlined. The relationship between early sensorimotor development and later intellectual development has been established. Piaget's theory clearly suggests that the path of cognitive development is the same for all people. A descriptive outline of cognitive and affective development has emerged and is summarized in Table 7.1.

SUMMARY OF INTELLECTUAL DEVELOPMENT

During sensorimotor development (0–2 years), an infant's reflexive behaviors gradually evolve into clearly intelligent behavior. Through maturation and active interaction with the environment (assimilation and accommodation), sensorimotor behaviors become increasingly differentiated through construction and progressively evolve into the first intentional behaviors. The infant develops means–end problem-solving behavior. By age 2, a typical child invents the notion of representation and is becoming able mentally to represent objects and events and to arrive at solutions to sensorimotor problems through representation (thinking). The schemata of a 2-year-old are qualitatively and quantitatively superior to those of a younger child. By age 2, affective development can be seen in children's likes and dislikes. During these early years, affect is largely invested in the self.

During preoperational development (2–7 years), intellectual behavior moves

137

TABLE 7.1 Summary of cognitive and affective development

Stage	Characteristics of the State	Major Change of the Stage
Sensorimotor (0–2 years)		Development proceeds from reflex activity to representation and sensorimotor solutions to problems. Primitive likes and dislikes emerge. Affect invested in the self
Period 1 (0–1 months)	Reflex activity only; no differentiation	
Period 2 (1–4 months)	Hand-mouth coordination; differentiation via sucking reflex	
Period 3 (4–8 months)	Hand-eye coordination; repeats unusual events	
Period 4 (8–12 months)	Coordination of two schemata; object permanence attained	
Period 5 (12–18 months)	New means through experimentation—follows sequential displacements	
Period 6 (18–24 months)	Internal representation; new means through mental combinations	
Preoperational (2–7 years)	Problems solved through representation—language development (2–4 years). Thought and language both egocentric. Cannot solve conservation problems	Development proceeds from sensorimotor representation to prelogical though and solutions to problems. True social behavior begins. Intentionality absent in moral reasoning
Concrete operations (7–11 years)	Reversability attained. Can solve conservation problems—logical operations developed and applied to concrete problems. Cannot solve complex verbal problems and hypothetical problems	Development proceeds from prelogical thought to logical solutions to concrete problems. Development of the will and beginnings of autonomy appear. Intentionality is constructed
Formal operations (11–15 years)	Logically solves all types of problems—thinks scientifically. Solves complex verbal and hypothetical problems. Cognitive structures mature	Development proceeds from logical solving of concrete problems to logical solving of all classes of problems. Emergence of idealistic feelings and personality formation. Adaptation to adult world begins

from the sensorimotor level to the level of representation. There is a rapid development of representational skills including spoken language, which accompanies, but is not the cause of, the rapid conceptual development of the period. Spoken language is *not* necessary for the development of reasoning, but facilitates it. A preoperational child's thought is egocentric in that he or she is unable to assume the viewpoints of others. The child believes that everything he thinks is correct. In conservation problems, he is unaware of transformations of states and tends to center on limited perceptual aspects of problems. Until age seven or so, thought is typically prelogical or semilogical. Conflicts between perception and reasoning are generally resolved in favor of perception. Internal representation and language development facilitate the development of truly social behavior and spark social learning. Moral feelings and moral reasoning make their appearance. Children begin to construct knowledge about rules and justice, although typically they have not yet developed fully a concept of intentionality.

The concrete operational child (7–11 years) develops the use of logical thought and moves beyond the prelogical reasoning of the younger child. Children can solve conservation problems and most concrete problems. Inversion and reciprocity come to be used independently in reasoning. During these years, the logical operations of seriation and classification typically develop. The child can think logically but cannot apply logic to hypothetical and abstract problems. The major affective developments that become possible at the concrete operational level are conservation of feelings, development of the will, and the beginning of autonomous thought and feelings. These developments are instrumental in the increased regulation and stability of affective thought. In addition, largely because of peer social interaction, children begin to become able to "decenter" and take the view of others. Construction of a concept of intentionality emerges and allows children to begin to consider the motives of others when making moral judgments. These factors alter, and are in turn altered by, the child's social interactions. Patterns of cooperation and mutual respect relations emerge.

With the development of formal operations (11–15 + years), cognitive structures (schemata) become qualitatively mature. The child (or adolescent) becomes increasingly capable of applying logical operations in reasoning to all classes of problems, including those that are hypothetical and abstract. The child with formal operations can operate on the logic of an argument independent of its content. Logic becomes firmly available to the child as a tool of thought. During adolescence, formal thought is initially characterized by its own form of egocentrism. The adolescent tries to reduce all reasoning to what is logical. At the same time, she has difficulty coordinating her emerging *ideals* with what is *real.* Personality formation continues when and if the adolescent begins to adapt the self to the adult world.

At each new level of cognitive development, previous levels are incorporated and integrated. The preoperational child does not discard earlier sensorimotor schemata and take up entirely new ones. Sensorimotor schemata are modified and improved during preoperational development. The processes of assimilation and accommodation ensure the continuous construction and reconstruction of cognitive and affective structures. Schemata are continually modified throughout life, from birth onward. Although changes in capabilities for logical reasoning cease after the development of formal operations, changes in content and function of intelligence continue. That is, after acquisition of formal operations, people continue to develop concepts, areas of content or new knowledge, and purposes to which their reasoning can be applied. Even though their *capability* for reasoning does not improve, adults typically have more to reason about (content and function) than adolescents with formal operations. Thus, adult reasoning can be very different from adolescent reasoning.

Early sensorimotor development is the foundation on which later conceptual development is built. The basic paradigm of cognitive development for Piaget is the assimilation and accommodation of experience, resulting in qualitative structural changes in cognitive and affective structures (schemata). All knowledge is constructed by the individual. In this sense, the child is truly father to the man.

CHARACTERISTICS OF COGNITIVE AND AFFECTIVE DEVELOPMENT

In this book, Piaget's theory is outlined as four major levels or periods along the continuum of development. Every major change in development within or between levels is one more step on the way to more advanced and more fully adapted intelligence. Each step represents a qualitative change in reasoning abilities. These advances always share certain characteristics:

1. Each advance, each new construction or reconstruction, is characterized by capability for qualitatively different reasoning. The reasoning of successive levels of development is always superior to the reasoning of the previous level.
2. Each reconstruction or improvement in reasoning permeates a child's total reasoning rather than only affecting reasoning about a particular event. For example, the child who constructs a concept that the length of objects does not change when the position of the object changes (conservation of length) can use this new reasoning in all situations where object length is relevant. Objects and space literally take on a new dimension for the child. Many structures are affected, not just one isolated structure.
3. Each new advance involves an integration and extension of the knowledge and reasoning of the previous level into "new" knowledge. Structures, or schemata, are changed (adapted), but prior formulations are never destroyed or eliminated. What was previously known remains, with some improvement in the quality of knowledge. Each new level of reasoning is a transformation of prior reasoning and as such is not totally new; rather, it is improved or is a better adaptation to reality.
4. The course of development is invariant. Formal reasoning cannot develop before concrete operations are developed. Concrete operations develop only after preoperational reasoning develops. Development always pro-

gresses from a less differentiated and less sophisticated level of reasoning to a more differentiated and more sophisticated level of reasoning.

5. Each advance in reasoning is accompanied by egocentrism in the initial use of new reasoning. Preoperational children initially view their thoughts as necessarily correct. This egocentrism of thought diminishes gradually as children recognize that peers and others they interact with have ideas that conflict with their own. Doubts are raised about the certainty of their own ideas. Those with formal operations are initially egocentric in that they judge the correctness of thoughts against a criterion of logic. This egocentrism gradually diminishes when (and if) the adolescent attempts to adapt his or her views to an adult role.

6. Intellectual development is self-regulated. The transformation (assimilation and accommodation) of experience attended to results in new constructions. This process is not directed from the outside, but from the inside. It proceeds not by internalizing the external in a direct way, but through disequilibration followed by assimilation and accommodation of experience selected. The outcome is constructed or reconstructed knowledge. The control mechanism is internal. In Piaget's theory, the most efficient and well-adapted construction occurs when the control mechanism is autonomous, or allowed to have its own way; that is, to respond to (assimilate) the source of disequilibrium. The control mechanism is affective, with unconscious feelings, tendencies, and inclinations functioning as gatekeepers for what experiences affect intellectual development. The process is one of self-regulation.

7. Intellectual development depends on social interaction and social experience. Piaget saw social interaction as one of the four primary variables in development. It almost goes without saying that social knowledge cannot be constructed without interacting with others. People are the only possible source of material for construction of social knowledge. At all levels, intellectual egocentrism (affective and cognitive) is called into question primarily as a consequence of confronting the ideas of others. Although construction of knowledge occurs in the mind of the child, it often occurs in a social context that is often necessary for any construction that occurs.

Social interaction is necessary for advancing the development of logical–mathematical knowledge. Beginning with the emergence of preoperational reasoning, arguments and intellectual confrontations with others are a source of cognitive conflict and disequilibrium. In the affective realm, the continued development of affective and cognitive autonomy and healthy self-regulation depends on the establishment of cooperation with others, including reciprocity of feelings and mutual respect relations. Social relations of cooperation begin to emerge from interactions with peers during preoperational development. Peer social interactions pave the way for potential mutual respect relations with adults in later development. Thus, ultimately, the development of the will (one's own set of values) and personality (as differentiated from the self), all presumably necessary for healthy social adjustment, depend on social interaction at all levels of intellectual development.[1]

INTELLIGENCE AND ADAPTATION

For Piaget, cognitive and affective development are the intellectual counterparts of biological adaptation to the environment. As we adapt biologically to our environment, we adapt intellectually. Through assimilation and accommodation, the external world one experiences is organized and given structure. Schemata are the products of the organization and construction. The organization is internal and may or may not bear a clear resemblance to what we call reality. The process is self-regulated and functions most authentically when it is autonomous, or self-directed.

Adaptation begins at birth with the exercise or sensorimotor reflexes. Differentiations via reflexes (sucking, grasping) are some of the first adaptations. As a child develops, the adaptations he or she makes become less exclusively related to sensory and motor behaviors and increasingly related to representations.

Adaptation is a motivational concept. Adaptations occur when there is a internal need or a value to the individual. Needs and values are affects. The major psychological expression of the need for adaptation is found in *disequilibration.* Adaptations, including intellectual adaptations, are neither automatic nor inevitable. In order for development to proceed, disequilibration must occur. The gate must be open, so to speak. The concept of adaptation has major implications for educational practice and will be discussed further.

VARIABLES IN INTELLECTUAL DEVELOPMENT

The critical variables in intellectual development outlined by Piaget are *maturation, experience, social interaction,* and *equilibration.* Piaget believed intelligence is neither solely inherited (maturation) nor learned (experience), maintaining that each of the four variables is necessary for intellectual development but that none alone is sufficient to ensure its occurrence. According to Piaget, the *interaction* of all four sets the course of development.

Whether children's experiences result in assimilation and accommodation is not

---

[1] A criticism of Piagetian theory often voiced is the assertion that the theory is entirely individualistic and does not appreciate the roles of social activity and social context within which construction of knowledge occurs. Piaget's writing is often contrasted with that of Vygotsky on this issue. (See the Introduction for a comparison of Piaget's and Vygotsky's theories.) It is clear that this criticism of Piaget's theory is a misreading or incomplete reading of his work. The role of the social is central to his theory. As has been noted previously, Piaget paid more attention in his research to the cognitive aspects of development, possibly creating the impression that social and affective contributions to intellectual development were not important, but this is not what Piaget said.

ensured without disequilibration, an internal process. The saying "You can lead a horse to water, but you can't make him drink" is appropriate here.

The question whether schooling (a form of experience and frequent social interaction) can affect structural development is an important one. Few would disagree that schooling affects cognitive content and function. Children acquire, as social knowledge, information (content) in school that they might not encounter otherwise (such as the study of history, science, and English grammar). Also, children generally develop skills in applying knowledge (function), such as computational skills in arithmetic. These can be acquired with *or without* comprehension, depending on the availability of the relevant structures necessary for comprehension at the time of "learning" the instruction. Regarding structure, most studies conclude that children attain concrete operations around age 6 or 7 independent of formal schooling. A number of studies report that the development of formal operations is much more related to schooling than are earlier levels of development. Thus, it may be that schooling, as it is traditionally carried out, plays a more important role in helping children acquire content and functions to which they can apply reasoning and knowledge (structures) than it does in aiding the development of structures and logical–mathematical knowledge. Also, the importance of schooling and experience in general in developing cognitive structures may be more important in later than earlier periods. These issues are discussed more fully in the next chapter.

KNOWLEDGE AND REALITY: A CONSTRUCTION

The developing child's construction or knowledge of the world (and reality) is not a copy of the "objective" world.[2] Each of us, over the course of our development, constructs knowledge that is an ever-closer approximation of what we call reality.

Physical, logical–mathematical, and social knowledge are not acquired directly but are constructed by the individual.

> The clearest result of our research on the psychology of intelligence is that even the structures most necessary to the adult mind, such as the logico-mathematical structures, are not innate in the child; they are built up little by little. . . . There are no innate structures: every structure presupposes a construction. All these constructions originate from prior structures. (Piaget 1967, pp. 149–50)

Some may question whether knowledge is a construction because they observe that most children around the same age appear to have similar concepts. Although it

---

[2] In Piaget's theory, there is no objective reality as such. There is, of course, a real world to be known, but every individual's knowledge of that world is *always* under construction and never fully constructed. Thus, what is called objective reality is never fully known. We know and live in our own constructed reality, which we are constantly revising.

is true that many people have similar concepts, this does not make the notion of construction less viable. The world we live in is a physical and social world containing a diversity of objects. For most children, wherever they live, the necessary physical ingredients are present to enable them to construct similar *physical* knowledge and identical logical–mathematical knowledge. For example, most children encounter trees and other plants. They have active experiences with trees, so physical knowledge of trees is constructed. Because there are certain physical similarities and differences among trees, children "discover" and construct similar schemata of trees. It is therefore reasonable to expect children who live in the same or a similar environment to construct similar physical knowledge. Children reared in different environments, where the raw materials for the construction of similar concepts are not present, cannot be expected to develop similar structures. For example, Eskimo children, raised in the Arctic, may never see a tree growing. If their only source of wood is driftwood washed up on northern shores, experience with driftwood may become the material from which concepts of trees are built. Thus, an Eskimo child or adult may have a concept of wood and tree as being rootless, leafless, and so on. Virtually any environment contains potential experiences and materials that permit the construction of logical–mathematical structures such as number, length, and volume. Number requires that children act on sets of objects. The objects can be checkers, stones, sticks, whatever. The particular materials are not important; what is important is that collections be available for exploration.

The greatest variability in constructed knowledge among people is probably found in their social knowledge. Cultural differences and local subcultural differences can be great. Children construct social knowledge from and within the sociocultural communities they live in and experience. The Chinese learn Chinese (as their first language) and Americans learn English. Chinese learn the history of China from a Chinese perspective. Americans learn Chinese history (and American history) from an American perspective. These perspectives and the constructions they engender are very different and necessarily result in Americans and Chinese constructing different social knowledge. On the other hand, as we have seen, differences between cultures in constructed logical–mathematical knowledge are minor in comparison.

The development of cognitive structures and knowledge is an evolutionary process that takes place within every individual. Construction occurs in the mind of the child and is manifest in the individual's schemata, which undergo revision when disequilibration occurs. The process of assimilation ensures that schemata are not copies of reality; accommodation ensures that constructions have a measure of correspondence to the real world (Elkind 1969).

AFFECT AND COGNITION

Piaget viewed intellectual development as a lifelong process that can be conceptualized as having cognitive, social, and affective aspects. Psychologists and educators have, over the past 30 years, attended to the role of cognitive concepts in Piaget's theory more than they have attended to affective concepts.[3] At least four plausible reasons can be brought forward to explain why this happened. First, Piaget did his research on and wrote primarily about the cognitive aspects of intellectual development and cognitive structure. Piaget recognized affectivity as important from his earliest writings (Piaget 1981b; Brown and Weiss 1987). It is clear that Piaget never intended this difference to be a value statement. It is likely that cognition created the most disequilibrium for him personally and thus received the most attention.

A second likely reason why Piaget studied cognition more than affectivity is that Piaget viewed the scientific study of affectivity as more difficult than the study of cognitive structure. It may have been that Piaget tried to solve what he saw as the more manageable questions first and thus dedicated a disproportionate amount of his energies to questions of cognitive structure.

A third reason for this state of affairs is that as psychologists and educators tried to understand Piaget's work, their constructions of his theory started off by assimilating what was available, which was primarily Piaget's writing about cognitive development. It has taken many of us some time to bring our constructions into line with the "reality" of the theory.[4]

These considerations aside, a careful reading of Piaget's writing makes clear that a view of intellectual development that includes only cognitive development without fully taking into account the affective aspects is incomplete.[5]

Lastly, affectivity (feelings, interests, values, etc.) in psychology is often associated with subjectivity and intellectual "mushiness". Many believe that feelings do not have a place in real science; thus, affectivity is suspect. Piaget from the beginning placed affectivity at the center of intellectual development.

When we ask the question "What does this child know?" we are asking what knowledge the child has right now; we are asking what the child's schemata look like; we are asking what type of reasoning the child is capable of. Each of these is a question about the child's cognitive status.

When we ask the questions "How did this child come to know what she knows?" or "How do children (people) acquire knowledge?" we are asking about the process of intellectual development and its cognitive and affective aspects.

In Piaget's theory, knowledge develops when children assimilate and accommodate experience. This can occur through actions that are thoughts in representation as well as through physical actions. In young children, construction occurs almost exclusively when they perform actions on objects. What starts the processes of assimilation and accommodation? Clearly, not all actions result in assimilation and accommodation. The key is disequilibration.

Disequilibration occurs when an experience or thought is inconsistent with what the child's schemata predict at the moment. Thus the experience or thought is selected to be attended to. It is the "attending to," an act of selection, that determines

---

[3] Piaget would argue, I believe, that attending to the cognitive more than the affective aspects of intelligence was an affective decision.

[4] Personal communication, William Gray, University of Toledo.

[5] See in particular Piaget 1981b.

which events provoke disequilibrium and result in cognitive development. These important decisions are made by the affective system. Affectivity, which includes feelings, interests, drives, tendencies (such as "will") and values, "constitute[s] the energetics of behavior patterns whose cognitive aspect refers to the structures alone. There is no behavior pattern, however intellectual, which does not involve affective patterns as motives" (Piaget and Inhelder 1969, p. 158). In Piaget's conceptualization of intellectual development, the affective and the cognitive both play key roles.[6] If Piaget is correct, affectivity decides whether ideas live or die, metaphorically speaking—what experiences are selected for construction (Brown and Weiss 1987). This gatekeeper role of affectivity has largely been overlooked by many interpreters of Piaget's theory. Those interested in the implications of Piaget's theory for educational or clinical practice are encouraged to attend to Piaget's affective as well as cognitive conceptions. Intellectual development is a unity of the two.

---

[6] Terrance Brown, known primarily as a translator of Piaget's work, has written about the role of affectivity in Piaget's theory (Brown and Weiss 1987). In a provocative analysis of this issue, Brown suggests that Piaget approached a full synthesis of the cognitive and affective but never fully developed it. Brown (1990) describes a functional model that can be used to conceptualize the selection or decision-making role of affectivity in intellectual development and affirms the viability of Piaget's views.

chapter **8**

The Implications of Piaget's Theory for Education: Principles of Constructivism

A student who achieves a certain knowledge through free investigation and spontaneous effort will later be able to retain it; he will have acquired a methodology that can serve him for the rest of life.

Piaget, To Understand Is to Invent

Piaget's theory of intellectual development should not be viewed as carved in stone. All psychological theories are organic and living and thus changing. Like other theories, Piaget's theory is still under construction. At this point it is a coherent description of how and why intellectual development proceeds. Although the theory is not a theory of education, it does provide a framework for analyzing educational practices and the extent to which they are consistent with developmental principles.

Piaget's constructivist theory makes clear that there are universals of development. There is a course to intellectual development, with reliable milestones and endpoints in the developmental sequence. As a part of adaptation to the world around them, children normally construct cognitive, affective, and social knowledge and seem to arrive at the milestones of development in a seemingly natural way. Edelstein (1992) calls this "natural learning," learning that is fully consistent with, and a part of, development. Of course, development or construction of knowledge is not automatic. Half of the adult population never fully develops formal operational reasoning. Although the course of development is the same for all, rates of development vary, some proceeding slower or faster than the average ages suggested by Piagetians.

Although all would agree that optimizing children's cognitive, affective, and social/ethical development is a worthy goal, development cannot be the only goal of education. Each child is asked by its culture to adapt not only to the developmental demands of life, but also to the expectations of the culture. Edelstein (1992) writes:

It is a common misunderstanding that in a cognitive–developmental formulation of educational aims, the formal universals of stage-specific competen-
cies in reasoning will substitute for more traditional formal (skill) or material (content) goals of instruction . . . [T]hey . . . represent much too narrow
a program for general education. After all, education is not concerned, or at
least not merely concerned, with what comes naturally with human development; rather, it is concerned with the content and skills implied in and
needed for individual development in a normative culture. (pp. 161–62)

Thus, education cannot be just about development but must also be about adaptation to the culture.[1] Education must necessarily be about skill acquisition and content learning as well as development. Currently, in most schools, education is almost
exclusively about skill acquisition and content learning and "learning in the schools is
organized in such a way that natural learning processes tend to be thwarted,
impeded, or subverted" (Edelstein 1992, p. 168). Development, so denied, often
results in closed gates, bad affect, boredom, and mindlessness among students *and*
teachers. Should it be so? Need it be? Constructivists think not.

The Piagetian/constructivist vision is that educational practice and development
need not and should not be at odds. The constructivist belief is that when compatibility exists, the learning of skills and content along with the child's natural development are enhanced. Constructions are more authentic. The compatibility between
development and the content and skill goals of school learning can be ensured only if
schools, and teachers in those schools, ensure it. It does not happen by accident.
Constructivist theory is a vision of how to accomplish this. What follows are the
author's view of the principles that guide Piagetian/constructivist thinking regarding
effective and responsible educational practice and the rationale for those principles.

Most of us who are interested in interpreting Piaget's work for educators consider the "cookbook" approach, one that attempts to tell teachers *what* to do, to be
inappropriate. Piaget's theory cannot be reduced to a set of operational procedures.
Piaget's theory is *one* perspective on which to reflect that can be used to aid teachers in understanding children and evaluate why they do or do not learn in school.
Educators who come to understand (construct) Piaget's work find their own
autonomously selected ways to integrate the principles into their dealings with children. Some work, some do not work and provoke further active reflection. The intellectual autonomy of teachers is *as* important as the autonomy of her students. With
this in mind, the principles and implications suggested here are more general than
specific.

---

[1] Adaptation to a culture does not mean automatically assuming all the values of the culture. It means
that after constructing knowledge of the culture and its values, and after constructing one's own values, one "decides" how to mesh one's own values and view of the world with one's constructed view
of the culture and its values. This, as we know, is neither a smooth nor predictable journey. But if one
comes to hold as a value cooperation, one is inclined to act on that value and seek cooperation in
social relations. This disposition necessarily increases mutual respect relations and moves one toward a
convergence of understanding with others.

HOW KNOWLEDGE IS ACQUIRED: EXPLORATION

American educational practice is generally based on the premise that knowledge is something that can be transmitted directly from teachers or books to students. The assumption is that "meaning" or comprehension can be carried by the spoken or written word and language is sufficient to transfer the word and meaning from a source (teacher, book) to the eagerly waiting student. When the knowledge or "meaning" is not acquired, it is often assumed that there is a problem with the student (such as a lack of motivation or cooperation) or with some component of the communication process (such as hearing or vision).

Children construct knowledge out of their exploratory actions on the environment. Actions can be physical (as manipulation of objects) or mental (such as wondering about something). Actions typically have two phases. The first phase involves exploration of an object or an idea. If the exploration of the object or idea provokes disequilibration, then exploration continues, but is focused on making sense of (assimilating) that which produced disequilibrium. This is construction of knowledge.

Physical knowledge is constructed through actions on objects. For example, relatively accurate (valid) concepts of oak trees are eventually constructed from children's actions on oak trees and trees in general. Concepts of oak trees and how they differ from other types of trees require assimilation and accommodation of relevant experience. Representations of oak trees, either pictures or words, cannot alone provide the necessary raw materials for the construction of accurate concepts or schemata.[2]

Logical–mathematical knowledge is constructed from exploratory actions on objects when the most important component is the child's action, not the particular object(s). Number, length, and area concepts cannot be constructed only from hearing about them or reading about them.

The construction of social knowledge depends on the child's exploratory action on, and interaction with, other people. Again, social knowledge cannot be directly transmitted only through words or other symbols; it must he constructed from active exploration.

Edelstein (1992) correctly says, "The overarching principle of instruction is the principle of *exploration* (often mistakenly overstated as *discovery*), leading to various forms or implementations of the construction process" (p. 169).

---

[2] Children can act on words or pictures in thought, but concepts derived exclusively from representations of objects are necessarily not the same or as complete as concepts derived from actions on the objects themselves. Does this mean that words or language have no role in construction of physical (and logical–mathematical) knowledge? No, words do have a role. If children have available only words to confront a concept to be constructed (such as an atom, Russia, oxygen), they can "act on" the words, and the language will be assimilated as best as it can. To the extent that the words children "act on" are meaningful to them from previous constructions, what they construct can have increasing relative accuracy. An important realization here is that written or spoken words (representations) do not have or carry meaning. Meaning is (or is not) contained in the minds of children (in schemata). The meaning of a word is the constructed concept we attach to it.

For educators, the basic implication is clear. If an objective of education is to enhance children's acquisition of knowledge, educational methods must be based on active exploration.

MOTIVATION: DISEQUILIBRATION

Nowhere are the differences between the traditional (empiricist) and constructivist views greater than in how they conceptualize motivation. For empiricists, the main mechanism of motivation is reinforcement. Motivation is viewed as external to the child. Constructivists, though not above using reinforcement in appropriate ways, recognize motivation for construction of knowledge to be largely an internal affair, responsive to the external environment but not directed by it. In Piagetian and related constructivist theory, children are motivated to restructure their knowledge when they encounter and attend to experiences that conflict with their predictions. Piaget called such an occurrence disequilibration and the result of it, disequilibrium. Some have called it cognitive conflict. Affect plays the central role in determining what is attended to. Affect is the gatekeeper and determines whether the gates are open or closed. Open gates invite attention and disequilibration; closed gates preclude attention and disequilibration. To the extent that educators are interested in helping children acquire knowledge, they must develop methods that encourage disequilibrium and permit children to carry out, in their own ways, the reestablishment of equilibrium through active methods (assimilation and accommodation).

Constructing knowledge efficiently is like being an enthusiastic detective. There is a question one is interested in exploring. In search of an answer, you follow your nose, wherever it leads, actively pursuing the mystery. The search path is neither planned nor time-constrained. You keep at it, testing hypotheses and hunches until you feel you have done the best you can for the time being. It is active detective work, driven by the enthusiasm associated with interest. Interest fuels the effort. The gates are open.

Children arrive at school with things they wonder about and want to make sense of. This disposition is often called curiosity. Curiosity is a form of interest and disequilibrium. A part of the constructivist teacher's job is to recognize what provides disequilibrium or curiosity for children and how to use that in a valid way. Another part of the job is creating disequilibrium where there is none. How can the teacher recognize and encourage disequilibrium?

Interests

Most of us recognize the power of our interests to spark efficient learning. When pursuing our interests, often outside of a school setting, we put great energy and enthusiasm into what we do and learn. As educators, we have not seriously pursued the potential of children's interests in schooling for facilitating the developmental goals and skill and content goals we want children to strive for. Dewey spoke strongly and compellingly to the educational value of interests (1913). Piaget similarly argued strongly for using children's interests for improved learning (1970b, 1981a). He wrote (1970b):

> The traditional school imposes . . . work on the student: it makes him work. And it is doubtless true that the child is free to put a greater or lesser degree of interest and personal effort into that work, so that insofar as the teacher is a good one the collaboration that takes place between his student and himself will leave an appreciable margin for genuine activity. But in the logic of the system the student's intellectual and moral activity remains *heteronomous* [not autonomous] because it is inseparable from a continual constraint exercised by the teacher, even though that constraint may remain unperceived by the student or be accepted by him of his own free will. The new school [constructivist school], on the contrary, appeals to real activity, to spontaneous work based on upon *personal need* and *interest.* This does not mean . . . that active education requires that children should do anything they want, . . . it requires above all that they should *will* what they do; that they should *act,* not that they should be *acted upon.* Need, the *interest* that is the resultant of need, . . . that is the factor that will make a reaction into an authentic act . . . The *law of interest* it thus . . . the *sole pivot* around which the whole system should turn. (pp. 151–152, my emphasis)

In an earlier book, I suggested that children should be permitted to explore many of their *interests* in educationally legitimate ways (Wadsworth 1978). Such interests, unique to the individual child, often reflect disequilibrium and are affectively charged sources of motivation. When children communicate a strong interest in something, they are often communicating to us as parents or teachers that the area of interest has generated cognitive conflict for them. It is of value in education to legitimize and make productive use of interests. Interests can be viewed as part of the child's emerging lesson plans for their personal development. Although children's interests and teachers' curricular goals rarely mesh neatly, creative autonomous teachers can find ways to allow students to pursue their interests and accomplish the teachers' goals as well. Innovative programs that make use of mentors often do exactly this. Mentors and teachers fashion an interdisciplinary set of educational activities in a child's area of interest so that the basics (such as arithmetic, reading, and writing) are covered. The difference from a conventional program is that the child's interests can drive their engagement and activity.

Cognitive Conflict

Cognitive conflict is created when one's expectations and predictions, based on one's current reasoning, are not confirmed. It is disequilibrium. *Critical exploration* is a method of questioning students that can be used by teachers (or parents) to help lead students into productive *cognitive conflict* and to produce disequilibrium. The method employs elements of Piaget's clinical interview used for assessing children's knowledge, but goes beyond it.

> Such a method [critical exploration] is adapted to educational purposes by questioning children about how they would approach a problem and how they arrived at their answers. The teacher presents children with further problems based on those the children have already solved (or not solved), to see what rules or generalizations the children have formed. Often the children are given a second problem, especially in mathematics, that, if solved by the procedure used to solve the first problem, would lead to an incorrect answer. Thus, by setting up a conflict situation, the teacher notes whether the disturbance causes an adjustment and consequent avoidance of future errors. (Gallagher and Reid 1981, p. 150)

The purpose of critical explorations is to determine what constructions (rules and generalizations) a student has regarding the content under discussion. The teacher can then pose questions designed to conflict with the reasoning underlying the child's constructions. For example, if a student is experimenting with sinking and floating objects, a teacher might ask the child which objects float and which objects sink, and why. Many children believe that objects such as wood float and metals sink. One might ask such a child, "What will happen if we put a needle on the water?" or "What will happen if we put a metal box in the water?" Children who believe that metals sink under all conditions will probably predict that the needle and box will sink. Trying out these beliefs, the child will find that they float. Experiences such as these, guided by teachers' questions, hold promise for producing cognitive conflict and disequilibrium and motivation for further exploration.

Social Interaction and Collaboration

Social interaction and collaboration among children in school are essential for the development and learning of children. Social interaction is the source of learning cooperation as well as a source of cognitive conflict and disequilibration. Even though the exact way in which the disequilibrium will arise and play out for an individual child cannot be known ahead of time, what is known is that when children (or adults) collaborate and interact over content and problems, different points of view arise. This is fertile ground for disequilibration of individuals' reasoning. Edelstein (1992) writes:

> Cognitive conflict is frequently, if not always, nested in interactional conflict, and social conflict generates cognitive conflict—the signal and function of collaboration. Collaboration . . . must be implemented in terms of developmental stage, subject matter, and problem at hand. There are many forms of collaboration—such as group instruction, project organization, team enterprise, learning by discussion, peer instruction, individual profile development, and differentiated group design—that can be engineered in view of a constructivist perspective as manifestations of a collaborative process serving to generate intraindividual cognitive conflict and decentering. (p. 169)

The views of peers become particularly important for cognitive development when a child becomes able to assimilate the viewpoints of others that are contrary to his or her own. This comes about when the egocentrism of preoperational thought begins to be dispelled, around age 6 or 7. Accordingly, peer interactions are of particular cognitive importance from the time the child enters school. Children learn to evaluate their egocentric thoughts by comparing them with the thoughts of others. Around age 6 or 7, most children become able to begin to consider the views of others. Thus, peer interactions can be a fruitful means of stimulating cognitive conflicts that can provoke an evaluation of one's own concepts as part of accommodation to the views of others.

Social knowledge, the form of knowledge created by humans, is constructed by children primarily out of their social interactions. Social knowledge cannot be acquired independently of other people (although physical and much logical–mathematical knowledge can). To the extent that educational programs purport to teach social knowledge, legitimate opportunities for social interaction must be provided.

One peer activity of great value that is often overlooked by teachers is children tutoring (or teaching) other children. Gallagher and Reid (1981) point out that benefits accrue to both the tutor and the tutee when students attempt to communicate their points of view. Tutors learn to clarify their thinking, and tutees often experience cognitive conflict from being exposed to the views of peer tutors.

Surprise

Another approach I suggested in earlier writings is for teachers to use surprise to induce disequilibrium (Wadsworth 1978). Teachers cannot predict what will function as a surprise for all students, but they can structure experiences to have outcomes that are not predictable by most students. The unknown and the unpredictable can generate cognitive conflict and disequilibrium.

When I was in elementary school, the teacher of our combined 5–8 class put our whole K–8 school (45 children) on a bus, and we drove off to see a whale grounded on a beach a few miles away (on Long Island Sound). None of us had ever seen a real whale before, and we were indeed surprised by this novel experience.

> We looked at it, we listened to it, we went up to it to touch it (it could not move much), we ran away from it when it opened its massive mouth, we threw water on it, we made faces at it—we did all sorts of things. From that day on we all knew exactly what a whale was. (Wadsworth 1978, pp. 54-55)

Motivation is an internal affair associated with disequilibration. Though not external, disequilibrium can be provoked by external events such as teachers' questions (cognitive conflict), surprising events, and intellectual confrontations with peers (social interaction and collaboration). These strategies all hold potential for provoking children's intellectual development. Children's interests reflect their disequilibrium and, in Piaget's view, merit being at the center of educational activity.

INTELLECTUAL AUTONOMY

Intellectual autonomy has a cognitive and an affective component. Both are important and they are functionally inseparable. Intellectual autonomy has to do with making intellectual choices for oneself, with learning how to make decisions. It is self-regulation. It is how a detective proceeds in pursuit of truth, following the leads as they appear, testing hypotheses, and deciding what to do next based on what is known at the moment. It is charting one's own course of inquiry and action by following one's disequilibrium.

Capitalizing on autonomy, allowing children to function more autonomously, requires teachers to give up some of their control of what course of action children pursue and what they actually do. Clearly it requires educators to have faith in value of autonomy. It implies that children know something the teacher does not know. The child, in one sense, knows better than the teacher what is best to do next. The child *feels* the interest. Also, the *process* of struggling with the question of what to do next is a formative one for the child. Although apparent errors may be made, it is how we best "learn to learn," something educators give a lot of lip service to. Interfering with or preventing children from developing cognitive autonomy discourages their efforts to learn how to learn. Autonomy is not about giving children license to do whatever they want or abandoning teacher control. Quite the opposite, it is about learning how to self-regulate, to control and direct the self efficiently, effectively, and responsibly.

Affective autonomy leads to cooperative social action and interaction based on the desire to do what is right, fair, just, and responsible for others and yourself. Affective autonomy incorporates one's constructed values and an accompanying sense of obligation (imposed by the formation of the will) to act on those values. A morality of cooperation comes to exist, not because it is imposed, but because it is a freely constructed value, a recognition at some level that cooperation works and is adaptive. Affective autonomy is the basis for what many call self-discipline because it is a guide for behavior selection that is grounded in one's constructed values and a sense of obligation to adhere to those values.

Affective autonomy arises out of mutual respect relationships. These relations are first established with peers and later with adults (if all goes well). Affective autonomy thus has its source in the social activities of children and are based on freely chosen cooperation.

Intellectual autonomy—following one's nose, so to speak—is important because it permits children (and adults) to learn how to most efficiently find paths for effective learning and development, to function as problem solvers. This, I believe, is what we mean by *learning how to learn*. It also works to create a disposition of self-confidence and thus to keep gates open to new possibilities. Clearly, and contrary to the views of some, Piaget's notion of autonomy is not an individualistic, nonsocial concept. Fully developed, it is a individual's disposition that values cooperation with others, mutual respect relations, and shared values made one's own.

WHAT CAN BE CONSTRUCTED?

Piaget stated that cognitive structures (schemata) are developed in an invariant sequence.[3] That is, the course of cognitive development, marked by the development of structures, is the same for all children, although the ages at which they attain particular structures varies with intelligence and the social environment (Piaget and Inhelder 1969). Research on the invariance of concept development, though not conclusive, supports Piaget's belief that acquisition of concepts is hierarchical and integrative in nature (Dasen 1977).

A word of caution: Piaget did not say that the sequence of cognitive development he described is the *only* possible sequence in which schemata can be acquired. In fact, Piaget indicated that other sequences are possible (Bringuier 1980). Piaget's theory is a description of intellectual development as he found it to be; it is not necessarily how it *must* proceed. Although Piaget did not preclude other possible sequences, any other sequence would have to meet the criterion that successive structures incorporate previous structures in an integrative and hierarchical fashion.

Assuming that concept acquisition is invariant, at least in Western cultures, it makes educational sense to use Piaget's model of invariance in determining *when* to expect children to be capable of learning *what.* Curriculum sequences should be designed with children's changing cognitive status in mind. If what children are asked to learn does not take into account children's levels of conceptual development, learning with comprehension is unlikely, if not impossible. Children cannot successfully construct if they have neither the prerequisite cognitive skills nor the educational support necessary to acquire the skills first.

At issue here is not just success in construction of knowledge, but also the affective consequences of nonsuccess or "failure." Directed to "learn" certain concepts that are over their heads, children try to do what is the impossible. When they are held accountable for this learning (as they are with tests and grades), they seek alternatives to understanding (memorization, test-taking strategies, and cheating) to get by, or they fail. Either way, the affective consequences are unhealthy. Children who fail repeatedly or do less well than their knowledge suggests they should come to dislike the content they are unable to understand. They develop negative feelings about the content and potentially about themselves as learners. At the worst, gates close. As with math-phobia, children can see the cause as hopeless and give up, and literally not allow certain content into their systems. Such an outcome for students also diminishes the relationship between the student and the teacher. To the student, his inability to understand necessarily signals either that he is limited or that his teacher is unable or unwilling to *respect* the child's development. Perceived respect begets respect and vice versa.

Readiness to learn is of particular concern to educators of elementary school children, although it should be of concern at *all* levels of education, including college

---

[3] Piaget never made any claim that his theory applied universally (Dasen 1977). The claim of universality of his theory is speculation by others.

and adult education. According to Piagetian theory, a child (or adult) is cognitively ready to construct a particular concept when, and only when, he or she has acquired the schemata and general level of reasoning that are necessary (prerequisites). Of course, there must be an internal reason to learn (motivation).

The problem of mismatch between curriculum and students is serious at all levels of education and largely unappreciated. Shayer and Adey (1981) in their extensive research on the cognitive levels of high school science students and the "cognitive demand" of the concepts embedded in courses (biology, chemistry, and physics courses) found that serious mismatches existed for even the most advanced students. They write:

> [B]ecause of poor cognitive matching the true potential of most pupils is not being fully stimulated and realised. . . . If you treat a mixed-ability class as if they were all able to understand something which you think is important for them to understand, then you will force those who cannot understand to define themselves as incompetent . . . Our view is that by understanding the difficulties of different learners, and taking that understanding into thinking about lesson planning you not only show respect for them as persons, but also very much increase the rate at which they are able to learn and the breadth of knowledge and skills that they can achieve. (pp. 139–40)

Robert Kegan, in *In Over Our Heads: The Mental Demands of Modern Life* (1994), articulates a similar message not only for students (high school and college) but also for adults just trying to exist in modern society. Kegan describes the consequences for most of us when we are confronted with curriculum that is over our head and the implications for school learning, parenting, work, and all forms of interpersonal communication. He writes:

> [P]eople grow best where they continuously experience an ingenuous blend of support and challenge . . . Environments which are weighted too heavily in the direction of challenge [cognitive demands too high] without adequate support are toxic; they promote defensiveness and constriction. Those weighted heavily towards support without adequate challenge are ultimately boring; they promote devitalization. Both kinds of imbalances lead to withdrawal or dissociation from the context. In contrast, a balance of support and engagement leads to vital engagement. (p. 42)

Kegan argues that students and adults can suffer when the cognitive demands they face are too high or too low. He also says that being in over one's head can be good if the proper supports are in place.

> [I]t is *not* necessarily a bad thing that adolescents are in over their heads. In fact, it may be just what is called for *provided they experience effective support.* Such supports constitute a holding environment that provides both

welcoming acknowledgement to exactly who the person is right now as he or she is, and fosters the person's psychological evolution. (p. 43)

Kegan clearly makes the point that learners without support cannot move far beyond where they are in their learning. Educators have a responsibility to know and take account of children's strengths and limits, engage them where they are, and invite them to step beyond that limit. Kegan has much more to say to educators and clinicians from his constructivist perspective.

Individual Differences in Intellectual Development

Piaget's research and theoretical work on intellectual development were primarily concerned with the universal aspects of children's construction of knowledge. His efforts were directed primarily at how structures evolve in people in general. Although content and function were central to his theory, he focused less of his research on these aspects of intelligence and its development. Piaget did not address the topic of individual differences or individual variations in construction of knowledge. Nonetheless, it is clear that large differences between individuals exist. It is not true that all children are capable of learning the same things at the same time.

Children's rates of intellectual development vary considerably. In *any* classroom, there is a wide range of difference among students in the knowledge they have constructed and their overall levels of intellectual development. Although this is most striking in classrooms with heterogeneous grouping, it is almost as true where there is some form of homogeneous grouping. From a constructivist perspective, there is little, if any, validity to traditional grouping procedures. We undoubtedly could do a lot better grouping students by their interests where grouping is necessary.

Among randomly selected 7- and 8-year-olds (probably second graders), one will find that the largest percentage are in or close to transition from preoperational reasoning to concrete operational reasoning. A smaller group will probably still be early preoperational, and another similar group will be late concrete operational. We will

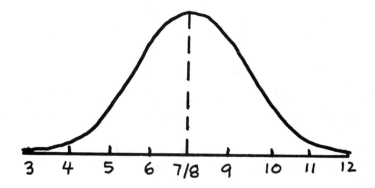

Hypothetical levels of intellectual development of 7–8 year olds

also find some students who are sensorimotor in their reasoning and a few who are developing formal operations. Thus, among children of the same chronological age, one can expect to find overall levels of intellectual development ranging from sensorimotor through early formal operational. The same ranging of, or variability in, Piagetian developmental levels is found at any chronological age group.

In a typical high school algebra class composed of 14-year-olds, most students are likely to be in the earlier steps of developing formal operations. Some will be in advanced formal operations. Some will be in concrete operations. Comprehension of algebra requires formal operations as its content is basically abstractions of abstractions. Assuming all students are motivated to learn algebra (which is unrealistic), those who are in a position to construct the relevant knowledge successfully are those with advanced formal operations and some of those with beginning formal operations. Certainly, children who are concrete operational will be at a loss, as will some of those who have entered but do not have sufficient development of formal operations. This assumes that instruction is ideal, which is not always the case. In any event, students who have slower than average rates of development are, as Kegan (1994) would say, "in over their heads" even when the cognitive demand of the material and the instruction is appropriate for the average student in their age group. Students with slower than average rates of development look like "slow learners."

Slow learners may well have the potential to develop formal operations as fully as students with average to above-average rates of development, but find themselves at risk because of their rates of development. In all likelihood they do poorly on tests and other measures of performance and suffer humiliation and self-concept-destroying consequences. It is ironic that the same student who could not do division two years ago and failed the division tests and who can do division today receives no positive strokes for that accomplishment, even if the child's learning is later in emerging than for most. Grouping by ages makes successful school learning and performance very difficult for these children.

The major factors in intellectual development presented at the outset of this book are maturation, experience, social interactions, and equilibration. Individuals differ with respect to the contribution of each of these variables in their development. Levels of intellectual development vary considerably among children.

Because development can be traced back to biological factors before birth, there can clearly be inherited biological differences that affect intellectual development. These can be manifest in different rates of the maturation of relevant physiological structures.

Experience is a second variable in development. No two children have the same experiences. The history of experiences is different for every human being. Even identical twins raised in the same home cannot be assumed to have had the same experiences. Accordingly, differences in prior experiences can contribute to individual differences in intellectual development.

As children have different histories of general experiences, so do they have different histories of social experiences, or *social interaction*. Clearly, one's history of interactions contributes to individual differences.

Children differ in their histories of maturation, experience, and social interaction, and they can differ in how these factors interact to govern intellectual development.

Bovet (1976) observes that one's rate of development can vary over life:

Both a slowing-up and an acceleration of the developmental rate has been observed in cross-cultural and learning studies. Slowing up may be caused by lack of stimulation, and acceleration can be achieved, within certain limits, by teaching methods which closely follow the normal course of development. (Bovet 1976, p. 277)

Individual differences are large. Children are certainly different in terms of the thinking, reasoning, and comprehension they bring to academic work and what they can be expected to learn and comprehend.

Problem Solving and Critical Thinking

Educators often discuss problem solving and critical thinking as if they are capabilities that are different from those that can evolve in the normal course of development of reasoning. From a Piagetian constructivist perspective, critical thinking is not fundamentally different from regular thinking. It is not a separate or unique type of thinking. Nor is the reasoning involved in problem solving unique. Critical thinking and problem solving capabilities are maximized by maximizing children's intellectual development, which includes nurturing the disposition, desire, and confidence to pursue problems.

From a Piagetian perspective, this is most likely to happen in environments where children's education is grounded in constructivist methodology, where exploration and construction of knowledge are valued and encouraged, and where gates are open and autonomy is the prevailing mode of functioning. Problem solving requires well-developed reasoning and relevant knowledge. It also requires an autonomous disposition, the desire to solve the problem, and the belief that one can succeed. Thus, affective conditions are as central to effective problem solving (and critical thinking) as are cognitive conditions.

These qualities are not best learned through passive educational practices that cover endless quantities of content (including exercises in problem solving), but through practices that nurture deep comprehension, personal autonomous construction, and self-confidence. Children and adults who learn to deal autonomously with problems and trust for guidance their own patterns of disequilibration acquire the most important tools for problem solving and critical thinking. What remains, then, is the desire, the perceived need (adaptation value) to solve a particular problem.

I believe that the developed habit of autonomous learning may be more crucial to effective critical thinking and problem solving than relevant cognitive knowledge. The autonomous learner lacking particular knowledge knows how to acquire that knowledge. On the other hand, simply having the necessary cognitive knowledge is not sufficient if autonomy and desire (the affective aspects) are not present. These cannot be learned quickly.

FOSTERING MORAL REASONING AND MORAL BEHAVIOR

Can parents and schools do anything to foster the development of moral judgment and moral behavior in children? Piaget has showed us how and under what conditions moral concepts are constructed. If the goals of education (at home and in school) include the development of sound moral reasoning and behavior, and if we agree with Piaget's views, we can conclude that the authoritarian model for the relationship between children and adults is a poor one.[4] If children develop moral judgment, cooperation, and self-discipline in an authoritarian environment, it can only be in spite of, not as a result of, their authoritarian relationship with adults.

> It is . . . absurd and even immoral to wish to impose upon the child a fully worked-out system of discipline when the social life of children themselves is sufficiently developed to give rise to a discipline infinitely nearer to the inner submission which is the mark of adult morality. It is idle . . . to try and transform the child's mind from outside, when his own taste for active research and his desire for cooperation suffice to ensure a normal intellectual development. The adult must therefore be a collaborator and not a master, from this double point of view, moral and rational. (Piaget 1965, p. 404)

Piaget recommended that schools foster active mutual respect between children, much in the way John Dewey (1963) described in the early 1900s. Authoritarian teachers need to discover ways to modify their authoritarian role so that a major portion of their interaction with children can be as collaborators and equals. Wright (1982) says, "The heart of moral development . . . can be defined as the prolonged and continuing experience of mutual respect relationships" (p. 216). The development of cooperation by a child, as well as the development of self-discipline (autonomy), can occur only in an environment that permits mutual respect to flourish.

As with other knowledge, children *construct* moral knowledge and reasoning out of their actions in the environment. Clearly, moral knowledge is necessary for moral reasoning and moral reasoning is necessary for moral behavior. It is also true that moral reasoning does not ensure consistent moral behavior. One does not act in a moral way only because one is intellectually capable of reasoning that way. In Piaget's scheme, moral behavior is very much under the control of the will, or one's permanent scale of values. If the individual has a strong will, then there is in place a strong sense of obligation to ones values. A strong will increases the likelihood that one will actually do what one's moral reasoning says is the right thing to do.

---

[4] This is not an argument against adults exerting their authority over children when appropriate. However, children cannot be expected to develop advanced moral reason while authority remains the dominant moral force in their lives.

[I]f we possess a permanent scale of values, the conflicts can be resolved, the solution of the conflicts consisting in a subordination of the actual situation to permanent values. . . . If these values are strong, then the regulation will result directly without the problem of adding a new force. And if these value are weak or incoherent, there will be no will. (Piaget 1962b, pp. 144–145)

Neither Piaget nor any other psychologist or educator can provide the teacher or parent with a ready-made plan that will ensure children's development of moral reasoning and behavior. Common sense suggests that educational practice at home and in school should be consistent with what we know about children and their development. What follows are several guidelines consistent with Piaget's theory:

1. Teachers and parents can assume mutual respect, nonauthoritarian relationships with young children for at least some of their time together and with high school students all the time. Teachers can encourage children to resolve issues themselves and develop autonomy. Teachers must respect children.
2. When punishment of children is necessary, it can be based on reciprocity rather than expiation. For example, the boy who refuses to clean up his room can be deprived of the things he does not clean up. The girl who hits other children can be denied interaction with other children.
3. Teachers can foster social interaction in their classrooms and encourage questioning and examining any issue children raise. There is intellectual value in dealing with children's spontaneous intellectual interests, and it is equally valuable to their moral development to deal with spontaneous moral questions.
4. Teachers can engage students, even at the preschool level, in discussions of moral issues. As children listen to their peers' views, they can experience cognitive disequilibration, which can lead to a reorganization of their concepts. Cognitive conflict is necessary for the restructuring of reasoning (development) to proceed.
5. Schools and classrooms can be restructured to allow students greater participation in the valid aspects of the school-governing process. Although many "educators" would like to think otherwise, responsibility, cooperation, and self-discipline cannot be transmitted to children authoritatively. Such concepts must be constructed by children out of their own experiences. Mutual respect relationships are essential. Teachers and parents are generally the ones who structure the social environment to which children adapt and from which they learn. It is questionable whether children can develop concepts of justice based on cooperation in environments in which justice is based only on authority.

chapter 9

Applications

PIAGET'S CONSTRUCTIVIST THEORY AND MATHEMATICS EDUCATION

As a traditional 7th-grade teacher in the late 1950s and early 1960s teaching in a self-contained classroom, I attempted to teach students arithmetic computation using the algorithms in the textbook. While introducing division of fractions one day, I went through the usual routine of "you invert one of the fractions and change the division sign to a multiplication sign, then multiply."

$$\frac{1}{2} \div \frac{3}{4} = \frac{1}{2} \times \frac{4}{3}$$

One of the brighter kids in the class, Jimmy Jones, shot his hand up and asked (insisted), "Why? That doesn't make any sense at all!" I thought for a minute, was embarrassed and said, "I don't know. But I'll find out." Later that day I asked the other 7th-grade teachers and they didn't know. I went and asked the 8th-grade teachers, figuring they must know more than the 7th-grade teachers. They didn't know either. I had heard there were two math teachers at the high school with doctorates. I was sure they would know. I went and asked them and the other high school math teachers. They didn't know either! At that point my intuitions told me that we were in serious trouble as teachers of mathematics; something was really wrong. Discovering Piaget several years later in graduate school began to help me make sense of these types of dilemmas. Thank you, Jimmy Jones.

It is my opinion that mathematics is the content area where traditional nonconstructivist methods (like those I used as a 7th-grade teacher) have had the most detrimental effects on children's school learning. Children arrive at school with their own, often well-developed and autonomously constructed "informal" arithmetic knowledge. (Baroody 1987; Ginsburg 1977; Kamii 1985, 1994). They can usually count and almost always have a intuitive understanding of addition and subtraction. Instruction begins with symbols and computation. All too often, even many developmentally advanced ("bright") students are more or less permanently handicapped by teaching methods and mathematics curricula they encounter. The main culprits are methods and demands that focus on direct transmission from teacher to student and on correct answers rather than on children's autonomous thinking and construction of mathematical concepts.

Most traditional arithmetic instruction is instruction in computation and encourages internalizing (memorizing)[1] standard algorithms. Such instruction forces children to abandon their own thinking. Because the reasoning behind algorithms is often "over the heads" of children and is not a product of their own thinking, they can make no sense of them (Kamii 1994). Isolated instruction in computation induces most children to believe that "real" mathematics is computation, and it is necessarily memorized. Children, prodded by instruction they cannot make sense of, can abandon their pursuit of reasoning about quantity. Thus, in mathematics instruction, rather than starting out with a "bridge" from children's informal or constructed knowledge, children often face a void they cannot make sense of.

Learning mathematical concepts is about thinking, reasoning, and construction. Computation is an important skill to be learned, but is best learned as a product of construction. Students generally construct the standard algorithms (or equally useful ones) in due time and they understand their constructions, and when and how to use them, and they do not forget them.

Learning mathematical concepts and procedures requires the application of concrete and formal operations to the content of mathematics. New or different forms of reasoning are not required. There is no special type of reasoning just for mathematics. Those who understand (have knowledge of) mathematics have constructed concepts out of their logical–mathematical reasoning, often despite the instruction they have received in school. The others are all too often lost. Being lost, if it persists, has serious affective (and thus intellectual) consequences. Those who cannot comprehend lose faith in themselves and often give up. Without a proper "bridge," or educational supports, they are at risk for learning to hate math. The gates are then closed.

This section presents the basic principles that must be present in arithmetic and mathematics programs if they are to be consistent with constructivist theory. The interested reader is encouraged to consult sources that go beyond what can be cov-

---

[1] The assertion that rote memory is not a kind of learning does not mean that rote memory is not valued, but that it is not the route to intellectual development from a Piagetian perspective. Rote memory is a valuable and useful skill to be encouraged for its own sake, but memorization and comprehension are not the same thing. The child who comprehends mathematical operations is intellectually different from the child who has only memorized computational procedures.

ered here. (See DeVries and Kohlberg 1987; Kamii 1985, 1994; Labinowicz 1985; Schifter and Fosnot 1993; Baroody 1987; Ginsburg, 1977). These principles are adapted from DeVries and Kohlberg (1987).

1. *Psychological structures must be developed before numerical questions are introduced.* If children try to reason about numerical issues before having acquired the logical–mathematical structures relevant to the mathematical concepts in the questions, the problems will have no meaning for them. Construction is interfered with.

2. *Psychological structures [schemata] must be developed before formal symbolism is introduced.* The symbolism or language of mathematics is a set of written or spoken numbers (1, 2, 3, etc.). These symbols are representations of concepts. Written numbers are not the concepts. The concepts are primary and give meaning to the representations. Ginsburg (1977) has made it clear that "children's understanding of written symbolism generally lags behind their informal arithmetic [concepts]" (p. 90). When children are asked to try to make sense out of written numbers (representations) before they have the underlying concepts, construction is impossible.

3. *Automatized knowledge should not be stressed before implicit logic is understood.* It is a strongly held belief by many that memorization of written number facts is absolutely necessary. Kamii (1984, 1985, 1994) and others have demonstrated that children can learn number facts without the usual rote memorization procedures if instruction is appropriate. Memorization before concept acquisition encourages memorization, not construction and understanding.

4. *Children must have the opportunity to invent [construct] mathematical relations rather than simply confront ready-made adult thought.* The importance of exploration and the autonomous construction of knowledge is a theme of this book. Successful instruction is that which leads to individual construction. Construction is the necessary criterion.

5. *Teachers must understand the nature of children's mistakes.* By definition, intellectual and mathematical development is full of errors. Errors are an inevitable part of construction in all areas. Systematic errors in mathematics often reflect the reasoning and constructed knowledge a child has used to solve problems.[2] For example, the following figure shows a child's (Peter's) responses to a series of renaming subtraction problems. All answers are incorrect. What is clear, though, is that the errors are not random, but systematic, indicating that a reasoning strategy was used. "Because borrowing did not make sense to Peter, he failed to learn the borrowing algorithm. When he encountered problems requiring borrowing, he fell

---

[2] Errors can reflect more than children's current knowledge. They can also reflect carelessness or emotional confusion and distress. Teachers who become familiar with looking at children's errors from a constructivist perspective quickly learn to tell which reflect constructions and which do not.

Example of errors

$$
\begin{array}{cccc}
11 & 12 & 16 & 20 \\
-4 & -8 & -9 & -7 \\
\hline
13 & 16 & 13 & 27
\end{array}
$$

$$
\begin{array}{cccc}
21 & 27 & 35 & 40 \\
-8 & -8 & -17 & -13 \\
\hline
27 & 21 & 22 & 33
\end{array}
$$

SOURCE: Baroody, 1987, p. 55.

back on the familiar procedure of subtracting the smaller digit from the larger. In effect, he invented his own incorrect method for coping with an unfamiliar task" (Baroody 1987, p. 55).

Peter's solutions to the problems are reasoned. His answers give us an idea of what he knows and what he does not yet know and what one needs to work with him on. Teachers should view errors as a source of information about children's reasoning and for understanding the nature of children's schemata. Kamii (1985), Labinowicz (1985), Ginsburg (1977), and Baroody (1987) are all helpful in developing more fully this important perspective on children's errors.

6. *An atmosphere for thinking must be established.* The typical form of mathematics instruction is some sort of direct effort by the teacher to pour into children mathematical facts and computational procedures. Typically, the students are passive participants. Children are forced to try to understand what the teacher is saying but most often are unable to make mental connections between what the teacher or textbook is saying and their constructed knowledge.

When intellectually blocked in this manner, students adapt as best they can (as did Peter). They use what knowledge they have constructed, however inadequate, to reason about the problems. When this is recognized as inadequate, they may try to memorize everything without comprehension. For some, this leads to passing tests. For some, it does not. For all but a few, there is no further construction of mathematical knowledge.

Children require classroom environments where they want to and are encouraged to try out their theories and strategies. It is helpful if students are encouraged to interact, share ideas, criticize each other's solutions, and intellectually debate how to do what. Peer interaction can facilitate individual construction by producing cognitive conflict, thus disequilibrium, the motivation for reconstruction of existing knowledge.

Most mathematics instruction focuses on computational procedures, not on methods that encourage autonomous construction of the mathematical concepts that underpin mathematics. Children strive to understand and make sense of things. When they cannot, they resort to memorization and other ineffective strategies. Students, even "bright" ones, may be persuaded by instruction that is "over their heads" to disregard their natural tendency to try to make sense of their experiences with mathematics.

Why do so many students hate mathematics? The clearest reason is that they do not understand it. It is not something most people make sense of, even though most have all the intellectual tools to do so. In the face of negative feelings, many avoid mathematics. The gates are closed. Constructivism seeks to keep the gates open.[3]

Infinity

One day in 1970, I visited a new private elementary school in Amherst, Massachusetts, called the Common School. It was started by a seasoned teacher, Mrs. Johnson. As I entered the run-down building, I saw four fourth graders in a small room with a large scroll of paper. One student appeared to be writing out numbers while the others watched intently. It was clear a large part of the scroll was full of numbers. Each number being written appeared to have about 25 digits, and each successive number was an increment of one over the previous number. The students were absolutely transfixed (as was I). I watched for a few more minutes and then set off to find Mrs. Johnson.

I found Mrs. Johnson and introduced myself. I mentioned the four students writing out numbers and asked whether she knew what they were doing. She said she did, and explained that their teacher, two days previously, during their math period, had been talking about the concept of *infinity*. It seems some of the students indicated they did not "get it" and argued that numbers had to end somewhere. Infinity, as the teacher was talking about it, did not make any sense to the students. During the discussion, several students suggested that they could write out all the numbers and get to the end. They asked to try. The teacher produced the scroll of paper and sent them off to try. They had been at it for two days when I arrived. They actually had teams of students spelling each other every few hours. Later I found out that they kept it up for another day and decided to stop.

Was this a worthwhile use of these students' time? It was not planned and was not part of the curriculum. Many students were out of class a lot for several days, missing whatever was going on in class. Some were thinking only about infinity. These students were actively engaged in constructing knowledge. The activity was prompted by disequilibration and was interest-driven. The actions were autonomous, cooperative, coconstructive and clearly worthwhile. Did they learn (construct) some-

---

[3] Mount Holyoke College in South Hadley, Massachusetts, offers summer graduate-level courses for elementary through secondary level teachers through its *SummerMath for Teachers* program. This nationally recognized program is explicitly based on constructivist principles and is of interest to any educator wishing to become more familiar with the application of constructivist principles to mathematics instruction.

thing about infinity?[4] Sure they did! To me, this is a nice example of a teacher's response to spontaneous interest and disequilibration.

Some might be tempted to think it might be a good idea to have all students (in teams) try to write to infinity and make it part of math instruction. Such a *required* activity would probably be a big mistake. This worked in this case because it sprang from children's disequilibration and teacher-guided autonomous action. To require this of students without authentic disequilibration would make it a meaningless task (Frank Murray, personal communication, 1992).

WHAT PIAGET'S THEORY SAYS ABOUT CHILDREN LEARNING TO READ AND WRITE

Only recently have authors attempted to look at reading through Piaget's theory (Chall 1983; Elkind 1981; DeVries and Kohlberg 1987; Wadsworth 1978). It is likely that the next decade will see an increased focus of Piagetian theory and research on issues related to reading.

Presented here are some guidelines derived from Piaget's theory. Piaget's theory does not lead directly to a methodology for teaching reading, writing, and spelling, but does offer a set of principles against which different instructional approaches can be evaluated.

1. Learning to read is clearly a part of coming to understand written language. Learning to read and reading are receptive aspects of dealing with written language. The other parts are learning to write and spell, which are expressive aspects of use of written language. For reading, writing, and spelling to be isolated from one another in a curriculum, as they typically are, makes no sense at all. The three must occur together, not as separate subjects.

2. Children need to construct an awareness that graphic symbols (written words) can be used to represent things. Most initial reading instruction assumes this understanding. Many children entering reading instruction do not have this understanding. Children who lack this understanding have difficulty making sense of any instruction.

3. Learning to read is different from reading. Reading for content and understanding is something one can do only after one has learned to read. Learning to read, like learning spoken language, can be viewed as a code-breaking process. For the motivated child, the task is to construct an understanding of the socially approved rules for written language. This requires active efforts by the child to assimilate and accommodate experience with

---

[4] Infinity is an abstract concept (or hypothetical construct) not knowable directly from one's observations. Most students do not construct the full concept of infinity before formal operations. Thus, it would not be realistic to expect most 9- to 10-year-olds to grasp the full meaning or hold them accountable for comprehending it. On the other hand, these students clearly had some concepts to bring to bear on the teacher's comments and some reconstruction of some of these notions came about

written language and the construction of progressively more accurate schemata about reading (and writing and spelling). The child's actions on written language are, therefore, central. Errors will abound and must be recognized as part of the construction process. Errors should be viewed as information about the child's constructions regarding written language and can form the basis for any instructional interventions.

Learning to read is a process of construction that occurs inside the mind of a child. Although the construction is individual, interactions with peers and adults about written language are essential. Written language is a form of social knowledge and is impossible to construct accurately without interaction with others.

4. "The content of the child's reading activity (during the learning to read process) should be meaningful *to the child.* That is, the child should have previously assimilated into structures the objects referred to by the written symbols [words] in the material he is learning to read" (Wadsworth 1978, p. 144). Children need to be able to attach meaning to symbols for things to make any sense. Where does meaning reside? Meaning resides only in the schemata that children have constructed. Words (written symbols) do not carry meaning. How can one ensure that the content of children's materials are meaningful to them while they are learning to read? The clearest way is to use children's language, not ready-made books, as the source of written material (see Ashton-Warner 1963).

5. Learning to read must be viewed from the perspective of adaptation and motivation. Piaget indicated that motivation is important in children's learning to read (Wadsworth 1978). Interest in reading is an indication of motivation to become engaged in figuring out what reading is all about. Interest is an important (maybe the most important) determinant of readiness.

It is unclear whether learning to read requires a particular level of cognitive development. Are concrete operational abilities required or are preoperational abilities sufficient? It may be that children at different levels can learn aspects of reading in many different ways. Learning to read progresses at various rates. Individualization is called for. An aspect of the teacher's job is to help maintain positive affect (keep gates open) throughout the process to prevent the motivation to construct from being turned off.

Why do children often experience so much more difficulty with learning to read than with learning to speak? One reason may be that learning to speak is *adaptive* from the first word learned. Learning to read a little bit is less clearly adaptive. One has to learn to read quite well for it to become a useful communication tool. Another reason may be that reading instruction often focuses on the mechanics of the reading process rather than on the child's active construction and code breaking. This can result in children's attention being deflected away from their own autonomously directed activities to those the teacher indicates are more important. This is disastrous for many children, as they do not construct what reading is about. This has only negative affective consequences for their willingness to continue.

Although Piaget's theory does not lead to a recommended reading method, I encourage interested readers to read Sylvia Ashton-Warner's book *Teacher* and reflect on the procedures she developed. It is not a perfect match with constructivism, but most of what she recommends regarding reading and writing can be viewed as consistent with Piaget's cognitive and affective principles (see Wadsworth 1978).

Many constructivists support a whole-language approach to reading, writing, and spelling, and Ashton-Warner's approach is one version of what might be called whole language. Some versions of whole language are theoretically sound; some are not. Unfortunately, I do not know of a good critique of different whole language programs, although DeVries and Kohlberg (1987) is well worth reading to develop a frame with which to evaluate programs. Not all are consistent with constructivist principles.

There is a very real population of children (and adults) who are unable to successfully construct the rules for "sounding out" written language. They appear to have significant language learning "disabilities." They make up as much as 15–20 percent of the population. They often have problems in learning to use spoken language, reading, writing, spelling, and foreign languages. They may be labeled *learning disabled* (or more specifically *dyslexic*) if no clear alternative hypothesis is clear from their histories. These are real people who are unable to respond to conventional approaches to learning to use language, including whole language methods. Many educators, including many constructivists, deny the existence of this population. Successful education for dyslexic students requires more than reading programs generally offer. More is said on this issue in the following section on learning disabilities.

CONSTRUCTIVIST THEORY AND LEARNING DISABILITIES

For many years I have regularly taught a constructivist-based course in educational psychology and a introductory special education course in the teacher preparation program at Mount Holyoke College. Though initially trained in educational psychology with no training in the education of extreme populations, I had the good fortune many years ago to work and study one summer with Newell Kephart, one of the early perceptual-motor theorists. I was truly impressed by his brilliance in clinical analysis of children's individual learning and performance issues and his efforts to examine these issues within a developmental framework. The experience with Kephart helped me to begin to understand how to determine effective educational assistance for students with severe learning issues. I went on to work part-time in a learning disabilities clinic in the 1970s at Mount Holyoke. Several years ago, I started and directed the support program for learning disabled and dyslexic college students at Mount Holyoke. In addition, I have evolved a clinical practice working with and advocating for learning-disabled students. Thus, my professional work has had two educational strands: Piagetian-based constructivist "regular" education and "special" education.

Constructivist education and special education have historically been two separate fields with little overlap with regard to philosophy and teaching strategies. In recent years, some constructivist educators (Harris and Graham 1994; Reid and Hresko 1981) have begun to question the separation and explore the potential utility of constructivist concepts in thinking about education of the learning-disabled and other "special" populations. To look at the intersection of the two seems to me to be a wise thing to do, not because I believe constructivism, as translated here for regular education, will automatically "save" special education, but because the disequilibration special education issues induce can enrich our thinking. I do believe that special education can benefit from constructivism.

I tell the students in my classes that *we are all more or less learning-disabled,* and I mean it. To be clearer, what I mean is that we all have strengths and weaknesses. In Howard Gardner's (1983) terms, some of our areas of intelligence are more developed than others. For a variety of reasons, we are good at some things and quite poor at others. Some of my strengths are excellent visual-spatial and motor skills, which help me a lot in art work, furniture making, building construction, and reading maps. One of my weaknesses is very limited musical ability (or musical intelligence). I have tried very hard to learn to play instruments with the most dismal results. My strengths and weaknesses have no clear explanation or "cause." They are part of the hand I was dealt. What we call learning disabilities are conditions where an individual has weaknesses that affect their school learning and performance. They also have strengths, but they typically are evaluated through their weaknesses. If the criterion for excellence as a person was musical ability rather than school grades, I would be correctly labeled as learning disabled. My strengths would count for naught. So it is with the learning-disabled.

The population of students who have significant differences in the way they learn and perform ranges from 15 to 20 percent (higher in some populations). The primary categories I will focus on here are learning disabilities (LD) and dyslexia, the most common "handicapping" conditions schools deal with (David Drake, personal communication, 1994). Learning disabilities are defined by exclusion. When a person is of normal intelligence, does not have a primary emotional problem, has had normal opportunities to learn, and is motivated, and there are no other factors or combination of factors that explain the low performance, the person is learning disabled. This means that he or she has one or more areas of weakness that interferes with learning or performance. *Dyslexia* is a learning disability in which symptoms cluster around use of language and suggest a fundamental language disability. Dyslexics often have some form of observable difficulty learning and using their native language (such as word searching and slow processing speed). They usually have reading and writing difficulties and almost always have difficulty learning a foreign language. They often have unusual strengths in some nonlanguage-related areas. It is important to me to ask what constructivist theory has to offer educators working with "special education" students. In addressing this question, I shall, for the moment, sidestep the important and problematic issues of diagnosis and identification, etiology, and such politically fraught issues as inclusion and mainstreaming. My comments here will address only the LD and dyslexic populations, although I believe their application is more general.

When one looks at instruction of regular and learning-disabled students, clear differences are usually seen. Instruction of LD students is often highly structured, skill-oriented, highly repetitive, and completely teacher-directed. Notions of disequilibration, construction, interests, and autonomy are rarely evident. Viewed from a Piagetian-constructivist perspective, such instruction seems at odds with developmental principles.

Construction of Knowledge and Comprehension

The keystone of Piagetian constructivism is the belief that knowledge is a construction and that the source of one's comprehension and reasoning is that constructed knowledge. Do learning-disabled students construct knowledge? Do they experience disequilibration and assimilate and accommodate experience? Clearly they do! Indeed, while having areas of weakness, LD students often have strengths that exceed those of non-LD students.

A recent graduate of Mount Holyoke College who was admitted as a known dyslexic with profound disabilities is such a individual. Her reading and writing levels were at the fourth grade level. For her four years of college, she required a student editor to help her with all her writing. She was a science major and completed a research thesis in her senior year (which was published). When she took the Graduate Record Exams (untimed) she did about average on the verbal and quantitative sections and received an 800 (perfect score) on the analytical section. She applied to and was accepted in the four top Ph.D. programs in the neurosciences. She is currently completing her dissertation. This young woman has profound handicaps in language usage and profound strengths in analytical reasoning and thinking. She is destined to become an exceptional scientist.

A common area of "weakness" of LD students is memory, often both short-term and long-term memory. When typical non-LD students are confronted with school content they do not understand and face a test or other performance demand, the strategy they use most often is to memorize what they can and, with some luck, pass the test. Of course, this is not a measure of what has been really learned (or constructed), but that is the way the traditional system works. LD students with weak memories do this less well, if at all. LD students can not rely on memory in the way non-LD students often can. In this type of situation, the difference in test performance between LD and non-LD students may be almost entirely memory ability. Indeed, a test on material not understood can become a test of memory. An implication of this is that on test performance, LD students can be more dependent on comprehension than are non-LD students.

Affectivity

Because LD students typically have learning and performance difficulties in school, they typically have lower self-esteem than non-LD students. Like their non-LD peers, they avoid academic tasks that they feel they cannot succeed at. There are lots of closed gates. In the very worst of cases, they see even limited success in school as hopeless. The affective system, in charge of what is permitted to enter into construction of knowledge, is often chaotic. They may be, in Priscilla Vail's terms, not "available for learning" (Vail 1987). The gates are closed. Gates become closed in mathematics, for example, not because of some innate hatred of mathematics or absence of mathematical aptitude but because of the inability of the student to make sufficient sense of mathematics and the affective ramifications of failure. Closed gates are kept closed by strong affective locks. The child's intention is not to reopen closed gates. In a Piagetian view, this is an understandable adaptation.

Of course, the possibility of learning school content while the gates are closed is nil. What is learned affectively is to dislike the content, often dislike the self, and not trust those who insist that they learn. A big question for educators, then, is whether closed gates can open, and if so, how can we facilitate that?

Opening Closed Gates

Both LD and non-LD students can have closed gates, although LD students surely do. A concern for teachers is how to help children keep gates open and how to help children open gates when they are closed. At the core, this is an affective issue. It is an issue of how students *feel*, not what they *know*.

Given that a student has closed gates, we can assume that their feelings about those areas are negative. These negative feelings reflect autonomously constructed values. The teacher who values mathematics may want the student to value it as well. The question, then, is how does one assist one who does not value mathematics (gates are closed) to come to value mathematics (gates are open)?

Autonomy and Self-Regulation

Central to Piaget's constructivist theory is the belief that learning and development that is autonomously directed is better than that which is externally directed. Autonomy or self-regulation in Piaget's theory refers to the inclination, susceptibility, and willingness or determination of the child to experience disequilibration and be open to experiences and, on experiencing disequilibration or allowing experiences in (to the process of knowledge construction), to pursue its resolution by active assimilation and accommodation and by selection of other experiences necessary to attain resolution. More simply stated, the child's affective system keeps the gates that control what enters the construction of knowledge process open and allows the child's adaptive learning procedures to follow their own direction, as would a detective.

Autonomous learning is seen as better because it efficiently and *surely* builds on the child's existing constructed knowledge and ensures that the outcome of reconstruction of knowledge will result in a qualitative advance and a better adaptation. Autonomously directed learning ensures improved comprehension and meaning.

It is well-known that most LD children in school are rarely autonomous or self-directed learners (Garner 1992; Palinczar and Klerk 1992; Drake and Wadsworth 1992). LD children usually lack strategies that are effective for figuring out how to proceed with many school tasks and typically have little confidence about regulating their own learning. They look outside for direction. Most programs for LD students structure the "control" with the teacher and program and do not have self-regulation as a goal for students. Deci et al. (1992) observe that programs for LD children and other special populations are typically control oriented (explicitly or implicitly). His research indicates that "[I]nternal motivation variables are important for the achievement and adjustment of these [learning disabled] students. . . .There is evidence that support of autonomy in the home and classroom environments . . . along with involvement on the part of significant adults promotes greater internal motivation, achievement, and adjustments" (p. 469).Thus, it is reasonable to ask whether LD children would be more effective learners if their learning was more autonomous and self-directed or whether autonomy should not be a goal for these students. If one decides that it is desirable to promote intellectual and affective autonomy in LD children (in all children), how does one proceed?

It is important to recognize that *all* children self-regulate their learning and development from birth.They are born self-regulators. Self-regulation is the norm and it remains the primary mode of regulation unless it is derailed. In school, the derailment is most often caused by repeated failure. After repeated bouts of failure, children subsume their own internal inclinations toward self-regulation to those external to them (i.e., the teacher) until they drop out.This is an understandable adaptation. How does one bring them back?

In Piaget's theory, the establishment of intellectual autonomy and full self-regulation requires the establishment of what Piaget called *mutual respect relations.* Such relations among peers can begin during the development of preoperational reasoning; mutual respect relations with adults (such as teachers) can begin to evolve during the development of concrete operations. Such relations always involve a notion of equality between the student and the teacher (or other adult), shared values, and a mutual appreciation. In my view, mutual respect relations necessarily translates into students' feeling someone cares about some of what they care about (values), cares about them, and seems to them to take seriously their interests and what they say.

Mutual respect and caring, when perceived as such by the child, are usually met by the child coming to care for and respect the adult. Reciprocal valuing and caring normally evolves into mutual respect relations and trust. I believe mutual respect relations and trust foster the willingness of the child to consider as possibly important the values of the co-carer even though those values may otherwise seem objectionable to the child.With mutual respect and trust intact, and with proper support, the teacher (or parent) is in a position to gradually persuade the child to consider opening some closed gates, to take a risk he might not otherwise take. Because the relationship is valued, the student trusts and believes that his or her best interests are being considered. If the gate opens even a crack, the teacher has one foot in the door. If followed by educational assistance or instruction that helps the child become a more effective learner in a legitimate sense (no easy task), then eventual success becomes a real possibility. It becomes possible for students to establish competence in an area previously avoided and move toward reestablishment of self-regulation (autonomy) as a workable strategy.

Piaget saw mutual respect relations as necessary for the development of students' autonomy and autonomy as necessary for the development of personality and full social development. Although Piaget did not use the word *caring* to describe these relationships, I believe his use of the terms *valuing, reciprocity,* and *trust* imply that the child, in a mutual respect relationship, feels valued, in a certain way equal to the adult, and thus cared for.

Mutual respect relations and trust (which Piaget asserts underlies development of autonomy and further affective and social adaptation) are often overlooked in education. It may be assumed that teachers respect and care for students. Indeed, many teachers are caring and respectful of students not because educational policy sets caring as a priority but because those teachers have autonomously decided to treat students that way. Nonetheless, educators usually seek unilateral respect from students and only rarely mutual respect with them. This goes double for LD children. I argue, as does Noddings (1992), that mutual respect relations and caring are essential to development of autonomy and further affective and social development, and should be central to the educational enterprise.

PIAGETIAN CONSTRUCTIVIST COMMENTS ON THE WHOLE LANGUAGE VERSUS PHONICS DEBATE

In some educational circles, the whole-language approach to reading instruction is properly associated with constructivist theory. Unfortunately, there are many different reading programs that identify themselves as "whole language," most of which are not fully consistent with constructivism. They often stray from constructivist principles or omit important principles from their programs (such as mutual respect and caring). In constructivist theory, whole-language reading instruction is not a set of proscribed procedures for teaching, but a set of principles one uses to guide that instruction. (see "What Piaget's Theory Says About Children Learning to Read and Write," this chapter).

Liberman and Liberman (1991), respected theorists in working with dyslexic students, take the whole language movement to task and argue that whole language is reckless and that code emphasis and decoding procedures are responsible. Much of the Libermans' criticism is accurate. Many children learn to read with a whole language approach. Many seem to learn to read regardless of the method, possibly despite the instruction. The Libermans suggest that 25 percent will not learn how to read with the whole-language approach and must be explicitly taught the alphabetic principle (how to decode) to proceed. I think they are basically correct and this reality is something that many whole-language teachers refuse to recognize. Whole language, however conceived, does not work all the time. Dyslexia is real and young dyslexics just do not catch on regardless of how hard they try. They need an educational bridge that works for *them.*

Although there is much the Libermans say that I believe to be true, their lack of appreciation of constructivist theory and development in general is apparent. The following sections draw attention to several principles of Piaget's constructivist theory that the Libermans missed and that many whole-language advocates have missed as well.

Construction

Knowledge is a construction. All agree that the mastery of spoken language (in the case of the deaf, sign language) is a prerequisite for constructing the alphabetic principle and learning to read. The Libermans' view seems to be that spoken language is fully biologically rooted and children's learning of spoken language occurs with ease. Although it does seem to come about easily for most children, what is omitted is that spoken language is a construction. That construction is neither automatic nor inevitable. Only as the child actively tries to break the code and progressively constructs the regularities and irregularities of spoken language does the knowledge yield. (For dyslexics, it may yield little). Similarly, breaking the code of written language, seemingly a more complex and difficult task, is also a process of construction. That spoken language and written language are constructions must be recognized by all those assisting children with reading. Whatever teaching methods are used for reading instruction, the criterion for progress must be whether the child is progressively constructing rules for reading.

Adaptation

Intellectual development is a form of adaptation in the biological sense. Many years ago, I worked on the case of a 3-1/2-year-old boy who had severely delayed spoken language. The parents were concerned. He did not speak much and had been diagnosed as retarded by a team of specialists. They recommended that he be placed in a special preschool program for retarded and language-delayed children. My interviews regarding the child's home life revealed little contact with other children or with adults other than the mother. The mother was a gem! She was always with the child, attentive, loving, and particularly skilled at anticipating what the child was going to want or need next. My constructivist hypothesis regarding the delayed speech was that the child had no reason to speak, so he didn't. He had a perfect communication system and speech did not offer anything better. There was absolutely no adaptation value for this child to learn speech at that time. At my suggestion, the child was placed in a regular preschool program and the mother was counseled to be less anticipatory toward the child. A few months later, he was a real chatterbox! There was no evidence that he was retarded or that he had a fundamental language disability (dyslexia). Not all language "problems" are dyslexia.

Autonomy

Autonomy is central to efficient construction of knowledge in constructivist theory. The child's self-directed struggle to understand and make sense of what is engaged is valued. Autonomy is as valued in learning to speak, read, and write as in all learning. Fortunately, in learning spoken language, the child's autonomy is usually ensured. Two- and three-year-olds do not go to school to learn how to speak. Adults and older children interact verbally with the child and from this most young children construct the rules for spoken language. They break the code, so to speak.

In a fundamental way, advocates for whole-language reading instruction believe in standing back and letting learning happen, choosing carefully when to interact as teacher with the child. But this approach works only some of the time. As the Libermans correctly remind us, 25 percent of children do not spontaneously construct the alphabetic principle and rules for decoding. In these cases, they argue, the children must be directly taught what they have not spontaneously figured out. This approach is used quite successfully in "reading recovery" programs. This is also the approach used in different versions of the Orton–Gillingham method for working with dyslexic children with reading difficulties. Direct instruction, as in reading recovery, seems to be effective for non-LD students who struggle excessively with decoding. Whether it is of value in the case of dyslexic students is less clear.

Sometimes autonomy does not work.

A FINAL WORD

> *"It all turns on affection now," said Margaret. "Affection. Don't you see?"*
> *E. M. Forster,* Howards End

There are lots of excellent schools and teachers who respect and value children and provide reasonably effective programs for them. These programs are not necessarily fully consistent with what we know about children's intellectual and social development, but, by design or by instinct they do enough that is positive. There are also many schools, too many schools, where students and teachers and are not valued, where the spirit is dead or dying, where what we hope for young minds is not happening. The reasons are complex and the answers are not simple. In some ways, we have lost our way.

Raymond Callahan, in *Education and the Cult of Efficiency* (1962) describes the pursuit of industrial-like "efficiency" in American education during the early part of this century and the devastating consequences of this path on the lives of students and teachers. This continues through today. Ted Sizer in *Horace's Compromise* (1984) identified many universal problematic aspects of American high schools: uniformity, mindlessness, negotiated inactivity, low expectations for students, depersonalization and lack of respects for adolescents, and the burdens of high school teachers. Part of what has eroded this century is the remembrance that children and their teachers are human and require certain human supports and connections: respect, autonomy, care, trust. Without the proper human connections, the spirit withers.

I am not going to argue that everyone who reads this book and seeks to become a teacher needs to model themselves as Piaget and constructivism suggest it should be. That cannot happen. The fact is that each of us constructs our own theory of education, which we modify through reconstruction. You already have a theory of education (probably based on how you were taught), a framework within which your actions are determined. Your theory may be unarticulated, but it is there. I hope your reading of this book provokes you to reflect on your theory and to evaluate your satisfaction with it. Our personal theories determine our efforts in many ways. How teachers conceptualize phenomena very much determines their behavior. A classic example is the nature–nurture controversy that has pervaded psychology for years. If a teacher conceptualizes intelligence (or the ability to succeed in school) as fixed, she or he is probably not going to be motivated to try very hard to help a student who is a poor performer in the classroom and has been for several years. On the other hand, a teacher who conceptualizes intelligence as developed, not fixed, is likely to be motivated to help the poor performer. How teachers conceptualize intelligence and learning, what their theory is, influences their actions. Teachers' expectations of how children can perform in the classroom are derived from their constructions.

I have found much in the Piagetian constructivist framework that gives me hope for the future of education. It does not hold all the answers, and it is not even a theory of education. What it can do is help us construct a more authentic understanding of children, how they construct knowledge, and the influence of affectivity and social activity on development. Ultimately, we hope for our children that they learn how to learn, have confidence in themselves, are respectful of others, and feel an obligation toward ideas, objects, and people. For constructivists, this is not just a matter of each new generation recapitulating the prior generation, but moving beyond it to a hopefully more adequate societal adaptation; an equilibrium between societal change and societal stability. Meacham (1993), in discussing this issue, made the case for constructivism this way:

> The solution, of course, is entirely consistent with Piaget's structural-developmental theory, namely, the strength of what the individual knows about society comes from the fact of children having constructed society for themselves, so that the child believes firmly in, desires, even loves his or her society. . . . In short, society reproduces itself not by transmission from one generation to the next, but instead by each new generation constructing a new society for itself. Because the child and subsequently the adult firmly believes in his or her own construction, the danger inherent in knowing structures as the fragile basis for society can be substantially contained, for the individual will act . . . to maintain and defend his or her own construction. (p. 259)

Suggested Readings

PIAGETIAN THEORY

Brainerd, C. *Piaget's Theory of Intelligence.* Englewood Cliffs, N.J.: Prentice-Hall, 1978.

Flavell, J. *The Developmental Psychology of Jean Piaget.* New York: Van Nostrand, 1963.

Forman, G., and D. Kuschner. *The Child's Construction of Knowledge: Piaget for Teaching Children.* Belmont, Calif.: Brooks-Cole, 1977.

Furth, H. *Piaget and Knowledge: Theoretical Foundations.* Chicago: University of Chicago Press, 1981.

Gallagher, J., and D. Reid. *The Learning Theory of Piaget and Inhelder.* Monterey, Calif.: Brooks-Cole, 1981.

Ginsburg, H., and S. Opper. *Piaget's Theory of Intellectual Development,* 2nd ed. Englewood Cliffs, N.J.: Prentice-Hall, 1978.

Gruber, H., and J. Vonèche, eds. *The Essential Piaget.* New York: Basic Books, 1977.

Kohlberg, L. *Child Psychology and Childhood Education: A Cognitive-Developmental View.* White Plains, N.Y.: Longman, 1987.

Piaget, J. *The Origins of Intelligence in Children.* New York: International Universities Press, 1952.

Piaget, J. *Six Psychological Studies.* New York: Vintage Books, 1967.

Piaget, J. *Genetic Epistemology.* New York: Columbia University Press, 1970.

Piaget, J. *Science of Education and the Psychology of the Child.* New York: Viking Press, 1970.

Piaget, J. *To Understand Is to Invent.* New York: Viking Press, 1973.

Piaget, J. *Intelligence and Affectivity: Their Relationship During Child Development.* Palo Alto, Calif.: Annual Reviews, 1981.

Piaget, J., and B. Inhelder. *The Psychology of the Child.* Translated by Helen Weaver. New York: Basic Books, 1969.

EDUCATION

Brooks, J., and M. Brooks. *In Search of Understanding: The Case for Constructivist Classrooms.* Alexandria, Va.: ASCD, 1993.

DeVries, R., and L. Kohlberg. *Programs of Early Education: The Constructivist View.* White Plains, N.Y.: Longman, 1987.

DeVries, R., and B. Zan. *Moral Classrooms, Moral Children: Creating a Constructivist Atmosphere in Early Education.* New York: Teachers College Press, 1994.

Duckworth, E. *The Having of Wonderful Ideas.* New York: Teachers College Press, 1987.

Elkind, D. *Child Development and Education: A Piagetian Perspective.* New York: Oxford University Press, 1976.

Forman, G., and F. Hill. *Constructive Play: Applying Piaget in the Preschool.* Monterey, Calif.: Brooks-Cole, 1980.

Fosnot, C. *Enquiring Teachers, Enquiring Learners: A Constructivist Approach to Teaching.* New York: Teachers College Press, 1989.

Furth, H. *Piaget for Teachers.* Englewood Cliffs, N.J.: Prentice-Hall, 1970.

Gallagher, J., and D. Reid. *The Learning Theory of Piaget and Inhelder.* Monterey, Calif.: Brooks-Cole, 1981.

Kamii, C. *Number in Preschool and Kindergarten.* Washington, D.C.: National Association for the Education of Young Children, 1982.

Kamii, C., and R. DeVries. *Physical Knowledge in Preschool Education: Implications of Piaget's Theory.* Englewood Cliffs, N.J.: Prentice-Hall, 1978.

Piaget, J. *Science of Education and the Psychology of the Child.* New York: Viking Press, 1970b.

Schwebel, M., and J. Raph, eds. *Piaget in the Classroom.* New York: Basic Books, 1973.

Shayer, M., and P. Adey. *Towards a Science of Science Teaching.* London: Heinemann, 1981.

Sheehan, D., ed. *Piaget: Educational Perspectives.* Oneonta, N.Y.: State University College at Oneonta, 1979.

Wadsworth, B. *Piaget for the Classroom Teacher.* White Plains, N.Y.: Longman, 1978.

ARITHMETIC/MATHEMATICS

Baroody, A. *Children's Mathematical Thinking.* New York: Teachers College Press, 1987.

Copeland, R. *How Children Learn Mathematics,* 2nd ed. New York: Macmillan, 1974.

Ginsburg, H. *Children's Arithmetic: The Learning Process.* New York: Van Nostrand, 1977.

Kamii, C. *Number in Preschool and Kindergarten.* Washington, D.C.: National Association for the Education of Young Children, 1982.

Kamii, C. *Young Children Reinvent Arithmetic.* New York: Teachers College Press, 1985.

Kamii, C. *Young Children Continue to Reinvent Arithmetic: 3rd Grade.* New York: Teachers College Press, 1994.

Labinowicz, E. *Learning from Children, New Beginnings for Teaching Numerical Thinking: A Piagetian Approach.* Menlo Park, Calif.: Addison-Wesley, 1985.

Piaget, J. *The Child's Conception of Number.* London: Humanities Press, 1952.

Piaget, J., B. Inhelder, and A. Szeminska. *The Child's Conception of Geometry.* New York: Basic Books, 1960.

Shifter, D., and C. Fosnot. *Reconstructing Mathematics Education.* New York: Teachers College Press, 1993.

SPECIAL NEEDS EDUCATION

Gallagher, J., and D. Reid. *The Learning Theory of Piaget and Inhelder.* Monterey, Calif.: Brooks-Cole, 1981.
Inhelder, B. *The Diagnosis of Reasoning in the Mentally Retarded.* New York: John Day, 1968.
Reid, K. *Teaching the Learning Disabled: A Cognitive Developmental Approach.* Boston: Allyn and Bacon, 1988.

SOCIAL AND MULTICULTURAL ISSUES

Edwards, C. *Promoting Social and Moral Development in Young Children.* New York: Teachers College Press, 1986.
Furth, H. *The World of Grown-Ups.* New York: Elsevier, 1980.
Inhelder, B., and H. Chipman, eds. *Piaget and His School.* New York: Springer-Verlag, 1976.
Ramsey, P. *Teaching and Learning in a Diverse World.* New York: Teachers College Press, 1987.
Wadsworth, B. *Piaget for the Classroom Teacher.* White Plains, N.Y.: Longman, 1978.

MORAL REASONING

Cowan, P. *Piaget with Feeling.* New York: Holt, Rinehart and Winston, 1978.
DeVries, R. and B. Zan. *Moral Classrooms, Moral Children: Creating a Constructivist Atmosphere in Early Education.* New York: Teachers College Press, 1994.
Gilligan, C. "In a Different Voice: Women's Conception of Self and of Morality." *Harvard Educational Review* 47 (1977): 481-517.
Hersh, R., D. Paolitto, and J. Reimer. *Promoting Moral Growth: From Piaget to Kohlberg.* White Plains, N.Y.: Longman, 1979.
Kohlberg, L. *The Philosophy of Moral Development: Moral Stages and the Idea of Justice.* San Francisco: Harper & Row, 1981.
Lickona, T., ed. *Moral Development and Behavior: Theory, Research and Social Issues.* New York: Holt, Rinehart and Winston, 1976.
Lickona, T. *Educating for Character: How Our Schools Can Teach Respect and Responsibility.* New York: Bantam, 1991.
Piaget, J. *The Moral Judgment of the Child.* New York: Free Press, 1965.
Piaget, J. *Six Psychological Studies.* New York: Vintage Books, 1967.
Piaget, J. *Intelligence and Affectivity: Their Relationship During Child Development.* Palo Alto, Calif.: Annual Reviews, 1981.

CLINICAL PSYCHOLOGY

Dupont, H. *Emotional Development, Theory and Applications: A Neo-Piagetian Perspective.* Westport, Conn.: Praeger, 1994.
Fast, I. *Event Theory: A Piaget-Freud Interpretation.* Hillsdale, N.J.: Erlbaum, 1985.
Greenspan, S. *Intelligence and Adaptation.* New York: International Universities Press, 1979.
Kegan, R. *The Evolving Self.* Cambridge, Mass.: Harvard University Press, 1982.

Kegan, R. *In Over Our Heads: The Mental Demands of Modern Life.* Cambridge: Harvard University Press, 1994.

Malerstein, A., and M. Ahern. *A Piagetian Model of Character Structure.* New York: Human Sciences Press, 1982.

Rosen, H. *Piagetian Dimensions of Clinical Relevance.* New York: Columbia University Press, 1985.

Weiner, M. *The Cognitive Unconscious: A Piagetian Approach to Psychotherapy.* Davis, Calif.: Psychological Press, 1975.

Wolff, P. "The Developmental Psychologies of Jean Piaget and Psychoanalysis." *Psychological Issues* 2. Monograph 5. New York: International Universities Press, 1960.

Bibliography

Alben, R. "David Elkind: Going Beyond Piaget." *APA Monitor* 11 (Nov. 1980).

Ashton-Warner, S. *Teacher.* New York: Simon & Schuster, 1963.

Baroody, A. *Children's Mathematical Thinking.* New York: Teachers College Press, 1987.

Bearison, D. "Role of Measurement Operations in the Acquisition of Conservation." *Developmental Psychology* 1 (1969): 653–60.

Bereiter, C., and S. Engleman. *Teaching Disadvantaged Children in the Preschool.* Englewood Cliffs, N.J.: Prentice-Hall, 1966.

Berry, J., and P. Dasen. *Culture and Cognitions: Readings in Cross-Cultural Psychology.* London: Methuen and Co., 1974.

Bloom, B. *Stability and Change in Human Characteristics.* New York: Wiley, 1964.

Bovet, M. "Piaget's Theory of Cognitive Development and Individual Differences." In *Piaget and His School,* edited by B. Inhelder and H. Chipman, New York: Springer-Verlag, 1976.

Brainerd, C. *Piaget's Theory of Intelligence.* Englewood Cliffs, N.J.: Prentice-Hall, 1978.

Bringuier, J. *Conversations with Jean Piaget.* Chicago: University of Chicago Press, 1980.

Brooks, J., and M. Brooks. *In Search of Understanding: The Case for Constructivist Classrooms.* Alexandria, Va.: ASCD, 1993.

Brown, T. Foreword. In *The Equilibration of Cognitive Structures,* by J. Piaget, translated by T. Brown and K. Thampy. Chicago: University of Chicago Press, 1985.

Brown, T. "The Biological Significance of Affectivity." In *Psychological and Biological Approaches to Emotion,* edited by N. Stein and T. Trabasso, pp. 405–34. Hillsdale, N.J.: LEA, 1990.

Brown, T., and L. Weiss. "Structures, Procedures, and Affectivity." *Archives de psychologie* 55 (1987): 59–94.

Callahan, R. *Education and the Cult of Efficiency,* Chicago: University of Chicago Press, 1962.

Carnegie Quarterly 23, no. 3 (Summer 1975).

Carroll, J., and J. Rest. "Moral Development." In *Handbook of Developmental Psychology,* edited by B. Wolman. Englewood Cliffs, N.J.: Prentice-Hall, 1982.

Chall, J. *Stages of Reading Development.* New York: McGraw-Hill, 1983.

Clements, D. H. "Effects of Logo and CAE Environments on Cognition and Creativity." *Journal of Educational Psychology* 78 (1986): 309-18.

Copeland, R. *How Children Learn Mathematics,* 2nd ed. New York: Macmillan, 1974.

Cowan, D. *Piaget with Feeling.* New York: Holt, Rinehart and Winston, 1981.

Crandall, V. C., W. Katovsky, and V. J. Crandall. "Children's Beliefs in Their Own Control of Reinforcements in Intellectual-Academic Achievement Situations." *Child Development* 36 (1965): 91-109.

Damon, W. "Conception of Positive Justice as Related to the Development of Logical Operations." *Child Development* 46 (1975): 301-12.

Dasen, P., ed. *Piagetian Psychology: Cross Cultural Contributions.* New York: Gardner, 1977.

Deci, E., R. Hodges, L., Pierson, and J. Tomassone. "Autonomy and Competence as Motivational Factors in Students with Learning Disabilities and Emotional Handicaps." *Journal of Learning Disabilities* 25 (1992): 457-71.

DeVries, R., and L. Kohlberg. *Programs of Early Education: The Constructivist View.* White Plains, N.Y.: Longman, 1987.

DeVries, R., and B. Zan. *Moral Classrooms, Moral Children: Creating a Constructivist Atmosphere in Early Education.* New York: Teachers College Press, 1994.

Dewey, J. *Interest and Effort in Education.* Edwardville: Southern Illinois Press, 1913.

Dewey, J. *Education and Experience.* New York: Colliers, 1963.

diSessa, A. A. "Phenomenology and the Evolution of Intuition." In *Mental Models,* edited by D. Gentner and A. Stevens, pp. 15-33. Hillsdale, N.J.: Erlbaum, 1983.

Drake, D., and B. Wadsworth. "Constructivist Theory and Learning Disabilities: Confluence and Disconnections." Paper presented at 43rd Annual Conference of the Orton Dyslexia Society, Cincinnati, Ohio, 1992.

Duckworth, E. "The Having of Wonderful Ideas." *Harvard Educational Review* 42 (May 1972): 217-31.

Duckworth, E. "Either We're Too Early and They Can't Learn It, or We're Too Late and They Know It Already: The Dilemma of 'Applying Piaget,'" Pt. 2. *Genetic Epistemologist* 7, no. 4 (1978): 3-7.

Duckworth, E. *The Having of Wonderful Ideas.* New York: Teachers College Press, 1987.

Dupont, H. "Affective Development: Stage and Sequence (A Piagetian Interpretation)." In *Adolescents' Development and Education: A Janus Knot,* edited by R. L. Mosher. Berkeley: McCutchan, 1979.

Dupont, H. *Emotional Development, Theory and Applications: A Neo-Piagetian Perspective.* Westport, Conn.: Praeger, 1994.

Dweck, C., and E. Elliot. "Achievement Motivation." In *Handbook of Child Psychology,* vol. 4., edited by P. Mussen, pp. 643-91. New York: Wiley, 1983.

Easley, J. "Four Decades of Conservation Research." In *Knowledge and Development,* Vol. 2, *Piaget and Education,* edited by J. Gallagher and J. Easley, pp. 139-76. New York: Plenum, 1978.

Edelstein, W. "Development as the Aim of Education—Revisited." In *Effective and Responsible Teaching,* edited by F. Oser, A. Dick, J. Patry, pp. 161-72. San Francisco: Jossey-Bass, 1992.

Elkind, D. "Children's Discovery of the Conservation of Mass, Weight and Volume: Piaget's Replication Study II." *Journal of Genetic Psychology* 98 (1961a): 219-27.

Elkind, D. "Quality Conceptions in Junior and Senior High School Students." *Child Development* 32 (1961b): 551-60.

Elkind, D. "Quantity Conceptions in College Students." *Journal of Social Psychology* 57 (1962): 459-65.

Elkind, D. "Egocentrism in Adolescence." *Child Development* 38 (1967): 1025-34.

Elkind, D. "Cognitive Structures and Adolescent Experience." *Adolescence* 2 (1967-68): 427-34.

Elkind, D. "Giant in the Nursery." *New York Times Magazine* (May 26, 1968): 25-27+.

Elkind, D. "Piagetian and Psychometric Conceptions of Intelligence." *Harvard Educational Review* 39 (1969): 319-37.

Elkind, D. *Child Development and Education: A Piagetian Perspective.* New York: Oxford University Press, 1976.

Elkind, D. "Is Piaget Passe in Elementary Education?" *Genetic Epistemologist* 7, no. 4 (1978): 1-2.

Elkind, D. "Stages in the Development of Reading." In *New Directions in Piagetian Theory and Practice,* edited by I. Sigel, D. Brodzinsky, and R. Golinkoff, pp. 267-80. Hillsdale, N.J.: Erlbaum, 1981.

Epstein, H. "Growth Spurts During Brain Development: Implications for Educational Policy and Practice." In *Education and the Brain,* edited by J. Chall and A. Mirsky, pp. 343-70. Chicago: University of Chicago Press, 1978.

Epstein, H. "Brain Growth and Cognitive Functioning." *Colorado Journal of Educational Research* 19 (Fall 1979): 3-4.

Erikson, E. *Childhood and Society.* New York: Norton, 1950.

Evans, R. *Jean Piaget: The Man and His Ideas.* New York: Dutton, 1973.

Ferreiro, E., and A. Teberosky. *Literacy Before Schooling.* Portsmouth, N.H.: Heinemann, 1982.

Flavell, J. *The Developmental Psychology of Jean Piaget.* New York: Van Nostrand, 1963.

Flavell, J. "The Uses of Verbal Behavior in Assessing Children's Cognitive Abilities." In *Measurement and Piaget,* edited by D. Green, M. Ford, and G. Flamer, pp. 198-204. New York: McGraw-Hill, 1971.

Forman, G., and D. Kuschner. *The Child's Construction of Knowledge: Piaget for Teaching Children.* Belmont, Calif.: Brooks-Cole, 1977.

Fosnot, C. *Enquiring Teachers, Enquiring Learners: A Constructivist Approach for Teaching.* New York: Teachers College Press, 1989.

Fowler, R. "Piagetian Versus Vygotskyian Perspectives on Development and Education." Paper presented at annual meeting of the American Educational Research Association, New Orleans, 1994.

Freud, A. *The Ego and the Mechanisms of Defense.* New York: International Universities Press, 1946.

Furth, H. *Piaget for Teachers.* Englewood Cliffs, N.J.: Prentice-Hall, 1970.

Furth, H. "The 'Radical Imagery' Underlying Social Institutions: Its Developmental Base." *Human Development* 33 (1990): 202-13.

Gallagher, J. "Reflexive Abstraction and Education: The Meaning of Activity in Piaget's Theory." In *Knowledge and Development,* Vol. 2, *Piaget and Education,* edited by J. Gallagher and J. Easley, pp. 1-20. New York: Plenum, 1978.

Gallagher, J., and D. Reid. *The Learning Theory of Piaget and Inhelder.* Monterey, Calif.: Brooks-Cole, 1981.

Gardner, H. *Frames of Mind: The Theory of Multiple Intelligences.* New York: Basic Books, 1983.

Garner, R. "Self-Regulated Learning Strategy Shifts and Shared Expertise: Reactions to Palinezar and Klerk." *Journal of Learning Disabilities* 25 (1992): 226-29.

Gelman, R. "Cognitive Development." *Annual Review of Psychology* 29 (1978): 297-332.

Gilligan, C. "In a Different Voice: Women's Conception of Self and of Morality." *Harvard Educational Review* 47 (1977): 481-517.

Ginsburg, H. *Children's Arithmetic: The Learning Process.* New York: Van Nostrand, 1977.

Ginsburg, H., and S. Opper. *Piaget's Theory of Intellectual Development,* 2nd ed. Englewood Cliffs, N.J.: Prentice-Hall, 1978.

Goodnow, J., and G. Bethon. "Piaget's Tasks: The Effects of Schooling and Intelligence." *Child Development* 37 (1966): 573–82.

Green, D., M. Ford, and G. Flamer, eds. *Measurement and Piaget.* New York: McGraw-Hill, 1971.

Greenfield, P. M. "On Culture and Conservation." In *Studies in Cognitive Growth,* edited by J. Bruner, R. Olver, and P. Greenfield, pp. 225–56. New York: Wiley, 1966.

Gruber, H. *Darwin on Man: A Psychological Study of Scientific Creativity,* 2nd ed. Chicago: University of Chicago Press, 1981.

Gruber, H., and J. Vonèche, eds. *The Essential Piaget.* New York: Basic Books, 1977.

Gruen, G. E. "Experiences Affecting the Development of Number Conservation in Children." *Child Development* 36 (1965): 964–79.

Hall, G. *Adolescence.* 2 vols. New York: Appleton, 1908.

Harris, K., and S. Graham. "Constructivism: Principles, Paradigms, and Integration." *The Journal of Special Education* 28 (1994): 233–47.

Heard, S., and B. Wadsworth. "The Relationship Between Cognitive Development and Language Complexity." Manuscript. Mount Holyoke College, May 1977.

Hersh, R., D. Paolitto, and J. Reimer. *Promoting Moral Growth: From Piaget to Kohlberg.* White Plains, N.Y.: Longman, 1979.

Hofmann, R. "Would You Like a Bite of My Peanut Butter Sandwich?" *Journal of Learning Disabilities* (Spring 1983): 174–77.

Hooper, I. H. "Piagetian Research and Education." In *Logical Thinking in Children: Research Based on Piaget's Theory,* edited by I. E. Sigel and F. H. Hooper, pp. 423–34. New York: Holt, Rinehart and Winston, 1968.

Hunt, J. McV. *Intelligence and Experience.* New York: Ronald, 1961.

Inhelder, B. *The Diagnosis of Reasoning in the Mentally Retarded.* New York: John Day, 1968.

Inhelder, B. "Outlook." In *Jean Piaget: Consensus and Controversy,* edited by S. Modgil and C. Modgil. New York: Holt, Rinehart and Winston, 1982.

Inhelder, B., and H. Chipman. eds. *Piaget and His School.* New York: Springer-Verlag, 1976.

Inhelder, B., and J. Piaget. *The Growth of Logical Thinking from Childhood to Adolescence.* Translated by Anne Parsons and Stanley Pilgram. New York: Basic Books, 1958.

Inhelder, B., and J. Piaget. *The Early Growth of Logic in the Child.* London: Routledge and Kegan Paul, 1964.

Kagan, J. *Carnegie Quarterly* 23, no. 3 (Summer 1975).

Kagan, J. "Emergent Themes in Human Development." *American Scientist* 64, no. 2 (March–April 1976): 186–96.

Kagan, J. "Jean Piaget's Contributions." *Phi Delta Kappan* (Dec. 1980): 245–46.

Kamii, C. "Autonomy as the Aim of Education: Implications of Piaget's Theory." In *Number in Preschool and Kindergarten,* by C. Kamii, pp. 73–87. Washington, D.C.: National Association for the Education of Young Children, 1982.

Kamii, C. "Autonomy: The Aim of Education Envisioned by Piaget." *Phi Delta Kappan* 65, no. 6 (1984): 410–15.

Kamii, C. *Young Children Reinvent Arithmetic.* New York: Teachers College Press, 1985.

Kamii, C. *Young Children Continue to Reinvent Arithmetic: 3rd Grade.* New York: Teachers College Press, 1994.

Kamii, C., B. Clark, and A. Dominick. "The Six National Goals: A Road to Disappointment." *Phi Delta Kappan* 76 (1994): 672–77.

Kamii, C., and R. DeVries. *Physical Knowledge in Preschool Education: Implications of Piaget's Theory.* Englewood Cliffs, N.J.: Prentice-Hall, 1978.

Kegan, R. *The Evolving Self.* Cambridge, Mass.: Harvard University Press, 1982.

Kegan, R. *In Over Our Heads: The Mental Demands of Modern Life.* Cambridge: Harvard University Press, 1994.

Kohlberg, L. "The Development of Modes of Moral Thinking and Choice in the Years Two to Sixteen." Ph.D. dissertation, University of Chicago, 1958.

Kohlberg, L. "Early Education: A Cognitive-Developmental View." *Child Development* 39 (1968a): 1013-63.

Kohlberg, L. "The Montessori Approach to Cultural Deprivation: A Cognitive Development Interpretation and Some Research Findings." In *Preschool Education, Theory, Research, and Action,* edited by R. Hess and R. Bear, pp. 105-18. Chicago: Aldine, 1968b.

Kohlberg, L. "Stage and Sequence: The Cognitive-Developmental Approach to Socialization." In *Handbook of Socialization Theory and Research,* edited by D. Goslen, pp. 347-408. Chicago: Rand McNally, 1969a.

Kohlberg, L. *Stages in the Development of Moral Thought and Action.* New York: Holt, Rinehart and Winston, 1969b.

Kohlberg, L. "Moral Stages and Moralization: The Cognitive-Developmental Approach." In *Moral Development and Behavior: Theory, Research and Social Issues,* edited by T. Lickona. New York: Holt, Rinehart and Winston, 1976.

Kohlberg, L. *Child Psychology and Childhood Education: A Cognitive-Developmental View.* White Plains, N.Y.: Longman, 1987.

Kohlberg, L., and R. Mayer. "Development as the Aim of Education." *Harvard Educational Review* 42, no. 4 (Nov. 1972): 449-96.

Kuhn, D., N. Langer, L. Kohlberg, and N. Hann. "The Development of Formal Operations in Logical and Moral Judgment." *Genetics Psychology Monograph* 95 (1977): 115.

L'Abate, L. "Frequency of Citation Study in Child Psychology Literature." *Child Development* 40 (1968): 87-92.

Labinowicz, E. *Learning from Children: New Beginnings for Teaching Numerical Thinking: A Piagetian Approach.* Menlo Park, Calif.: Addison-Wesley, 1985.

Langer, J. *Theories of Development.* New York: Holt, Rinehart and Winston, 1969.

Lawler, R. W. *Computer Experience and Cognitive Development: A Child's Learning in a Computer Culture.* New York: Halsted Press, 1985.

Lester, J. "Piaget and Vygotsky," unpublished manuscript, 1994.

Liberman, I, and A. Liberman. "Whole Language vs. Code Emphasis: Underlying Assumptions and Their Implications for Reading Instruction," *Readings for Educators,* pp. 51-76. Baltimore, Md.: The Orton Dyslexia Society, 1991.

Meacham, J. "Where is the Social Environment? A Commentary on Reed." *Development in Context: Acting and Thinking in Specific Environments,* edited by R. Wozniak and K. Fisher, pp. 255-68. Hillsdale, N.J.: Erlbaum, 1993.

Mermelstein, E., and L. Schulman. "Lack of Formal Schooling and the Acquisition of Conservation." *Child Development* 38 (1967): 39-52.

Neimark, E. "Adolescent Thought: Transition to Formal Operations." In *Handbook of Developmental Psychology,* edited by B. Wolman. Englewood Cliffs, N.J.: Prentice-Hall, 1982.

Noddings, N. *The Challenge to Care in Schools,* New York: Teachers College Press, 1992.

Overton, W., and J. Newman. "Cognitive Development: A Competence-Activation/Utilization Approach." In *Review of Human Development,* edited by T. Field et al., pp. 217-41. New York: Wiley, 1982.

Palinczar, A., and L. Klerk, L. "Fostering Literary Learning in Supportive Contexts." *Journal of Learning Disabilities,* 25 (1992): 211-25+.

Papert, S. *Mindstorms: Children, Computers, and Powerful Ideas.* New York: Basic Books, 1980.

Pea, R., and D. Kurland. "On the Cognitive and Educational Benefits of Teaching Children Programming: A Critical Look." *New Ideas in Psychology* 1 (1984a).

Pea, R., and D. Kurland. "On the Cognitive Effects of Learning Computer Programming." *New Ideas in Psychology* 2 (1984b): 137–68.

Phillips, J. *The Origins of Intellect: Piaget's Theory.* 2nd ed. San Francisco: Freeman, 1969.

Piaget, J. *Recherche.* Lausanne, Switzerland: La Concorde, 1918.

Piaget, J. *The Language and Thought of the Child.* New York: Harcourt Brace Jovanovich, 1926.

Piaget, J. *Judgment and Reasoning of the Child.* New York: Harcourt Brace Jovanovich, 1928.

Piaget, J. *The Child's Conception of Physical Causality.* New York: Harcourt Brace Jovanovich, 1930.

Piaget, J. *The Child's Conception of Number.* London: Humanities Press, 1952a.

Piaget, J. "Autobiography." In *History of Psychology in Autobiography,* edited by E. G. Boring et al., pp. 237–56. Worcester, Mass.: Clark University Press, 1952b.

Piaget, J. *The Origins of Intelligence in Children.* New York: International Universities Press, 1952c.

Piaget, J. *The Construction of Reality in the Child.* Translated by Margaret Cook. New York: Basic Books, 1954.

Piaget, J. "The Genetic Approach to the Psychology of Thought." *Journal of Educational Psychology* 52 (1961): 275–81.

Piaget, J. *Play, Dreams and Imitation in Childhood.* New York: Norton, 1962a.

Piaget, J. "Will and Action." *Bulletin of the Menninger Clinic,* 26 (1962b): 138–45.

Piaget, J. *The Child's Conception of the World.* Paterson, N.J.: Littlefield, Adams, 1963a.

Piaget, J. "Problems of the Social Psychology of Childhood." Translated by T. Brown and M. Gribetz. Manuscript. Originally published in *Traité de sociologie,* edited by G. Gurvitch, pp. 229–54. Paris: Presses Universitaires de France, 1963b.

Piaget, J. *The Psychology of Intelligence.* Paterson, N.J.: Littlefield, Adams, 1963c.

Piaget, J. "Three Lectures." In *Piaget Rediscovered,* edited by R. E. Ripple and U. N. Rockcastle. Ithaca, N.Y.: Cornell University Press, 1964.

Piaget, J. *The Moral Judgment of the Child.* New York: Free Press, 1965.

Piaget, J. *Six Psychological Studies.* New York: Vintage Books, 1967.

Piaget, J. *The Mechanisms of Perception.* New York: Basic Books, 1969.

Piaget, J. *Genetic Epistemology.* New York: Columbia University Press, 1970a.

Piaget, J. *Science of Education and the Psychology of the Child.* New York: Viking Press, 1970b.

Piaget, J. "The Theory of Stages in Cognitive Development." In *Measurement and Piaget,* edited by D. Green, M. Ford, and G. Flamer, pp. 1–7. New York: McGraw-Hill, 1971.

Piaget, J. "Intellectual Evolution from Adolescence to Adulthood." *Human Development* 15 (1972a): 1–12.

Piaget, J. *The Principles of Genetic Epistemology.* New York: Basic Books, 1972b.

Piaget, J. *To Understand Is to Invent.* New York: Viking Press, 1973.

Piaget, J. "Need and Significance of Cross-Cultural Studies in Genetic Psychology." In *Cultures and Cognition: Readings in Cross-Cultural Psychology,* edited by J. Berr and P. Dasen, pp. 299–309. London: Methuen, 1974a.

Piaget, J. *Understanding Causality.* New York: Norton, 1974b.

Piaget, J. "The Affective Unconscious and the Cognitive Unconscious." In *Piaget and His School,* edited by B. Inhelder and H. Chipman, pp. 63–71. New York: Springer-Verlag, 1976.

Piaget, J. *The Development of Thought: Equilibrium of Cognitive Structures.* New York: Viking, 1977a.

Piaget, J. "Problems in Equilibration." In *Topics in Cognitive Development,* Vol. 1, *Equilibration:*

Theory, Research and Application, edited by M. Appel and L. Goldberg, pp. 3–13. New York: Plenum, 1977b.

Piaget, J. *Les formes élémentaires de la dialectique.* Paris: Gallimard, 1980.

Piaget, J. "Creativity." In *The Learning Theory of Piaget and Inhelder,* edited by J. Gallagher and K. Reid, pp. 221–29. Monterey, Calif.: Brooks-Cole, 1981a.

Piaget, J. *Intelligence and Affectivity: Their Relationship During Child Development.* Palo Alto, Calif.: Annual Reviews, 1981b.

Piaget, J., and B. Inhelder. *The Child's Conception of Space.* London: Routledge and Kegan Paul, 1956.

Piaget, J., and B. Inhelder. *The Psychology of the Child.* Translated by H. Weaver. New York: Basic Books, 1969.

Piaget, J., B. Inhelder, and A. Szeminska. *The Child's Conception of Geometry.* New York: Basic Books, 1960.

Pinard, A., and M. Laurendeau. "A Scale of Mental Development Based on the Theory of Piaget: Description of a Project." *Journal of Research in Science Teaching* 2 (1964): 253–60.

Pulaski, M. *Understanding Piaget.* New York: Harper & Row, 1971.

Ramsey, P. *Teaching and Learning in a Diverse World.* New York: Teachers College Press, 1987.

Reid, K., and Hresko, W. *A Cognitive Approach to Learning Disabilities.* Austin, Tex.: Pro-Ed, 1981.

Resnick, L. "Constructing Knowledge in Schools." In *Development and Learning: Conflict or Congruence,* edited by L. Liben, pp. 19–50. Hillsdale, N.J.: Erlbaum, 1987.

Rosenthal, R., and L. Jacobson. *Pygmalion in the Classroom.* New York: Holt, Rinehart and Winston, 1968.

Schifter, D., and C. Fosnot. *Reconstructing Mathematics Education.* New York: Teachers College Press, 1993.

Schwebel, M. "Formal Operations in First Year College Students." *Journal of Psychology* 91, no. 1 (Sept. 1975): 133–41.

Schwebel, M., and J. Raph, eds. *Piaget in the Classroom.* New York: Basic Books, 1973.

Selman, R. L. "The Relation of Role-Taking to the Development of Moral Judgment in Children." *Child Development* 42 (1971): 59–91.

Selman, R. L. "Social-Cognitive Understanding: A Guide to Educational and Clinical Practice." In *Moral Development and Behavior: Theory, Research and Social Issues,* edited by T. Lickona. New York: Holt, Rinehart and Winston, 1976.

Shayer, M., and P. Adey. *Towards a Science of Science Teaching.* London: Heinemann, 1981.

Sheehan, D., ed. *Piaget: Educational Perspectives.* Oneonta, N.Y.: State University College at Oneonta, 1979.

Sigel, I. E. "The Attainment of Concepts." In *Review of Child Development Research,* Vol. 1, edited by M. L. Hoffman and L. V. Hoffman, pp. 209–48. New York: Russell Sage Foundation, 1964.

Sigel, I. E., and F. H. Hooper, eds. *Logical Thinking in Children: Research Based on Piaget's Theory.* New York: Holt, Rinehart and Winston, 1968.

Sinclair, H. "Piaget's Theory of Development: The Main Stages." In *Piagetian Cognitive-Development Research and Mathematical Education,* edited by M. Rosskopf, L. Steffe, and S. Taback. Washington, D.C.: National Council of Teachers of Mathematics, 1971.

Sinclair, H. "Conflict and Congruence in Development and Learning." In *Developmental Learning: Conflict or Congruence,* edited by L. Liben, pp. 1–17. Hillsdale, N.J.: Erlbaum, 1987.

Sizer, T. *Horace's Compromise.* Boston: Houghton Mifflin, 1984.

Smedslund, J. "The Acquisition of Conservation of Substance and Weight in Children." In

Readings in Child Development and Behavior, edited by G. Stendler. New York: Harcourt Brace Jovanovich, 1964.

Sullivan, E. V. "Computers, Culture and Educational Futures: A Meditation on Mindstorms." *Interchange* 16 (1985): 1–18.

Tursman, C. "Computers in Education." *School Administrator* (April 1982).

Uzgiris, I. "Situational Generality of Conservation." In *Logical Thinking in Children,* edited by I. E. Sigel and F. H. Hooper, pp. 40–52. New York: Holt, Rinehart and Winston, 1968.

Vail, P. *Smart Kids with School Problems.* New York: Dutton, 1987.

Vygotsky, L. *Thought and Language.* Cambridge: MIT Press, 1962.

Wadsworth, B. "The Effect of Peer Group Social Interaction on the Conservation of Number Learning in Kindergarten Children." Ed. D. dissertation, State University of New York at Albany, 1968, p. 7.

Wadsworth, B. *Piaget for the Classroom Teacher.* White Plains, N.Y.: Longman, 1978.

Wadsworth, B. "Piaget's Concept of Adaptation and Its Value to Educators." In *Piagetian Theory and the Helping Professions,* pp. 210–15. Eighth Annual Conference Proceedings. Los Angeles: University of Southern California, 1979.

Wadsworth, B. "Misinterpretations of Piaget's Theory." *Impact on Instructional Improvement,* 16 (1981): 1–11.

Wadsworth, B., and J. Cody. "Frequency of Citation in *Child Development* in 1974." Manuscript. South Hadley, Mass.: Mount Holyoke College, n.d.

Wadsworth, B., and K. Page. "The Relationship Between Choice of Major and Type of Moral Reasoning." Manuscript, 1987.

Wallach, L., J. Wall, and L. Anderson. "Number Conservation: The Roles of Reversibility, Addition, Subtraction, and Misleading Perceptual Cues." *Child Development* 38 (1967): 425–42.

Wohlwill, J., and R. Lowe. "Experimental Analysis of the Development of Conservation of Number." *Child Development* 33 (1962): 153–68.

Wright, D. "Piaget's Theory of Moral Development." In *Jean Piaget: Consensus and Controversy,* edited by S. Modgil and C. Modgil, pp. 204–14. New York: Praeger, 1982.

Youniss, J., and W. Damon. "Social Construction in Piaget's Theory." In *Piaget's Theory: Prospects and Possibilities,* edited by H. Beilin and P. Pufall, pp. 267–86. Hillsdale, N.J.: Erlbaum, 1992.

Zimiles, H. "The Development of Differentiation and Conservation of Number." *Monograph Society for Research in Child Development* 31 (1966): 8.

Zimmerman, B. "Commentary," *Human Development,* 36 (1993): 82–86.

Index

Abstraction, reflective, 117–119
Accidents, how children develop concepts of
    concrete operations and, 107
  preoperational development and, 81–82
Accommodation, 17–19
Action, cognitive development and, 22, 149
Active experience, cognitive development
    and, 29
Adaptation
  to culture, 148
  intellectual organization and, 13–20,
    142
Adey, P., 156
Adolescence
  cognitive development in, 128–134
  moral development in, 125–128
Affect
  cognition and, 144–146
  in coordination of schemata period, 47
  in first differentiations period, 40–41
  in reflex activity period, 37
  in representation period, 53
Affective development
  characteristics of, 140–142
  concrete operations and, 101–109
  description of, 30–32
  emergence of reciprocity and moral feel-
    ings, 77–79
  formal operations and, 123–128
  preoperational development and, 77–88
Analogies, 118–119

Ashton-Warner, Sylvia, 170
Assimilation, 17
  reproductive, 41–42
Autonomy
  concrete operations and, 104–106
  defined, 79n.13
  intellectual, 154
  in learning disabled, 173–175

Baroody, A., 166
Behaviorists, 128
Behavior modification, 4
Binet, A., 6
Biological development, intellectual
    organization and, 13–20
"Biology and War" (Piaget), 6
Borderline conservers, 76n.11
Bovet, M., 159
Brown, Terrance, 92n.4, 146n.6

Callahan, Raymond, 177
Causality
  concrete operations and, 100
  in coordination of schemata period, 46–47
  in experimentation period, 49–50
  in reflex activity period, 36–37
  in representation period, 52–53
  in reproduction of events period, 43
Centration
  concrete operations and, 94
  preoperational development and, 68–69